WHEATON PUBLIC LIBRARY
3 5143 00887782 8

D1385261

OUT OF CHAOS

OUT OF CHAOS

Hidden Children Remember the Holocaust

Edited by Elaine Saphier Fox

Introduction by Phyllis Lassner

Northwestern University Press
Evanston, Illinois

Northwestern University Press
www.nupress.northwestern.edu

Printed in the United States of America

10 9 8 7 6 5 4 3 2 1

Library of Congress Cataloging-in-Publication Data

Out of chaos : hidden children remember the Holocaust / edited by Elaine Saphier Fox ; with an introduction by Phyllis Lassner.
p. cm.
ISBN 978-0-8101-2911-5 (cloth : alk. paper)
1. Hidden children (Holocaust) 2. Holocaust, Jewish (1939–1945)—Personal narratives. 3. World War, 1939–1945—Jews—Rescue. 4. Righteous Gentiles in the Holocaust. I. Fox, Elaine Saphier. II. Lassner, Phyllis.
D804.48O98 2013
940.531835083—dc23

2013002304

∞ The paper used in this publication meets the minimum requirements of the American National Standard for Information Sciences—Permanence of Paper for Printed Library Materials, ANSI Z39.48-1992.

We dedicate this anthology
to the one and one-half million children
whose lives were cut short and who are,
therefore, unable to tell their stories.

Contents

PART 3. Hidden with Parents

Belgium

PART 4. Hidden with Rescuers

Belgium

France

Illustrations

Acknowledgments

From the Authors

This book speaks in different voices because each of us has different experiences as a witness and a survivor. Yet even as we thank the contributors to this anthology for allowing each of us to speak for ourselves, we recognize that because we have given each other that freedom, we are actually speaking in one voice. We could not have accomplished this task individually or without the support and encouragement of each other as we relive these monumental memories.

It is now twenty years since the Hidden Children/Child Survivors Chicago group was founded. When we first started meeting at the Spertus Institute for Jewish Learning and Leadership, which we thank for its generosity, we shared these stories, which are so painful and difficult to revisit. It took a long time for us to feel comfortable with one another. We discovered that many of us had never told our stories before.

Some of us had been told that the events that had happened to Jewish children during the Holocaust were not important enough to tell. Yet as we met and began to trust one another with these dreadful memories, we became stronger and more confident. We began to sense not only the validity of our experiences, but also the obligation to share them beyond our group and beyond our generation. Eventually, we felt that we had to reach out to our children, to other relatives, and to a wider audience. We decided to show that this is about more than just our individual journeys; it is about values and how people enact them in their lives. Our stories say that people can act with respect for other human beings, they can act negatively, or they can stand by and do nothing, and that each of those choices has consequences for other human beings and themselves. The choices made by ordinary individuals, who stood up for their values under great duress, are what saved us.

Thus, what we have done in this book is simply to stand up—for ourselves, for each other, for the millions who were murdered in the Holocaust, and for those honorable individuals who stood up and risked everything for us. We thank our parents, both biological and adoptive, and our rescuers. In telling our stories we are seeking to honor them as we hope we have done with our lives—the lives their sacrifices made possible for us. As the parents of one of us told their daughter as she was saying good-bye just before her successful escape from the Radomsko Ghetto, "If the war ends and we don't make it, tell the world what happened to us and the Jews."

From the Editor

In addition to the authors' acknowledging their biological and adoptive parents, and their rescuers, this anthology would never have been possible if it were not for several people. I want to thank my dear friend Chaya Horowitz Roth, with whom I have had a multidecade friendship, for introducing and encouraging me to become involved with the Hidden Children group's desire to tell and publish their stories in an anthology. I have her to thank for meeting and working with this most incredible group of people whom I now consider friends. I further thank my newfound friends for trusting me with their feelings and emotions.

I also thank my friend Judge Carole Bellows for putting me on the right track to getting this book on the road to publication and initiating a new friendship. When I casually mentioned my project to Carole, she immediately said, "You have to meet my friend Professor Phyllis Lassner, who teaches Holocaust literature and film among other topics at Northwestern University." Through Carole's initiation, I met Phyllis, who has become my mentor, teacher, and support throughout this entire process. Although I have had professional work published before and have taught legal writing in law school, I had never worked with a group of novice authors to write personal stories suitable for publication. I thank Phyllis for the guidance and professional advice she has given that helped polish the manuscript. I also thank her for the friendship that this relationship has inspired.

I realized that if I was interested in creative nonfiction writing, distinct from professional writing, I had to learn not to write like a lawyer. Therefore, I took writing classes at Newberry Library in Chicago and Northwestern University in Evanston. I thank my colleagues in these classes who encouraged and helped me understand writing fundamentals, which improved my skills and helped me teach and work with the authors of this book.

My sincere gratitude goes to my law firm, Seyfarth Shaw LLP, for all the help and support it has given me to make this book a reality. I thank my colleague Bart Lazar, an intellectual property lawyer, who on a pro bono basis reviewed and advised me on the contract with Northwestern University Press. Most of all, the authors and I are grateful and highly indebted to my assistant, Carla Bryant, for all her time and devotion to this project. Along with us, she worked endlessly and willingly on all the rewrites and other clerical matters that only she understood. But even more amazing was the interest and understanding that she exhibited for the authors and their history. In many ways she became an integral part of our group.

We recognize and thank Professor Elliot Lefkovitz, who provided us with a World War II timeline. We also gratefully acknowledge and appreciate the United States Holocaust Memorial Museum's assistance with and providing the timeline and maps denoting the Nazi occupation of Europe.

Finally, I am indebted and thankful to my parents, of blessed memory, for encouraging and inspiring me throughout my life to care about others and do my best. To my wonderful children, I thank them for their moral support. Most of all I thank my incredible husband, Alan, who is my rock. He has supported, motivated, and helped me throughout this process in numerous ways. Alan is a concise and clear writer, so I have often consulted him on a passage's clarity. When I have been immersed in working on the manuscript, Alan has willingly taken over chores usually done by me.

Apart from the efforts of the authors and myself, the success of our project was dependent on the assistance and support of many others to whom we are grateful.

—*Elaine Saphier Fox*

A Thank You to Elaine Saphier Fox

Growing up in the United States in the late 1930s, '40s, and '50s, Elaine Saphier Fox was encouraged to be seen and to speak up. Her family let her know that even if she was a child, her thoughts and opinions were valued. At the same time, we, the contributors to this anthology growing up in Nazi-occupied Europe, intuitively knew that our very survival depended on us being neither heard nor seen. We had witnessed the danger of being noticed, of being singled out. We knew that our lives depended on blending in, not calling attention to ourselves, and making ourselves invisible. We learned to disappear in order to survive.

As we hidden children and child survivors of the Holocaust matured in the safety of America, we still tried to remain invisible. Our cultural history reminded us that there was just one way to make sure that our survival was ensured: keep quiet, don't talk, and don't be noticed. We married, had children, and became productive citizens, yet we continued our silence. Finally, our grandchildren began to inquire about our early years. Our group, Hidden Children/Child Survivors Chicago, recognized the importance of our stories for posterity, for those whom one of our members calls "Fellow travelers in the future reality."

We became aware that not only are we the last and youngest eyewitnesses of the Holocaust, but also that little research had been devoted to us as a group and to how these experiences had influenced and guided our lives. Our group decided to write about our experiences, and we decided that we needed an outsider to guide us through the process. But whoever we chose would need special and unique qualifications. The person would have to have come of age at the same time as most of us. She would need to have been affected by the Holocaust, but not firsthand. She would have to have read about survivors and to have heard survivors speak. She would be knowledgeable about the mechanics of writing. Most important of all, she would have to be aware of our idiosyncrasies, sensitivities, and pain. Enter Elaine Saphier Fox.

Elaine possessed all the skills and qualifications that were needed to undertake this difficult project, and she recognized two facts: first, that we could add a different dimension to Holocaust writing that was important for people to know, and second, that it was important for us to come out of hiding. Even though many of us have written speeches, most of us had not written for publication and did not realize a reading audience required a different process of writing. Print has a permanence that is not attributed to speaking.

Elaine was also aware that for some of us English was our third or fourth language and that we thought in our native tongues. Elaine also suspected something that most of us had not even thought about because to do so might end the project before we even began it. Elaine knew that for the reader to gain a better understanding of our ordeal, we would have to relive it as we wrote it. We would once again experience the pain of not being wanted and the fear of being abandoned. But at the same time that we went deep into the marrow, we might also come out of the journey no longer feeling that we needed to be invisible. Even realizing all the difficulties that this project would encompass, Elaine willingly took on this formidable task.

To paraphrase the song "Dayenu" ("It Would Have Been Enough") from the Haggadah that we read each year at the Passover seder:

> If all you had done was to agree to be our adviser
> But not allowed us to share our writings,
> It would have been enough.
>
> If all you had done was to allow us to share our writing,
> But not quietly given suggestions for improvement,
> It would have been enough.
>
> If all you had given us were suggestions for improvement,
> But not have encouraged the group to respond,
> It would have been enough.
>
> If all you had done was to give us encouragement to respond,
> But not have given the writer the final word,
> It would have been enough.
>
> If all you had given the writer was the final word,
> But had not found us a reader,
> It would have been enough.
>
> If you had found us a reader,
> But just distributed her comments,
> It would have been enough.
>
> If you had distributed the reader's comments,
> But not worked with each of us to incorporate them into our writing,
> It would have been enough.
>
> If you had worked with each of us individually,
> But had not had us bring pictures and documents,
> It would have been enough.

But, Elaine, you did all of this and more. In the process you helped us become better writers and free ourselves from the trauma of our childhood. You helped us outgrow our tendency to remain silent. You did all of this in a gentle, respectful, and nonthreatening way. You allowed each of us to speak in our own voice so that the finished product was authentic and reflected our pain and growth. And from the beginning you knew exactly why our stories are worthy of preservation. You helped us make them live for our readers now and in the future.

—*Hidden Children/Child Survivors Chicago*

Introduction

Phyllis Lassner

"The Story of Adam Paluch" begins with the doubt that arises from a forgotten Holocaust past:

> My name is Adam Paluch, but it was not always so. There are those who say I was born in 1942; others say I was born in 1939. I am a strong, athletic male: a former part-time professional boxer and wrestler. But the paperwork says that I was a girl. I was taunted for being Jewish before I knew that I was Jewish. I was told that I am the child of a childless woman. I was told that my search for my identity was hopeless—that I was "digging in the ashes."

So a Jewish childhood is lost and as his search continues, a Polish man unearths his Jewish future.

Adam contributed a single story to this volume, but nine other authors wrote more than one story or poem. Their pieces appear in different chapters because the chapters are arranged thematically. Aaron Elster is one of these authors. Aaron ends his first story, "The Marketplace," with fear and hope: "My father grimly looks at me as he orders '*Loif, Arele, loif.*' Run, Aaron, run." So a childhood is lacerated and a child is saved from the Gestapo and its roundup of the Jews in Sokołów, Podłaski, Poland. Sometimes, as in Judith Levy Straus's story "My Grandfather's Watch," the facts are lost, but even the most fleeting feelings of parental love and anxiety can become indelibly shaping forces:

> It all started in 1938 or 1939. I cannot remember which. I was five or six years old—an only child—and we lived in Amsterdam, Holland. . . . There was tension in our house. My parents and uncle and some of their friends would gather in the living room to discuss "things," but the door was always closed. I did not know or understand what they were talking about; I just knew it did not feel good; it made me afraid.

The twenty-four child survivors who composed the stories and poems that comprise this anthology search for their childhoods as they write. What they find and transmit to us are the manifold forms and paths that memory and its language of expression take. No matter how partial, fragmented, and discontinuous, the memories encapsulated by these stories and poems create a graphic panorama of Holocaust experiences, responses, and memories. Altogether, this collection creates a chronicle of the survival of hidden children in Nazi-occupied Europe. I should say *survivals*—plural—because of their many types of hiding places and rescuers, the interspersed moments of deceptive calm, of authentic caring and cruelty, and of various risks, terrors, and hopes.

As the passage of time has created a sense of urgency about gathering Holocaust testimony from survivors, collective and individually written memoirs have proliferated along with audio and video testimony projects. Now that some video testimony archives have been digitized and acquired by university and Holocaust museum libraries, they are even more readily available. All these projects have proved significant to survivors and their families and communities as well as to scholars and teachers of the Holocaust. While historians have grappled with questions of authenticity, corroboration, and relationships to documented history, other scholars have studied the narrative forms and ethical and psychological issues that arise from close readings of the testimonies. Most scholars agree that even when testimony and memoirs fall short of precise historical validation, we learn a great deal about singular experience and responses from the survivors' struggle to tell their stories. We find distinctive voices and responses in survivors' chronological gaps, lapses of memory, inability to find the concrete language of expression, and other forms of narrative disruptions. In turn, as we respond to Holocaust representation, there is a mirroring effect in that we confront the problem of finding the language and forms in which to articulate our own struggle to understand experiences for which there are no analogies in our prior knowledge.

Out of Chaos: Hidden Children Remember the Holocaust was made possible by the incalculable support of Elaine Saphier Fox, who edited it as well. Elaine worked with Hidden Children/Child Survivors Chicago for several years, defining and enacting her role as encouraging members to write, develop, and revise their stories to create individual responses. This was not a simple or easy task, as issues of absent and painful memories often overwhelmed the desire to testify. As Elaine and the group persevered, as she guided it through revision after revision, each time adding graphic details and painfully visceral reactions, each writer found his or her way into and through the story that was waiting to be told. One of the great achievements of *Out of Chaos* is its sense of each writer's struggle with language and memory, features that comprise such an important part of the anthology's contribution to Holocaust representation and memorialization.

The anthology is exceptional for several important reasons. Unlike those composed of testimonies that are uniform in length, form, and focus, this anthology presents stories and poems constructed in a variety of forms, lengths, and narrative structures. The authors discover their individual voices and forms of expression in such genres as brief vignettes, tableaux, poems, stories, and an imagined dialogue between two lost mothers.

In all, the anthology expresses these survivors' memories and reactions to a wide range of experiences as they survived in so many European settings. The sites of their experiences range from Holland, Belgium, Italy, and Germany to Greece, Yugoslavia, Poland, and France. The writers recall being on the run between countries, escaping over mountains, hiding and even sometimes forgetting their Jewish identities in convents and rescuers' homes and hovels, basements, and attics. Some were left on their own; others found themselves embroiled in rescuer family conflicts. Each of these stories is complete in itself even as it represents brief or elongated moments, fragments of memory and experience—what the great Holocaust writer Ida Fink called *A Scrap of Time*. Some writers chose to write story clusters, each one capturing a moment or incident and often disconnected by memory or spatiotemporal divides. Some stories offer introductory contexts and footnotes to establish as precisely as the authors can the historical frameworks of their personal experiences and reactions, including the exact locations of their childhood homes in *shtetlach* and city neighborhoods that mark the writers' social class, religious observance, and affiliation. Whereas historical surveys overlook such details, the stories' evocations of home become symbols of personal and cultural identity, reminding us that survivors and their extended families once belonged to vibrant Jewish communities with rich cultural and social lives. If those places are gone, they have been restored to view in the affectionately conceived details of vivid writing.

Where memory permits, some stories recount defining moments of prewar life with family and community while other authors admit to the emptiness they feel at having no memory of that time before terror defined their lives. The occasional photographs of childhood places attest to the end of meaningful Jewish life when Poland was invaded on September 1, 1939. The stories and poems capture moments of anxiety, joy, relief, fear, disillusionment, and loss. Some authors have chosen to write about their lives after the Holocaust while others end their stories in moments of traumatic rupture, encounters with the unknown, and inexplicable occurrences and feelings. Connections between past and present register as life stories that defy all platitudes about "happily ever after." Instead, their individual responses reveal how the burdens of memory and loss affect the rich lives they all built in the aftermath. We see how memory and loss figure in the present in the stunning vignette "A Dog" by Ahlyce Goldman Kaplan, who narrates an event that takes place entirely in the present but, without any explicit reference, resonates with an impassioned Holocaust memory. One contribution, "A Passion to Tell" by Chaya Horowitz Roth, is an autobiographical essay that reflects on the transmission of Holocaust memory to the second and third generations while expressing how the process affected family relationships. Precisely because of this variety of perspectives, experiences, and responses, this anthology represents a rich, complex, and original contribution to the growing canon of Holocaust memoirs and testimony.

The anthology is organized thematically, according to the nature of the group's experiences: being on the run, hiding in plain sight, hiding with rescuer families, in convents, and with their own families, as well as in the concentration camps. Some recount less familiar events such as the Nazi invasion and occupation of Greece while others participate in those that are well known, such as the ghetto roundups. Each chapter shows how in many cases being on the run, hiding in plain sight, and being hidden overlap. But given the writers' distinctly constructed forms and voices, there is no repetition. Some poems speak directly to a reader in the present while others show the personal process of putting words to experiences that took place so long ago, oceans apart, and in another language. The poem that opens this anthology, "Child Survivors" by Marguerite Lederman Mishkin, creates a collective voice that responds defiantly to the sense that being hidden did not produce the suffering experienced by those in the concentration camps. Instead *Out of Chaos* becomes an ironic riposte to such doubt by including a searing list of hiding places in which the good luck of survival also meant a childhood of imprisonment. There is a startling sense in these poems and stories of retaining a sensory experience of personal self amid the vast unsettling terrain of the Holocaust and its memories. Altogether the anthology is a profound testament to lost and found lives that are translated into compelling reading.

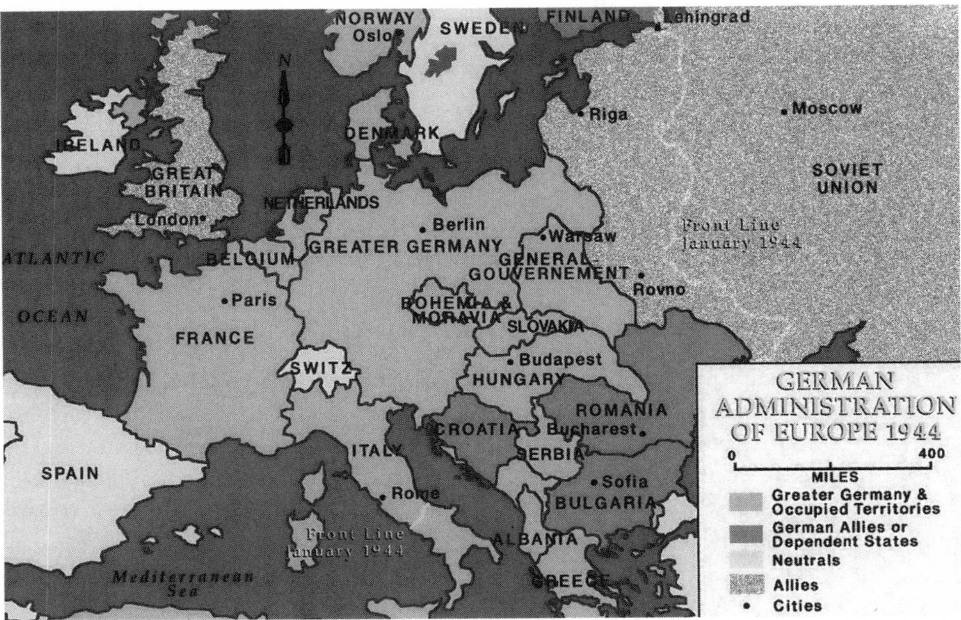

Figure 1. Map of the German administration of Europe in 1944.

OUT OF CHAOS

Child Survivors

Marguerite Lederman Mishkin

You say we are not survivors
We were not in a concentration camp
We were too young
We did not suffer
We did not understand
We don't remember
We were not affected
We are the lucky ones.

We hid in homes
We hid in convents
We hid in orphanages
We hid in basements
We hid in cellars
We hid in haystacks
We hid in barns
We hid in cabinets
We hid in fields
We hid in holes
We hid in sewers
Yet we were not in concentration camps.

We saw what no child should see
Our eyes betrayed us
We saw people wearing yellow stars
We saw people being killed
We saw people being humiliated
We saw people being beaten
We saw people being forced onto trains
We saw our parents being taken away
We sought to be invisible
We learned not to look and not to see
Yet we were too young.

We heard what no child should hear
Our ears betrayed us
We heard screams in the middle of the night
We heard screams of pain
We heard harsh words flung at us
We heard words of hatred

We heard words of disdain
We learned not to hear
We learned to scream in silence
Yet we did not suffer.

We learned to answer to foreign-sounding names
We unlearned our religion
We learned new customs
We learned to tolerate unknown food
We learned to pretend
We learned to deceive
We learned to be charlatans
We learned different ways of praying
We learned to call strangers by names reserved for family
We learned new languages
Yet we did not understand.

We felt abandoned
We felt unloved
We felt deserted
We felt unwanted
We felt we deserved what was happening to us
We felt stupid
We felt ugly
We felt dirty
We felt scared
We felt like damaged merchandise
We felt unready
We felt undeserving
We felt powerless
Yet we don't remember.

We lost our parents
We lost our relatives
We lost our religion
We lost our identity
We lost our innocence
We lost our childhood
We lost our security
We lost our trust
We lost our country
We lost our language
We lost our confidence
We lost our sense of self
Yet we were not affected.

In hunger we tasted our favorite food once again
In thirst we drank cool spring water
In rags we dressed in our finery
In cold we covered up with the feather bed that our mother had made
In loneliness we invented imaginary friends
In church we heard the Hebrew prayers
In boredom we read our most beloved books
In sadness we remembered joy
In drabness we envisioned beauty
In silence we heard music
In the air we wrote our life stories
In the depth of winter we planted spring flowers
In fear we felt our parents' love
In our time of need we learned to comfort ourselves
Yet we are the lucky ones.

We may not have been in a concentration camp
But we were not too young
To understand
To remember
To suffer
To grieve
To imagine
To be changed into strangers to our former selves
Lucky perhaps but
Transformed in the crucible
Of survival.

PART 1

In the Beginning

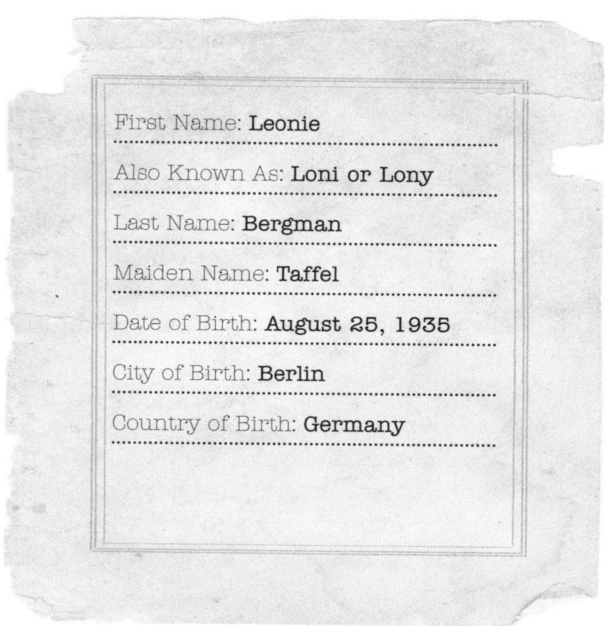
First Name: Leonie
Also Known As: Loni or Lony
Last Name: Bergman
Maiden Name: Taffel
Date of Birth: August 25, 1935
City of Birth: Berlin
Country of Birth: Germany

Earliest Memories: A Walk in the Park

Leonie Taffel Bergman

I am nearly three years old. It is a beautiful spring day in Berlin. My parents and I are taking a walk through the park close to our home, by Alexanderplatz. Many people are doing the same. It must be a Sunday, a day when people do not work and often look forward to that time for socializing, relaxing, and going visiting. The event—this walk—has an air of formality: an occasion to "look nice" in public. These walks are familiar to me.

Being the only child, I walk between my parents, holding the hand of each. There is talk between them, and I, as a child, also talk when I have some comment to make. I am careful when I speak: not in what I say but how I say it. I do not want to cause anything bad to happen.

Recently I have been warned by my parents not to speak Yiddish, the home language, when in public. It is dangerous to let others know that you speak that language. They may hurt us! I don't know why. It is only when I am with my parents that I can speak the way we speak at home. Wanting to be obedient, I try to be very careful.

Our promenade continues. People are sitting on benches, stopping and talking to those they greet, casually strolling. It is most pleasant. I continue to chat with my parents, in a low voice, using the home language.

I notice my shoelaces are untied. I let go of my parents' hands and stop to tie the laces. As I do so I look and see where my parents are and notice them walking ahead slowly. When I finish tying the shoe, I run forward, go between two sets of hands, and hold on to those hands. As we are walking I explain, in my nearly three-year-old way, what I was doing, using home language: "*mayn shikhele hot zikh ge-efnt*" (my shoe was open). I look at the hands I am safely holding. Suddenly, I look up at the faces that go with these hands. These people are not my parents!

I have a terrible sense of dread. I quickly let go and run to my parents, who are directly ahead. I fear for us—for me and for them. I have spoken Yiddish to strangers, and this will bring immediate danger to our family. I feel so scared.

In retrospect the whole episode with the strangers lasted such a short while, and they were probably surprised, pleasantly I expect, that a child should suddenly join them, and I had nothing to fear. Maybe they didn't even focus on what I was saying because little children often do not speak clearly; possibly they didn't distinguish between the sounds of German and Yiddish. Maybe they themselves were Jewish. These things I do not know.

But the fear I felt immediately, both of endangering my family and of having done something wrong, is still with me today, some seventy years later. I am often ready to blame my inability to foresee negative consequences that could occur when a serious event happens in my life. This might include a move, a change in family status, a serious medical situation. I will feel that if I had been more alert, I might have anticipated possible difficulties and therefore prevented, or lessened, them.

In August of that year, 1938, three days before my third birthday, we arrived in Brussels, Belgium, having left Berlin. I am unable to recall anything about that journey.

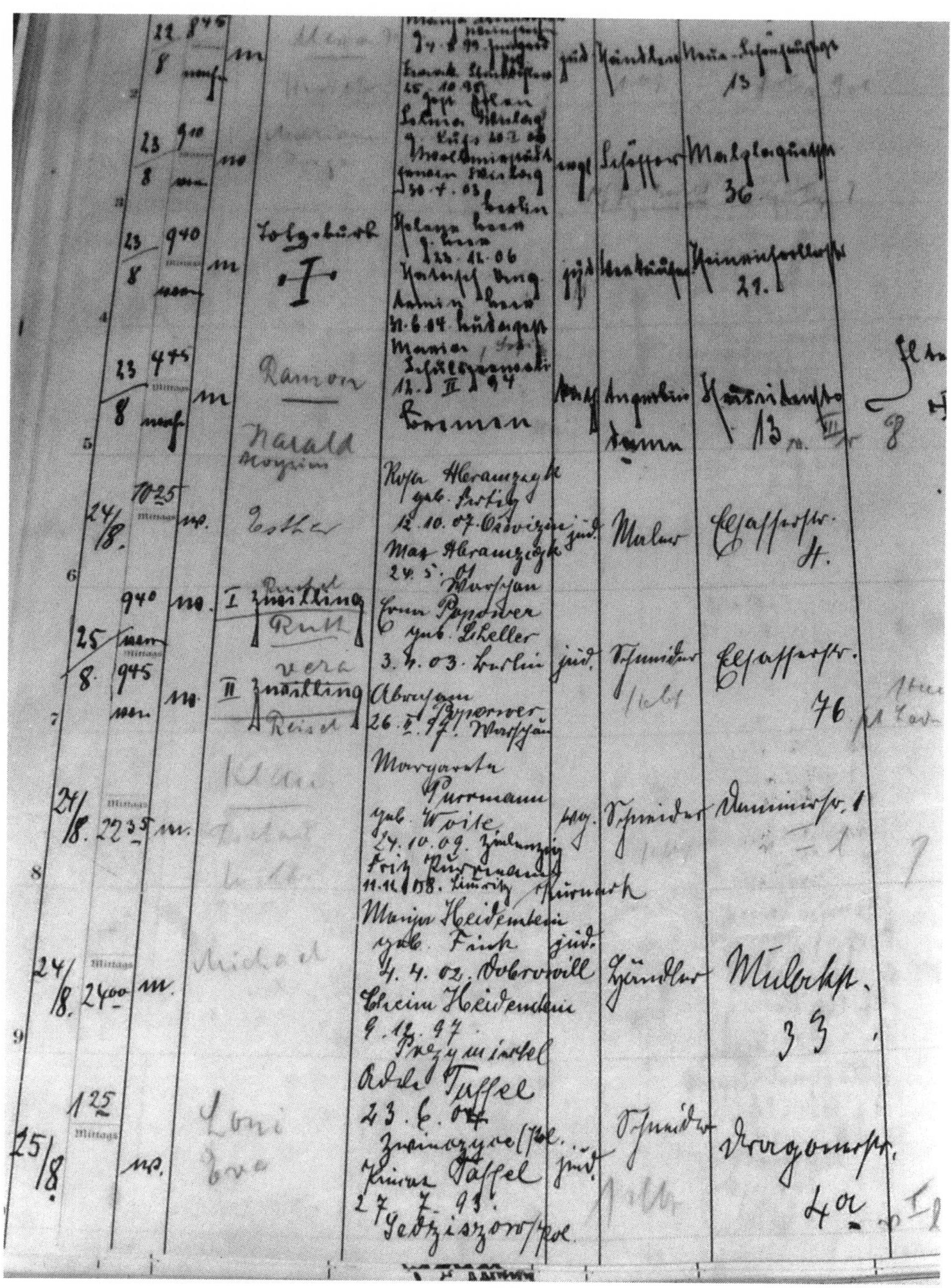

Figure 2. The last entry is Leonie Taffel's birth registration in Berlin, Germany, August 25, 1935.

First Name: **Chaya**

Also Known As: **Chayale, Helene Daveau, Elena Kantor**

Last Name: **Roth**

Maiden Name: **Horowitz**

Date of Birth: **September 30, 1934**

City of Birth: **Berlin**

Country of Birth: **Germany**

The Megillah: 1937

Chaya Horowitz Roth

You are with me still
My small hand melts in yours*
You reach for the drawer in the big brown buffet
And take out a shiny black tube
Unfurling the parchment you begin to chant.
I do not see the grogger
I do not know the story
Yet I remember well
The warmth of your enveloping hand . . .

*The author remembers standing with her father on the eve of the Purim holiday when she was three years old, holding his hand, not quite understanding the nature of the holiday; but she remembers her father, who would be brutally taken away three years thereafter.

Figure 3. Chaya and Gitta Horowitz's father, Aron Jakob Horowitz (1898–1939). He was born in Lucawicza, Poland.

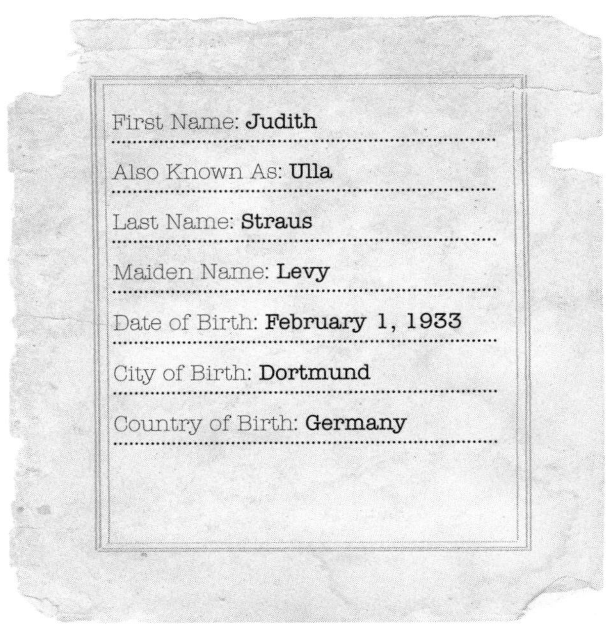
First Name: **Judith**
Also Known As: **Ulla**
Last Name: **Straus**
Maiden Name: **Levy**
Date of Birth: **February 1, 1933**
City of Birth: **Dortmund**
Country of Birth: **Germany**

My Grandfather's Watch

Judith Levy Straus

It all started in 1938 or 1939. I cannot remember which. I was five or six years old—an only child—and we lived in Amsterdam, Holland. "We" consisted of my parents, my uncle Ludwig Falkenstein (I called him Dada), and my grandfather Moses Falkenstein. Our home used to be in Germany, but in 1933, when Hitler came to power, my father was immediately dismissed from his position as an electrical engineer working for a government agency because he was Jewish. My parents and I moved to Holland, and my grandfather and uncle joined us in 1937 or 1938, just before the start of World War II, and two years before the Nazis invaded Holland.

There was tension in our house. My parents and uncle and some of their friends would gather in the living room to discuss "things," but the door was always closed. I did not know or understand what they were talking about; I just knew it did not feel good; it made me afraid. My grandfather was kept out of the living room discussions as well. Apparently he was too old, and I was too young. And so we kept each other company, my grandfather and I.

I would always feel better after sitting on his lap for a while. He told me stories, he let me comb his hair, and he would pull out his pocket watch. It was a very special watch—the most beautiful golden watch I had ever seen. It was a shiny, pinkish gold, and it had my grandfather's initials and the year 1900 engraved on its back. The face of the watch was covered by an exquisitely ornamented cover with a swirling floral design, and when you pushed a button, the cover would open and you could hear the "tic-toc, tic-toc"—so steady, so dependable—like a heartbeat. My grandfather would let me push the little button, and I would listen. And I would feel protected and at ease.

In March 1943, my grandfather was picked up by the Nazis and transported "east" to Sobibor, where he was murdered upon arrival. My uncle went into hiding—underground, and with him, it appears, went the watch. My father, David Levy, my mother, Alma Falkenstein Levy, and I were sent to Westerbork, a transit camp, where we stayed for a little over a year. From there we were transported to Theresienstadt. In September 1944, my father was sent from Theresienstadt to Auschwitz, where he was also murdered upon arrival. My mother and I survived.

My uncle survived the war, and so did the watch, and so did the memory of my grandfather and me sitting together and listening to its steady beat. The watch is now under a dome on one of my bookshelves. It is more than one hundred years old, and it still has a steady beat. And I still push the little button, and listen, and remember.

Figure 4. Judith Levy and her "Opa" (Grandfather) in Amsterdam, Holland, 1941.

The School Lessons

Leonie Taffel Bergman

I am in class. My desk is wood; it has an inkwell, and I am holding a pen over my penmanship book. The teacher is showing us, again, how to write our letters. "Make the circle; don't lift the pen; continue the circle and make it larger; it will turn into an oval; don't leave any spaces between the circle outlines." We are to measure carefully the ink on our points, shake off what is too much, and begin to form the shapes that she shows us. I try hard—but my pages are always messy. The teacher stands near me, corrects my hold on the pen, positions the notebook, and helps me form my letters. I hope for improvement, and so does she. After all, she has tried in her firmest, yet unorthodox, way to have me focus on improving my penmanship, and she expects it will now have had an effect on me. It does, but not what she had hoped for.

Not more than a few weeks earlier she had me stand on a table at the door where all the children were leaving to go home. I stood there, in full view of every student walking out of school, holding my penmanship book wide open so all the ink blotches and red marks could be seen by them. She hoped my embarrassment would force me to write better. It did not work. I was embarrassed, but my penmanship did not improve.

I am six years old in 1941, and in the first grade of a public elementary school in Schaerbeek, Brussels.

It is in this same classroom, some weeks later, on a typical school day, when another lesson is introduced. As the class is doing some reading work, a messenger comes in and confers with the teacher. After the messenger leaves, the teacher calls me to her desk. She tells me to take my things and put on my coat. I have to leave. My mother is coming to get me. After waiting for over an hour, ready to leave with my mother, I see another messenger come into the classroom. She approaches the teacher, and soon after the teacher tells me that it isn't necessary for me to leave. I do not know why this change occurs. The teacher seems relieved, though she never explains anything to me. The rest of the day does not seem unusual.

About a month later, with much more urgency, my teacher tells me to take all my belongings and to go to the principal's office immediately. I become very fearful at that news and at the rush and suddenness of this command. What will my mother think? Will I be able to go outside again? Or must I now stay shut in, within the limits of "safe walls"? What place is safe? Can I be told again to leave? I ask, but I do not know. I ask, but I cannot understand.

I was then taken home by someone. And that was the end of my public schooling for over four years.

Soon the years of hiding would begin.

Figure 5. Leonie Taffel and Chaya Horowitz in a first-grade classroom in Brussels, Belgium, 1941. Leonie is in the second row near the bookcase, with a bow in her hair. Chaya is to the left of the teacher in the back row. Photograph courtesy of Chaya Horowitz Roth.

PART 2

On the Run

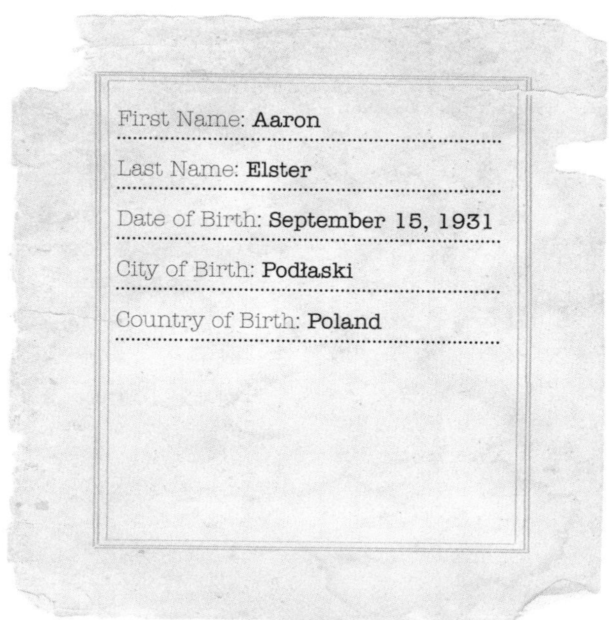
First Name: **Aaron**

Last Name: **Elster**

Date of Birth: **September 15, 1931**

City of Birth: **Podłaski**

Country of Birth: **Poland**

The Marketplace

Aaron Elster

My mother shakes me awake from a deep sleep and sternly orders me to dress in a hurry. I am confused and scared. Is this the day rumored about our death? The last few months neighbors sat around our kitchen table and talked about the gas chambers at Treblinka, our being deported there, and the certain death to follow. As a child, sitting on the floor listening and not able to participate in adult conversation about the death camp, I was afraid of dying a painful death. Fear takes hold of me. I silently beseech God to save me as we are being rushed into our hiding place on the first floor. To get there, we have to go upstairs and enter through a disguised covered opening and then climb down a ladder. Almost forty men, women, and children are prodded to hurry and descend the ladder down into a secret, small, empty room where we are all crushed against one another. The painted dark green window keeps anyone outside from seeing us in this room. Children cry, and mothers are urged to keep them quiet.

Ripping open our hiding place, the Gestapo and their collaborators find us. Screams and shootings force us out. They chase us up a small hill from Ulica Piękna toward the town's marketplace on Ulica Rogofska in Sokołów, Podłaski, about fifty miles east of Warsaw. Unable to keep up with the rest of us, our neighbor, the old tailor, falls to the cobblestones. The Ukrainian guard, a German collaborator, swings his rubber truncheon and begins pounding Shepsel the tailor about the head and body until he stops screaming. The smirking collaborator soon reappears in the marketplace. Once in the marketplace our whole group is forced to sit in a square facing a green-uniformed Gestapo officer pointing his automatic weapon at us, both the young and old. We are awaiting deportation in the cattle cars to Treblinka.

On this September day, the shining warm sun surrounded by bright blue skies and white clouds creates a painful dichotomy. I am horrified of my death in the gas chambers.

Bloody bodies from previous groups that were shot or beaten to death are still in the marketplace. An elderly woman lying in my line of sight has a blood-soaked dress that covers the lower part of her body. Old men reciting the *Shema* and praying to God for deliverance, the mournful cries of little children, the distraught mothers still clutching babies to their breasts, and the Gestapo's screams and beating of anyone not lined up to their exact specifications, all tell me these are my final hours. No one will come to our rescue. The Nazis have full power to kill us at will. Trembling overtakes me. I am terrified. I pray to God to spare me, but if he won't, I believe it is in his power to open this blood-soaked earth and swallow these murderers.

I look at my little sister Sarah, who clutches some dried farfel wrapped in a handkerchief in her little hand. Her eyes are ablaze with fear as she sits squeezed into my father's bosom. Father's hopeless look, gaunt face, and sad eyes express all that words could not.

My father grimly looks at me as he orders: "*Loif, Arele, loif.*" Run, Aaron, run.

Figure 6. Aaron Elster's father, Chaim Sruel, in Sokolów, Podłaski, Poland, 1940.

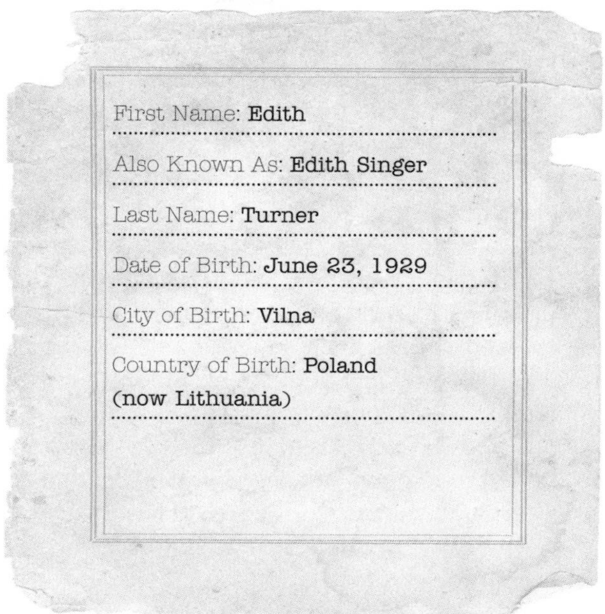
First Name: **Edith**

Also Known As: **Edith Singer**

Last Name: **Turner**

Date of Birth: **June 23, 1929**

City of Birth: **Vilna**

Country of Birth: **Poland (now Lithuania)**

Shema Yisrael

Edith Singer Turner

I was born in Vilna, Poland (now Vilnius, Lithuania), in 1929. I had a wonderful childhood surrounded by my family, good friends, and excellent schools. It all changed abruptly when I was ten years old. Germany attacked Poland in September 1939. Within two weeks, Poland lost the war. My father, Nachem Singer, had experience from the First World War, and he believed that it was safer to live in a small town during wartime. So we left our lovely home and the beautiful, cultural city of Vilna and moved to a small town called Święciany. Within a few weeks, Germany and the Soviet Union entered into an agreement whereby the Soviet Army occupied the eastern part of Poland. Święciany became part of the Soviet Lithuanian Republic.

On June 22, 1941, just before my twelfth birthday, the Germans attacked the Soviet Union. I remember the day when the German tanks entered and the soldiers wearing helmets marched in. It was a sunny June day, but to me it looked dark, like a black cloud descending on us. Shortly after, the Nazi terror began against the Jews.

Three months after the Germans invaded, the SS rounded up the entire Jewish population of our town and sent us to Poligon, which was an extermination site. Then the Germans moved Jews from small towns and villages to the Poligon Camp. There were about eight thousand Jews in the camp. Lithuanian police and SS surrounded and guarded the camp. Conditions were brutal. Men, women, and children were squeezed into three small barracks, practically one on top of the other. We had no food or water. The latrines were in front of the barracks. It was hot and the stench was terrible. If anyone tried to escape, they were shot on the spot.

My mother, Miriam Singer, was a nurse. She joined a few doctors and nurses who formed a semi-emergency tent to treat many injured and sick patients. Talking to several people, she learned that the Lithuanian commandant could be bribed, and she found a man who knew him. During the roundup, she gave this man a diamond ring, earrings, and a beautiful gold watch surrounded with diamonds to bribe the commandant to let us go. The commandant believed that sooner or later we would be caught, so he let us go. My parents, sister Alice, fifteen years old, and I escaped with four more people, who my mother claimed were our family. They ran in a different direction, and we never saw them again. A couple hours after we had escaped, the Germans shot and killed all eight thousand Jews.

After walking all night, we hid in the barn of decent Christians, the Mishkela family. They kept us for four weeks, but we had to leave because it was too dangerous for the Mishkelas to hide Jews. Not knowing which place would be safer for us, we left to join my father's family in Głębokie, Poland (now in Belarus). The trip to Głębokie was frightening and exhausting. Avoiding SS and police stations near the town of Postawy in Belarus, the wonderful Mr. Mishkela and his son Juzek led the way. It took us four cold November nights. I was scared walking in the dark and hearing dogs barking. We carried bread, water, and cooked potatoes. Mr. Mishkela brought us to the home of his reliable Christian friends who allowed us to rest near the warm oven, and they gave us hot soup.

As soon as we got to Głębokie, the Gestapo forced the Jewish population to give up their homes and move into a small, crowded area of the town, which became the Głębokie Ghetto. An electrified fence with a big iron gate surrounded the ghetto, guarded by Germans, local police, and German shepherds. The Gestapo counted the Jews, who worked as forced laborers for the German Army, as the Jews went in and out of the ghetto.

In the summer of 1942, a tragic massacre took place in the ghetto. The SS divided the ghetto into two parts; one was for the older people and the other for the younger people who were assigned to work and carried colored work permits indicating the importance of their job. My paternal grandparents, Sarah and Yirmiyahu Singer, were forced to move to Ghetto Number One. My unmarried Uncle Mula decided to move in with them. I felt bad and guilty about this separation from my grandparents and uncle. We were forcibly separated and couldn't do anything about it.

The SS and the local Belarus police entered the two ghettos. They forced all the older people out of their homes. In the second ghetto, where I was, they took two thousand young Jews, whose work they considered less important, out of their homes. We learned from the few people who had escaped that they marched the Jews to a nearby forest called Borok. They forced them to undress and to dig their own graves, and shot them dead. My father, mother, sister Alice, and I hid in a cellar for two days. When we came out from hiding, we realized that more than half of the people who lived in the two ghettos were still alive. A Belarus policeman told my Aunt Cyla that Uncle Mula, who was a very strong man, was forced to take the old, sick people off the wagons and carry them to their grave. He was the last to be shot.

I was devastated—emotionally drained by this tragedy. I was always frightened and feared that someday I would be shot in the back. My father kept telling us to run if we got surrounded by SS or police, as this may give us a chance to escape.

During the years in the Głębokie Ghetto, my father was forced to work in a wool factory for the German Army. Sometimes he was sent to load heavy sacks of flour, coal, or timber on army trains. The Germans forced Alice to work in the marmalade factory. Mother and I were ordered to work in the gardens and hothouses for the Nazi governor on the outskirts of Głębokie. I had to learn how to work in gardens because, before the war, I just went to school, studied French privately, and took ballet lessons. I was not used to manual labor; however, it was a question of survival. Each day someone was shot and killed. All I could think about was how not to get killed.

In March 1943, we heard rumors that SS commandos would be coming by train to liquidate the Głębokie Ghetto. It was unlikely that we would survive the second round of killings. While we were in the ghetto, my father had contacted some young Jewish people who had organized themselves in a group. They sought to establish contacts with Russian partisans to help them fight the Nazis in this area. The partisans hid deep in the Belarus forests and were difficult to find. We were lucky that my father had been in the lumber business before the war. Therefore, he was familiar with the surrounding forests. He offered to take the young people to the partisans, provided that our entire family came along. The young men reluctantly agreed, and a plan was made.

We were part of the group that worked outside the ghetto. Our work took us to different places. On the day of our planned escape, instead of returning from work to the ghetto, we left our separate workplaces, met at a preappointed spot, and removed our identifying yellow Jewish star from our coats. Removing the Jewish star was risky and punishable by death. The preappointed meeting spot was the house far beyond town where Jews, including my mother and I, worked in gardens and hothouses for the *Gebitskommissar* (governor). He liked to have fresh vegetables and fruit for his table. We hid there in the bushes until nightfall. Late at night we all started to run toward the woods, but police saw us and started shooting. We escaped.

During the day, we hid in small forests to avoid the Germans and the local police. We slept on wet ground. One of us would go to local farmers and beg for food. We walked at night. After a few nights' walking, we suddenly came upon a large lake near the village of Nieviery in Belarus that we had to cross. My father, the leader of our group, organized the crossing. A small dinghy that was taking on water was at the shore. It could accommodate only three people at a time. Because the Germans and Belarus police were close by, we had to move fast and quietly.

My father went back and forth helping people across the lake. I remember crossing with my mother and my sister Alice. It was in March 1943, a cold and dark night. We held each other, shivering. Uncle Moshe and my Aunt Chana Mirman were the last people to cross. We knew that they could not swim. I can still see my father in his brown sheepskin jacket as he accompanied them. As they started to cross, the boat took on water and started to sink. It turned over. My uncle and aunt fell into the water and started to drown. As he felt he was going under, my Uncle Moshe, a religious man, cried out, "*Shema Yisrael . . .*" (Hear O Israel, the Lord our God, the Lord is one). It is one of our most important Jewish prayers.

My feeling was of despair. We came so far. We escaped the massacres in the ghettos. We walked days and nights in the cold, always afraid that the Gestapo or police would find and shoot us. Now that we were almost at the destination where we might find the partisans, we would be caught. But my father was a good swimmer and a quick thinker.

Seeing that they were frantic, he quickly swam toward them. He pulled them out of the water and swam with them to shore.

Every time I attend services at my synagogue and I recite the *Shema,* the whole scene is before my eyes, and shivers run down my spine.

Figure 7. Edith Singer's family at dinner in their home, Vilna, Poland, 1934 or 1935.

Figure 8. The Singer family at their summer home in Podbrodie, Poland, 1939.

Figure 9. Edith Singer, *second from left, with the yellow star on her coat,* and other members of her family in the Głębokie Ghetto in Poland, working for the German *Gebitskommissar* in a hothouse garden, 1943.

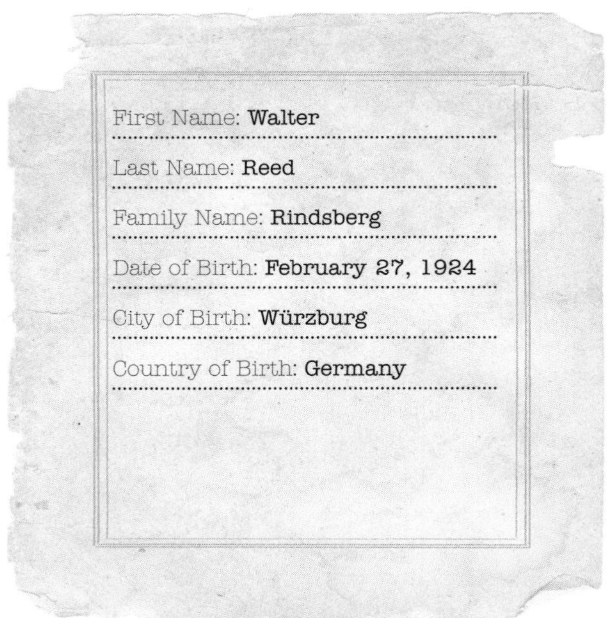
First Name: **Walter**
Last Name: **Reed**
Family Name: **Rindsberg**
Date of Birth: **February 27, 1924**
City of Birth: **Würzburg**
Country of Birth: **Germany**

A Holocaust Composite

Walter Reed

November 10, 1938

In the northern Bavarian village of Mainstockheim the signs of winter approaching were everywhere. On the hillside behind the village of 1,050 inhabitants the leaves in the vineyards had turned color and began to fall. The grapes had been harvested several weeks before.

In the early morning hours not many people were on the cobblestone streets. It could have been an ordinary fall day.

But at about seven A.M. a commotion occurred in front of the Rindsbergs' house (No. 58) and then shouts of "*raus, raus,*" "get out!!" When my father, Siegfried Rindsberg, looked out from his second-floor window, he saw a truck and a group of shouting brown-shirted SA thugs, and they were knocking loudly on our front door.

They shouted that he and his fourteen-year-old son Werner (that's me) needed to come out "and we mean now!"

I really don't remember, seventy years later, who the SA men were or who else was already on their truck. But for more than six years we had often watched SA men march through our village streets shouting antisemitic slogans and scaring young boys like me. The occupants of the truck were all the other Jewish men from our village. Where were they taking us and what was the reason, of course, was uppermost in my mind. And even more, what would they do—beat us, kill us? And why? They gave no explanation, but their hostile demeanor was not reassuring, to say the least.

The truck soon delivered us all to the county jail in Kitzingen, three kilometers away. There we found other Jewish men (and one other boy like me) from the villages and towns of the whole area. We still didn't know what triggered their frightening hostility or what might be in store for us. Nor did we know that the Kitzingen synagogue, just three blocks away from the jail, was then going up in flames.

The label "Kristallnacht" was invented much later to describe in a single word, quite inadequately, what was happening to us that morning. We had no idea that our arrest and treatment were inflicted on thirty thousand other German and Austrian Jewish men that day and that some one thousand other synagogues all over Germany and Austria were being desecrated and burned down by Nazi thugs. Even today it is unthinkable that these atrocities could have happened in the land of Beethoven, Brahms, and Goethe.

After two nights in the jail, overcrowded with frightened Jewish men, I was sent home to my mother and two younger brothers Herbert and Kurt. Apparently children should not have been arrested. It took quite a while before we became aware that the same type of atrocity had been organized from the top of the Nazi regime all over Germany and Austria in a trumped-up retaliation for the murder of a German diplomat in Paris by a Jewish teenager.

In fact, what was happening elsewhere was overshadowed by the rumor that our beloved father, Siegfried, may have been transferred from the jail in Kitzingen to the feared Dachau Concentration Camp. Indeed he was, along with many of the other Jewish men from our area and thirty thousand other Jewish victims from the entire country who were deported to various places similar to Dachau.

Fortunately, I do not remember the anguish over the treatment and fate of our father and can now only imagine my mother's fear and terror. After all, none of the Jewish men so incarcerated had committed any crimes or offenses. In my father's case, he was very popular in our village, had cofounded the local adult soccer club in the 1920s, and served as its treasurer for a number of years.

After about five weeks at Dachau he was released and returned home, hardly recognizable. He looked about twenty years older, had suffered jaundice, and was still visibly ill. When we asked him about Dachau, he replied that it was made clear to him that if he ever talked about it, he would be brought back for an even longer stay. Although he didn't talk, his gaunt face and sunken eyes told their own story.

It is interesting to note that I can write this story today only because my father had been incarcerated in Dachau. In fact, I believe that if he had not experienced Dachau, I would not have survived the war.

The events of Kristallnacht and my parents' traumatic experiences drove them to the probably heart-wrenching decision to send me away to save my life. It seems that they had learned that a rescue committee in Belgium was accepting young Jewish children from Germany and Austria. So they applied and sent me off to Brussels in June 1939, at age fifteen. Thanks, so to speak, to Kristallnacht and Dachau, I was able to escape the Nazi death machine. Unfortunately, my parents and brothers became their victims three years later.

May 10, 1940

It was late spring in Brussels and the sun rose early for what would be a very pleasant day at the Home Speyer, an orphanage for some fifty Jewish refugee boys who had been able to flee from Germany and Austria following Kristallnacht. But by the time we came down to breakfast, the sound of airplanes overhead (not common in those days) got everyone's attention. They were German reconnaissance and bomber planes, and the radio soon brought word that the Nazis had invaded Belgium, Holland, Luxembourg, and France.

For all the populations of these northwestern European countries this was frightening news because many remembered the horror of World War I in their home areas, a little over twenty years before. For the boys at Home Speyer it was even more upsetting, for all of us had successfully escaped the Nazi persecution in Germany and Austria the year before, thanks to the Belgian rescue committee that gained our admission to Belgium and took care of us at Home Speyer and at various other locations.

The group of about fifty boys at Home Speyer were all under seventeen years old, some as young as five. We older boys were the most anxious because we knew what was in store for us.

Four days after the Germans invaded, and forty-eight hours before they entered Brussels, the rescue committee members and the adult staff leaders of Home Speyer and of a separate Jewish refugee girls' home managed to squeeze ninety-three of us onto two cars of a refugee freight train. More than a million frightened citizens were streaming south, and to find space for all ninety-three of us on one of the scarce trains was yet another fortunate circumstance at a frightening time.

Our train departed during the night of May 14 and seemed to meander aimlessly all over northern and northwestern France to an unknown destination. Our freight train made many stops, but no one knew where we were headed or, more important, where the Germans were and whether they had been repulsed, a fervent but unrealistic hope, as it turned out.

After we had spent four days and nights lumbering all over northwestern and central France on the seemingly aimless freight train, it halted in Toulouse and went on to a tiny rural station, some eighty miles from the Spanish border. All the roads and means of transportation going south were jammed with over one million refugees. There we were unloaded and taken to one of the more remote rural spots in southern France, a village called Seyre, which then had fewer than fifty farm family inhabitants. It turns out that the French government, expecting the possibility of war and fleeing populations from the north, had designated certain facilities for refugees, if such a spontaneous mass evacuation should occur.

This is how our group of Jewish refugee children came to live in a large barn building in Seyre. There were no beds, no running water, no toilets, no kitchen, and nearly one hundred boys and girls aged six through seventeen. It was like a primitive summer camp, but it was forever. Our Belgian adult leaders organized the colony as best they could, with the older boys and girls "managing" the younger ones at play and, in improvised classes, teaching them math and French. Best of all, the remote village location gave us a sense of security when the new Vichy French government began to decree antisemitic Jewish laws and regulations.

Conditions were very harsh (there was no heat in the cold winter), food was scarce, and soon lice and infections made life uncomfortable for all—but we had all escaped Nazi persecution for a second time.

Fall 1940–June 1945

Much has been said and written about the "bad Swiss" in connection with the Holocaust. Fortunately for me, and for our entire children's refugee colony, the "good Swiss" came to the rescue in many ways and under great danger to themselves. They saved many of our lives.

By the fall of 1940, one of our Belgian committee rescuers, who had also fled to Vichy France with her husband, connected our refugee colony with the leaders of the *Secours Suisse aux Enfants* (Swiss Aid to Children), which assisted many victims interned in Vichy France camps and managed other children's colonies there.

Through the Swiss caretakers our colony obtained blankets, powdered milk, Swiss cheese, and Swiss staff leaders, an important advantage over the existing Jewish personnel in an increasingly anti-Jewish Vichy regime willing to collaborate with the Nazis. Because Switzerland remained neutral throughout the war, their young leaders at our colony had more influence with the Vichy authorities than did our Jewish caretakers from Belgium. The Swiss staff also connected most of us with Swiss wartime godparents who sent mail and packages to their selected children at our colony.

After the difficult months of the severe 1940 winter, the *Secours Suisse* rented an abandoned château closer to the Spanish border and moved our colony there in the spring of 1941. It was called the Château de La Hille, and from then on the colony became known as the Children of La Hille. At La Hille, young Swiss caretakers supplemented and then replaced the management personnel who had brought us from Belgium.

By the summer of 1942, the Nazi "Final Solution" had encompassed France, and the big roundup in Vichy France brought thousands of Jewish victims to internment camps and then to Drancy near Paris for deportation to the murder camps in Poland.

A year later, after I had left for the United States, forty La Hille boys and girls, then above the age of seventeen, and several adult Jewish personnel were arrested and brought to the Le Vernet assembly camp from which all Jewish prisoners were sent north and then to the gas chambers.

Maurice Dubois, the Swiss director of *Secours Suisse* in Vichy France, succeeded in lobbying the top officials in Vichy to release all the La Hille children and adults and brought them back to La Hille. All other inmates were deported.

When the Germans occupied all of France in November 1942 and intensified the hunt for Jewish victims, their Swiss caretakers encouraged and assisted many of the La Hille teenagers in saving themselves by crossing the Swiss and Spanish borders illegally, always with the help of their Swiss leaders. Several were dismissed by their superiors in Bern who opposed their rescue efforts.

At least five of the Swiss La Hille supporters were later honored as "Righteous Among the Nations" at Yad Vashem. Fortunately, I had been able to obtain a USA visa in mid-1941 and was already safely in New York when these events of 1942–43 occurred. Incidentally, many of my companions had relatives in the United States who had provided guaranties for their U.S. visa applications. Only a few were granted a visa, and I have never learned how I became one of the lucky recipients.

July 1945

The war against Germany had ended in May 1945, and I found myself, now a staff sergeant in Military Intelligence of the U.S. Army, in northern Germany. It was more a time of relief that three years in the wartime military were over than euphoria over having defeated the Nazis.

But the lack of information about the fate of my family, last heard from in Mainstockheim in 1941, prompted me to drive a jeep back to my home village as soon as I could obtain permission from my company officer. Now it was not the teenage Jewish Werner Rindsberg coming to question the villagers but Staff Sergeant Walter Reed, U.S. Army—in uniform, wearing a steel helmet, and carrying a carbine slung over my shoulder, driving a jeep. (I had changed my name when I became a U.S. citizen in 1943. I decided to change my name to sound more American but keep the initials of my former name. It was purely a coincidence that I chose the name of a famous army surgeon.)

Having considerable experience in interrogating German prisoners at the front, my main assignment as a GI, I did not hesitate to question the village residents about the fate of my family and that of other Jewish former residents. (I had left at age fifteen and was now an adult aged twenty-one, so I probably was not remembered by many.)

The best I could determine from local residents at that time was that my parents and brothers "had been sent to the east several years before, to a labor camp." That was the Nazi fiction, which they were telling the victims and also the German population. The locals were telling me that, and I believe that was all they knew because at that time the Nazis had kept the deportations and destinations secret. Of course, their relatives had not been sent away, though many of them were killed or wounded in the conflagrations ignited by their government all over Europe and in North Africa.

It was much later that I learned all the gruesome details. Siegfried, Rika, Herbert, and Kurt Rindsberg were assembled in nearby Kitzingen on March 23, 1942, and, with more than a thousand other Jewish German residents of that region, they were sent to Izbica near Lublin, Poland. Their traceable fate ends there, but they were all murdered in gas chambers either in nearby Belzec or in Sobibor, probably in 1942.

June 2007

If closure were possible, it would have come that month. But closure is neither needed nor possible.

In early 2007 one of the many friends my family and I have today in my original home area notified us that local German government officials, including mayors and town council members, were planning a journey of commemoration in honor of all the Nazi victims from their area and would place a memorial monument in a public square in Izbica, Poland, the victims' last known internment place in 1942.

This is how it happened that I, my wife, Jeanne, and our son Andrew accompanied fifty-five German officials, plus twenty-five high school students, all from my home region in Bavaria, on a commemorative journey of five days to the last known place of "residence" of my family and their fellow victims. During this pilgrimage with German citizens, whom we had already met in recent years, we became friends. We are now close and value them as personal friends.

I was asked to speak at the unveiling of the monument, as did other leaders of the pilgrimage. I believe that a copy of my remarks on that occasion may be a suitable conclusion to this review of my Holocaust experiences.

Here is the text:

> Permit me to express my personal feelings at this place—a place so saddening for so many innocent human beings.
>
> Not many weeks before the German domination of Poland in the month of September 1939, my parents had sent me to Belgium in order to save my life. Only because of their courageous decision and a foreboding of what was to come am I not among those whom you are honoring and commemorating here today.
>
> I heard the name "Izbica" for the first time in the month of July 1945. It was then that I returned to Lower Franconia as an American soldier, and the inhabitants of Kitzingen and the nearby area responded to my search for my parents and two brothers with the statement that all the Jewish residents had been sent to work camps in the east two or three years earlier. That was the lie told by the Nazis, and the local population believed that lie.
>
> I still have here the notebook in which I wrote the following information at that time: "Izbica a/w Block III/435, District Lublin." That, apparently, was the "work camp." It was much later that I learned the true and so horrible story of what was really going on here.
>
> This real story means that my dear parents would never get to know their daughter-in-law Jeanne, nor their three grandsons, among whom Andrew is here with us today.
>
> We have come together here today to recall these inhuman misdeeds and to honor the memory of the poor victims. I would like to emphasize that in this place it was not thousands of innocent victims who were

tormented and murdered. No, they were INDIVIDUALS—each with the right to have a good life; they were fathers, mothers, grandparents, and many young children. And what was probably even far worse—these human beings were hated, slandered, and tormented for nine years in their Franconian homeland before the so-called Final Solution.

The German government had offered me restitution, as it did to all other Holocaust survivors. Naturally, many accepted that offer and they surely are entitled to it. [This statement as used in the speech is incorrect. Restitution had to be requested and often required lengthy negotiations by the survivors.]

I, however, declined this restitution. For the only thing that I *wanted* to obtain was the return of my parents and of my two brothers—and that even the German government could not accomplish.

Also I had never wanted to come here, for that too would not bring about the impossible restitution of my murdered family. But when I learned from our friend Dr. Schwinger of your intention to gather here

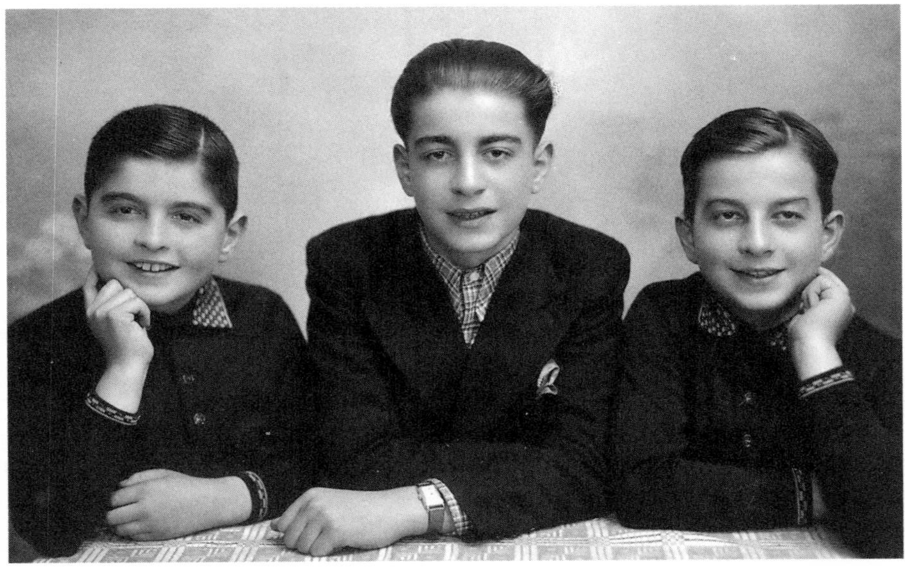

Figure 10. Werner Rindsberg (later called Walter Reed), *center*, and brothers Kurt and Herbert, Germany, about 1934. Both brothers were murdered in Poland in 1942.

Figure 11. Werner Rindsberg (later Walter Reed), *front left,* with older boys at La Hille, a children's refugee colony in France, 1941.

Figure 12. United States Army Sergeant Walter Reed at Ameln (near Aachen), western Germany, with the Ninety-Fifth Infantry Division, early 1945.

for this tribute, we decided immediately that we needed to join you for this occasion.

What are my thoughts and feelings at this emotion-filled place?

Forget—That is impossible and we MUST not forget.

Understand—That we must attempt, though it is not easy to do so.

Forgive—That is impossible, for what occurred here is unforgivable.

Reconcile—That is exactly why we are gathered here and we must indeed do so; otherwise no hope would remain.

Honor the victims—That we wish to do, and not only the six million murdered Jewish people but also the millions of German and Allied soldiers, as well as the many millions of the civilian population throughout Europe who fell victim to the lunatic and inhuman vision for a "thousand-year empire."

Regrettably the unfortunate human beings from Franconia and all the other fellow sufferers of this dreadful time will not be able to be comforted by your love and by your sympathy for them. But for all of us, and especially for the young people of Germany and of Poland, the fact that you are gathered here today gives hope and a truly meaningful "restitution."

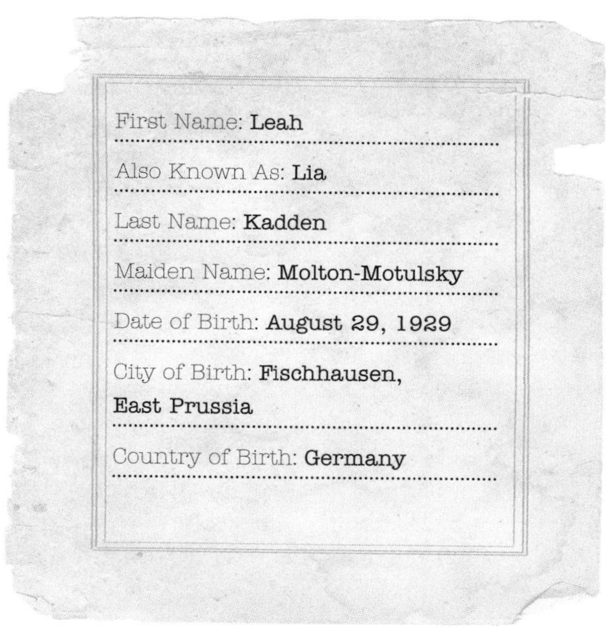
First Name: **Leah**

Also Known As: **Lia**

Last Name: **Kadden**

Maiden Name: **Molton-Motulsky**

Date of Birth: **August 29, 1929**

City of Birth: **Fischhausen, East Prussia**

Country of Birth: **Germany**

My Voyage on the SS *St. Louis* and After

Leah Molton-Motulsky Kadden

I was born on August 29, 1929, the youngest of three children in Fischhausen, East Prussia. My parents owned a dry-goods store that my paternal grandfather had established. Few Jews lived in this small town of about six thousand inhabitants. There was no synagogue. My parents, observant Jews, kept a kosher home. In 1933, a religious teacher came to our house weekly to teach my brothers, Arno, ten years old, and Lothar, seven years old. Because I was only four, I had no religious instruction.

In 1933, the Nazis came to power and anti-Jewish incidents occurred. Our store windows were smeared with swastikas. By 1937, the Germans gave my father's business and property to a German Christian. My parents were able to keep their personal property. My paternal uncle had immigrated to Chicago two years earlier, and we had hoped to join the family there. Intending to immigrate to the United States, my parents moved to a large apartment at 39 Hegestrasse in the port city of Hamburg, where we lived for two years. My paternal grandfather came to live with us there. But in August 1938, the Germans arrested my father and sent him to Sachsenhausen, a concentration camp thirty-five kilometers north of Berlin. By then the Nazi policy sought to create a Germany that was *Judenrein,* free of Jews—let Jews leave Germany but never return.

Our relatives in the United States arranged to get my father out of Germany, but only Cuba was open to immigrants at that time. He received a visa to Cuba with the condition that he never return to Germany. In November 1938, my father arrived in Havana. Due to the restrictive United States immigration policies that prevented us from getting to the States immediately and our fear of the war, my family decided to join my father in Cuba. He was able to secure Cuban landing permits for my mother, my fifteen-year-old brother Arno and twelve-year-old brother Lothar, and me. I was nine when we boarded the ship.

The Hamburg America Hapag Line advertised that passage could be booked for Cuba. My mother told us later that she paid for four passages and also had to pay an additional sum, a contingency fee, fully refundable, that might cover a return voyage to Germany should unforeseen circumstances arise.

I don't remember much about leaving our apartment in Hamburg and boarding the ship. Life on the ship was a real joy for all the passengers after leaving Hamburg harbor. I do remember a magnificent, large dining room that was also used to show movies. I had never seen a movie. I saw Nelson Eddy and Jeanette MacDonald in the musical *Maytime*. To this day, I can still see the beautiful blonde in a white fluffy dress singing the high coloratura songs. I remember learning to swim in the little swimming pool on deck. There were organized play activities for children as well, but I don't remember them.

I do remember my mother insisting that we do English lessons together every day. We sat on the ship's deck. Mother would read me German words, and I would copy them from an English dictionary into a small notebook. I felt quite proud to have had this advantage over my brothers. Not long ago, I found this notebook of my daily vocabulary lessons among my mother's papers.

Although I was unaware of it at the time, but learned years later, an internal power play was taking place in the Cuban government. A Cuban immigration officer, Manuel Benitez, had sold the landing certificates to the Hapag Line manager in Hamburg and had made a fortune for himself. He failed to inform any other government officials. He did not support the current Cuban president, Laredo Brú. A week before our ship sailed, Brú had issued an order invalidating all of Benitez's landing certificates. The decree stipulated that only with written authorization from the secretaries of State and Labor and a $500 bond would Cuba accept refugees.

The SS *St. Louis* pulled into Havana Harbor on May 27, 1939, with horns blasting at four A.M. We passengers awoke and had breakfast by 4:30. By daylight, however, passengers on deck became aware that something was wrong. The ship was still in the harbor and had not tied up at the dock. The next day, Captain Schroeder received a cable from the Hapag Line representative in Havana. The cable instructed him not to come alongside. President Brú stood firm behind his decree and made it plain to the Hamburg authorities. Various officials, including Milton Goldsmith of the Havana Jewish Relief Committee, Captain Schroeder, the Hapag Line director, and the Cuban officials, tried to negotiate, but President Brú refused. The landing certificates were invalid and passengers could not set foot in Havana. There were twenty-eight passengers who had the required, valid entry papers and were allowed to disembark. Nine hundred and nine passengers were left on board. While the ship was anchored outside the harbor, I and the other hundreds of passengers were crowded on the deck.

Many small boats surrounded our ship. My father had rented one. Passengers crowded on deck and shouted greetings to their relatives down in the little rowboats in the water alongside. One day I went to our cabin and looked through the open porthole and waved to him. I was excited to see him waving back at me.

Spending several days in the harbor, we passengers were not given any information as to why we could not land. The officials answered our questions about when we could land with the routine answer, *mañana,* tomorrow. As the ship remained anchored in the harbor, passengers became anxious. One afternoon, a passenger, afraid to be sent back to Germany, stood at the ship's railing, slashed his wrists, and jumped overboard. He was immediately rescued by an SS *St. Louis* sailor and was taken to a Havana hospital where he recuperated and remained in Cuba.

Various international reporters had come to Havana to report on the ship's arrival and the refugees' plight. On Friday, June 2, I heard over the loudspeaker that Milton Goldsmith came aboard to assure us that everything possible was being done to let us disembark. Years later when I read Arthur Morse's book *While Six Million Died,* I learned *St. Louis* Captain Schroeder did not want to take us back to Germany because he knew what fate awaited us. There was no change. Goldsmith returned to his office. The next four days, the ship treaded water between Cuba and Florida, twice sailing so close to the American mainland that we could see the Miami skyline.

I cannot recall the somber and anxious mood of the passengers after it was announced that we could not land in Havana, nor can I recall my reaction to this news. My mother did not talk to me about why we could not land, and my brothers didn't include me in their conversations. During that time, I participated in shipboard activities for children. Swimming lessons were given in the small swimming pool where I had learned how to swim. We played games, and I was part of a small group who played together.

On June 3, President Brú allowed the ship to land if the Joint Distribution Committee would post a bond of $500 per passenger, a total of $453,500. On June 4, the JDC made a counteroffer, but by June 6 the Cuban government declared the negotiations for the passengers terminated. The only hope left for us was the United States, but that was not to be.

On June 6, Captain Schroeder received a cable ordering him to return to Hamburg immediately. In the meantime, the JDC European director, Morris Troper, was able to persuade first Belgium, then France, Holland, and England each to take a percentage of the ship's refugees. England's acceptance was, in part, brokered by Joseph P. Kennedy, the American ambassador to England.

A week after the *St. Louis* had headed back and exactly a month since leaving Hamburg, Troper cabled the ship from Paris with the news that arrangements had been completed. The Belgian, French, Dutch, and English governments had agreed to accept the Jewish refugees and that everything possible was being done to keep us safe.

We sailed into the estuary leading to Antwerp, Belgium, on Saturday, June 17. After nine in the morning, Troper and representatives of the four countries took a tugboat to our ship. A line of children, including me, were waiting to greet Troper.

One little girl, who was celebrating her eleventh birthday that day, thanked him and said, “We thank you with all our hearts. I am sorry that flowers do not grow on ships, otherwise, we would have given you the largest and most beautiful bouquet ever.” A crowd of passengers moved to shake the man’s hand. In the ship’s social hall Troper and his colleagues decided which passengers would go to which country. England had agreed to take 288, France 224, Belgium 214, and Holland 181.

After the SS *St. Louis* landed in Antwerp, Belgium, JDC representatives met us and put us on a train destined for Brussels. There, again, the JDC looked after us and had arranged to move us into a small apartment and provided us with food. The JDC continued to give us financial support. Hebrew Immigrant Aid Society (HIAS) provided a weekly stipend of American money for spending. During the next year, my brothers and I attended school. I attended the École Publique numéro 2 for one year. Here for the first time I was bullied because I was German and not because I was Jewish. I don’t know where my brothers went to school. My mother made every effort to obtain immigration visas to the United States. In March 1940, our visas arrived, and we only had to book passage on a ship.

Then came May 10, 1940. The Germans invaded Belgium. Very early in the morning I awoke to loud noises. Airplanes were zooming over our houses. I could see them flying in formation. I remember my brother Arno sitting in an armchair reading the newspaper, which said that the Belgian authorities issued a proclamation that all German nationals would be arrested. Arno, age seventeen, told my mother to pack some clothes for us in a suitcase in case we would be arrested by Belgian police. A few hours later, a local policeman rang our doorbell and told us to come with him. Following him, he took us to the same local school that I had attended and brought us to a large hall filled with many people standing. The school was an assembly place for everyone arrested that morning.

At this point, it was announced that men and boys over the age of sixteen had to move to another room. Women and children could leave. Mother and the three of us started walking out of the hall when my eldest brother, Arno, was stopped and asked his age. He told the truth, seventeen. He was detained. My mother grabbed me and my brother Lothar and hurried us out of the hall.

Mother and we two children returned to our apartment. We later learned that the detained men and boys had been sent to a concentration camp in southern France. My brother stayed in the French camp for almost a year. My father had arrived in Chicago in the fall of 1939. His brother had arrived in the States two years earlier. They both obtained the necessary documents to allow Arno to emigrate. He arrived in Chicago in April 1941. Subsequently, the U.S. Army drafted him.

By mid-June 1940, the German military occupied and governed Brussels. Later they ordered Jews to wear the yellow star whenever Jews were on the street. School was out for the summer, and I was free to go wherever I wanted. I remember feeling grown-up wearing my flannel blazer with the yellow star sewn over the left breast pocket, covered with my pretty handkerchief. I was not afraid to be out alone. Then more stringent Nazi occupation forces took over, and by August 1942, the roundup of Jews in Brussels began.

As registered Jews, we received a letter ordering us to report to the train station for transport to the east. When Mother read the letter, she became agitated and broke down. She kept crying without a stop and went to bed, where she stayed for several hours. Not understanding what was happening, I was scared and felt helpless. Lothar had the good sense to take over and decide that we should not report and to hide instead. It meant leaving the apartment and staying at other addresses. Mother contacted some Christian friends for help.

Lothar was sent to a farm outside the city to be a farm helper. I was sent to an older woman who had white hair and lived in the neighborhood. She had a lovely apartment. She welcomed me warmly and helped me feel secure. She spent time teaching me to play solitaire and introducing me to English mystery stories. I stayed with her until Lothar, Mother, and I were reunited in Brussels. Mother reached some people active in helping Jews escape. They obtained false identity documents and train tickets for the three of us to leave Brussels. We left Brussels in October 1942, fleeing to Switzerland.

Once on the train, in the event one of us would be caught by the authorities, my brother sat in a different compartment from Mother and me. Our false documents showed that we were from Alsace. Because Mother didn't speak French well, we decided that I would speak for her and explain when necessary that she was deaf. We traveled through Belgium and France to reach the Swiss border. We had been told that when we reached our destination, we were to go to the station restaurant and wait. Someone would meet us there. We waited and waited. The restaurant emptied. The three of us were the only ones left. Finally, a man came up to Mother and explained that he was the guide and he would take us to the border.

We started walking and arrived at a meadow. The guide stopped and pointed his finger toward a hill quite a distance away. He told us to cross the road at that point, and we would be in Switzerland. Mother did not believe the man. She argued with him to take us all the way to the point where we were to cross. After a long time, he agreed. I remember standing at the top of the hill. The guide explained that the road we could see below was the border, patrolled by German soldiers. We had to watch for the patrol to pass before starting down the hill. As we started downhill, I remember the cowbells clanging, and, suddenly, I started sliding down the hill, making noise. I was frightened that the Germans would hear me. Somehow we three crossed the road without any mishap. In the meantime, night had fallen. Darkness surrounded us.

Standing at the edge of the other side of the road, we saw light. We decided that it must be a house. Lothar went ahead to investigate. He reported that he had heard French spoken. We took a chance that in fact we had, indeed, safely crossed the border. Together we walked to the house, which appeared to be on a Swiss farm. Lothar knocked on the door. A man opened the door, and we explained who we were. He kept us for the night and took us to the attic, where we slept in beds with big *Federbetten* (huge down comforters). I was happy to sleep in such a wonderful warm bed. The next morning he gave us some bread and milk and directions to the train station. The town was La Chaux-de-Fonds. At the train station Lothar bought three tickets for Zurich. We did not have any Swiss francs, but Mother had some dollars, and they were accepted.

Because Mother had our American visas, her idea was to get to Zurich and go to the American Consulate. As the three of us were standing on the platform, a gendarme stopped her and asked for her papers. Because she could not provide any proof of legal entry, we were taken to the local police station and kept overnight. We were assigned to a cell, Mother and I together and Lothar in another one. We did not have to stay in cells during the day but were allowed to sit in a sunny and bright dayroom. Food and drink were provided, and we were treated kindly. We spent about three or four days in that police station. During that time, they questioned Mother and finally they told us that we would be going to a refugee camp in Büren an der Aare.

The camp had been established to house Spanish Civil War prisoners. The barracks were wooden, the bunks had straw mats, and the men and women were kept in separate parts of the grounds. There was a daily roll call in the central square. We received adequate food and were treated well. After about a month's stay, the Swiss relocated the refugees to internment camps.

Mother was sent to a women's camp in Liestal, Basel-Land. There the women did mostly housekeeping and wove rugs from rags. I was sent to a children's camp, Kinderheim Waldeck, which took in youngsters from age twelve to eighteen years old. We had to keep house, as well as work in the kitchen and the gardens. I attended classes in English and German. The American YMCA and the worldwide Jewish organization ORT provided the textbooks. My mother's camp and mine were in the same small village in the Basel Oberland. We visited weekly. Lothar was sent to a youth work camp in the south of Switzerland, Davos. He became part of a group of young men who labored on the area roads.

During the summer of 1943, when I was fourteen, Kinderheim Waldeck closed. We were all dispersed to different places. A family in Basel Stadt took me in. Mr. Schrenck, a pharmacist, and his wife treated me like family. They had two daughters—Esther, who was my age, and Beatrice, who was two years younger. Esther and I became good friends. I lived with the Schrenck family until the end of the war. Even after the war and we got married and had families, we stayed in touch, visiting each other, and as recently as October 2010, our families vacationed together at a resort.

During the years we were in Switzerland, Mother had contacted the U.S. Consulate in Zurich and registered. She presented our U.S. visas issued in 1940, now expired, as evidence that we were to immigrate to the United States.

When the war ended in May 1945, Mother asked the U.S. Consulate for new visas. Once we obtained the new visas, Mother sought HIAS's help. HIAS helped Jews in need, and it provided us with the necessary funds to book passage. Mother gave HIAS our United States relatives' names who had sent small sums of money toward covering our travel costs. After seeking help from many travel agencies in Zurich, my brother finally was able to get three tickets on a small ship, which took some freight, and was leaving from Bilbao, Spain, in the beginning of December.

HIAS arranged the necessary train transportation from Basel to Bilbao. We left Switzerland in November 1945. The trip took several days, but I have little memory of it. I do remember arriving in Bilbao and a local HIAS representative greeting us

Figure 13. Leah Molton-Motulsky, *in circle,* with other children on the SS *St. Louis* en route to Havana, Cuba, May 1939.

Figure 14. Leah Molton-Motulsky's mother, *in circle,* as the SS *St. Louis* returns from Cuba and docks in Antwerp, Belgium, June 17, 1939.

and taking us to a lovely hotel. We had dinner and musicians played. The next day we boarded a small ship and we had a small cabin, but I remember nothing else.

The ship made a five-day stop in Cuba. My brother told me that we were not allowed off the ship because our papers declared us German. For four days they tried to get permission to go ashore. Finally, after negotiations with the Jewish Agency, the Cubans relented and my mother and brother were allowed off the ship to walk around the Havana Harbor.

On January 1, 1946, an official holiday, the ship finally landed in New York Harbor. We had to wait another day before we were allowed to land and stand on the New York pier. After spending a few days in New York getting acquainted with family we had not seen for so many years, and especially meeting with my father again, we arrived in Chicago to begin a new life.

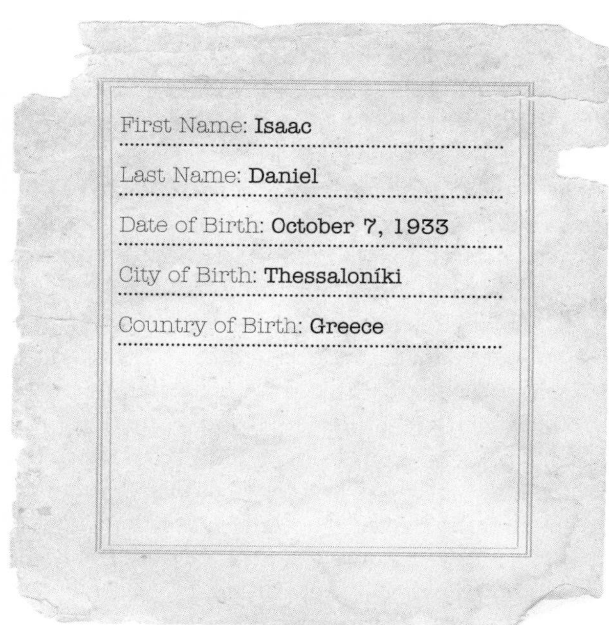
First Name: Isaac

Last Name: Daniel

Date of Birth: October 7, 1933

City of Birth: Thessaloníki

Country of Birth: Greece

Zamboni's List

Isaac M. Daniel

I was born in Salonika (Thessaloníki), Greece, in 1933, the second of four children of Mordochai Daniel and Bella Modiano Daniel. Before the war we moved to the town of Veria (Veroia), my father's hometown, about seventy-two kilometers west of Salonika. Veria had an over two-thousand-year uninterrupted Jewish history. The Jewish community of approximately eight hundred people out of a total population of about fifteen thousand had one synagogue and a single Jewish school. The synagogue is said to be the same one that Saul of Tarsus (Saint Paul) visited around the year 50 C.E. to preach to the community. Exiles from Spain in the fifteenth and sixteenth centuries transformed the community into a Sephardic, Ladino-speaking one. Almost the entire community lived within a walled ghetto around the synagogue. The ghetto had two gates that in old times used to be locked every night as well as during epidemics in the town.

In September 1939, I entered the Jewish school just as the war started and before I turned six years old. The school covered the regular secular curriculum of the Greek public schools supplemented by religious Jewish instruction. I studied Greek, history, geography, arithmetic, art, and calligraphy. I remember the angry outburst of my Greek teacher when she discovered that I spoke only Ladino and didn't understand Greek well. "How can they raise children in this country without knowing the language?" I do not remember how, but before the end of the school year I learned to speak, read, and write perfect Greek.

In October of 1940, Greece was invaded by the Italians under Mussolini, but the Greek Army managed to hold and even push back the invaders into Albania. One of the first casualties of that war was the highest-ranking Jewish officer in the Greek Army, Colonel Mordechai Frizis. The Germans came to the rescue of the Italians through Yugoslavia and invaded Greece in 1941. All of Greece fell to the Axis powers and was divided into three occupation zones: German in the north, Bulgarian in the east, and Italian in the south. Salonika and Veria fell in the German zone; Athens was in the Italian zone.

It was in late 1942 when rumors started circulating that the Germans were going to relocate all Jews to near Kraków, Poland, to establish an independent Jewish state. The faithful saw it as a sign of the coming of the Messiah; others were apprehensive but never suspected anything really dangerous. I remember only an old senile woman in the ghetto screaming, "*mos van a matar a todos*" ("they are going to kill us all"). "Shush, old lady," they said to her. A few skeptics, like two of my uncles, moved their families to the villages in the surrounding mountains. We stayed in our house because we were hoping that my mother's Italian citizenship would help us. We were ordered to wear the yellow star (*concarda*).

It was the last day of Passover in 1943. I was in the synagogue with my father. During the service, three armed Greek policemen, accompanied by a Jewish collaborator from Salonika, came and blocked the front door. My father grabbed me by the hand and led me through the women's section (*snoga*) and out by a side door that was not guarded (miracle number one). My Uncle Joseph, whose family was already in the mountains, also escaped by the same route. My father, my uncle, and I were the only three people from that synagogue service who survived.

We ran to our house just outside the ghetto and hid in the basement with the rest of the family. We decided in a panic that my father, with my twelve-year-old brother Anri and me, would try to escape to the mountains and send somebody from the village later to bring my mother, my six-year-old sister Sarica (Sarah), and my two-year-old brother Samico (Sam). We walked for hours and came to the Aliákmon River. We approached the bridge to cross it, when a peasant came out of nowhere and recognized my father. "Don't go there," he shouted, "German soldiers are guarding the bridge and checking papers" (miracle number two).

Frustrated to find our last escape route blocked, we turned back. We started walking slowly back, on the one hand disappointed but on the other hand worried about my mother, Sarica, and Samico. We were eager to join them, but Anri was not in a hurry. He said he was tired and wanted to rest for a while under a tree. After a short rest we continued on our way. When we got home, we found my mother was hysterical. The Gestapo had just come minutes before, searched the house, but did not discover her and the baby who was crying in the crib in the basement apartment. Had we returned a few minutes earlier, we would have run into the Gestapo. That short rest stop had saved us this time (miracle number three).

It was then that we realized that Sarica was missing. We thought she had stayed home with my mother, and my mother thought that she went with us. Our wildest fear was that she was caught and locked up in the ghetto. We stayed hidden in total ignorance and despair. A few days later we got a message that my uncle, after the roundup at the synagogue, had grabbed my little sister and escaped with her separately toward the mountains. He also came to the Aliákmon River but, with the help of some peasants, managed to ford it at some other point away from the bridge. We had no choice but to stay hidden in the basement apartment until the next opportunity to escape.

All six hundred fifty Jews remaining in the town—men, women, and children, the healthy and the invalid, including over fifty of our relatives—were rounded up within hours and locked in the ghetto. A few days later they were all shipped to the Baron Hirsch Transit Camp in Salonika and from there to Auschwitz and the crematoriums. Not a single one of them survived. In a matter of a few weeks, a Jewish community with over two thousand years of continuous history in Greece was wiped out.

We remained hidden in the basement apartment for over a month, avoiding the windows during the day and staying in the dark at night. Our friend Stavros would come and bring us food and pretend to be living there. My mother wrote letters asking for protection as an Italian citizen and sent them by messenger to the Italian Consulate in Salonika. We got no reply. One day the local police came to arrest us. They had known about us for some time and had hoped we would have escaped by now, but they were worried that somebody might betray us and get them in trouble with the Germans. They loaded us like cargo on a horse-drawn carriage and took us for interrogation to the German command. The commander seemed furious that we had the audacity to go into hiding, and he reminded us that the penalty for that was going to be summary execution of the entire family. (We found out later that they had executed fourteen others caught hiding.) My mother bypassed the interpreter, who did not seem to be translating correctly and even interjected his own bias, and she told the commander in her meager German that she was born an Italian citizen. The commander seemed to calm down a little. However, we were told that my mother had lost her Italian citizenship when she married my father, a Greek citizen; therefore we were all subject to German occupation law.

I was only nine years old when they took and locked all five of us in a tiny jail cell the size of a closet, with no beds or furniture, for the night. On the way to prison they allowed my mother to send a telegram to the Italian Consulate in Salonika with a brief and desperate message: *Ayuto urgente*—urgent help. To our relief, we were not shot in the morning as they had threatened to do, but we were sent to the Baron Hirsch camp in Salonika. We were scheduled to be sent on the next convoy to Auschwitz.

The Baron Hirsch camp was a ghetto conveniently near the railroad station. It was fenced in with barbed wire and turned into a transit camp for deportations to Auschwitz. Between March and July of 1943, nineteen convoys of trains, with cattle cars each carrying approximately three thousand people, left this camp for Auschwitz. When we got to the camp most of the deportations had already taken place. They were gathering the remnants of the Jews caught hiding for the last convoys. We were interrogated again, but not too harshly.

There was a tall, thin officer standing in the back holding the telegram that my mother had sent to the Italian Consulate. He didn't say a word. I have a strong suspicion that he was the Austrian intelligence officer named Kurt Waldheim working for the German commander. After the war he claimed that he had never heard of these deportations until much later (1986). He admitted that he was stationed in Salonika but for a short time—coincidentally, between March and July 1943.

I have vivid memories of our brief stay at Baron Hirsch. It seemed deceptively normal except that we were given only one meal a day. The meal consisted of beans, a liter of soup, or spaghetti, and sixty grams of bread. One time they served salami, but we couldn't eat it because we thought it contained pork. One early morning, a Jewish kitchen worker saw me on the street. He took me to the food storage room and gave me a huge chunk of bread with marmalade. It was such a treat. I brought it home and shared it with the rest of my family. One day my father managed to find some money. He went by the barbed-wire fence and bought some cheese pies from a Greek vendor. Strangely enough I felt some relief at being able to walk and run on the street again with other Jewish kids and see street names like Moses Avenue, Palestine Street, Bialik Street. We even managed to play and have some fun. We had races with baby strollers. There were lots of abandoned baby strollers around.

One of our camp neighbors was Mr. Frizis. He was the brother of the hero of the Albanian war, Mordechai Frizis. He had been arrested hiding in a village. One day I saw a dignified looking old man sweeping the streets of the camp. I was told he was the former Chief Rabbi Habib. I also remember seeing the latest and controversial Chief Rabbi Zvi Koretz, always walking alone, forlorn looking, and shunned by most. The Germans had brainwashed him. He had collaborated with them by urging us to comply and not resist the Nazis. He turned over all the Jewish community records to the Germans. Mountains of Hebrew religious books were being burned in a big bonfire in the middle of the street. I managed to rescue a little prayer book from that pile that I have kept to this day. It belonged to a young student. I can still make out her faded name on the inside cover, Leah Shiby.

There were a few other families in the camp in the same situation where the mothers had been Italian citizens. We were told again that would be of no avail. In fact several such families, including my mother's sister Julie and her family, had already been deported and murdered. One day, an order came to release all women who were born Italian citizens along with their children under the age of twelve, but not their husbands or older children. The bitter irony of all this was that my mother's name was not on the list. They had not found her name in the archives of the Italian Consulate. One of the released women, my mother's cousin Ida Modiano, promised to move heaven and earth to locate my mother's name. She was allowed to search through the files of the Italian Consulate until she found my mother's birth registration. Soon after we too were released, but without my father. All men in this category were Greek citizens and were subject to deportation. My mother and the other women mounted a relentless campaign to plead and petition for the men's release.

The next convoy to Auschwitz was imminent. The day before the train left, my father and the other men in the group were separated, locked up in a small synagogue in the camp, and placed under guard for their protection. To our great joy my father was finally released. He came out of the camp holding a piece of paper, a certificate saying "*Suditanza Italiana Provisoria*"—Temporary Italian Citizenship. It was an artificial device, which the Germans hated, but they respected it because the Italians were their allies. We were all together and free (miracle number four). This was just the first chapter of our dramatic adventures.

We were all sent to Athens, which was under Italian control. We were unmolested and free to move about for a short time until Italy surrendered to the Allies, on September 8, 1943. The Germans came and occupied Athens and all of southern Greece. All Jews were ordered on penalty of death to present themselves to the community offices and register.

We obtained false identity cards with Christian names and moved to an isolated country house on the outskirts of Athens. However, we were betrayed. In March 1944, the Gestapo came to our house to arrest and deport us. Realizing that the Gestapo agents were local collaborators, my father pleaded with them and bribed them with a bag of gold coins. That pacified them. They left, planning to return and arrest us later. As soon as they left, all six of us grabbed whatever we could carry and went on a long, several hours' journey on foot to another Athens suburb. There a friend of my great uncle put us up in a closed one-room taverna. About a month later, we moved to a basement of an unfinished house in the suburb of Nea Smyrni.

While hiding our identity, we tried to blend in with our new neighbors. The Greek Resistance started growing, and the Germans organized a Greek militia to combat the Resistance. One day a member of the militia discovered our family in the basement and wanted to arrest my father and take him to the German command for interrogation. When he discovered that we were Jewish, he said that he had to follow orders and take all of us. He feigned pity for us children and accepted my father's bribe. He returned soon for another bribe for his commanding officers as well.

Days later, there was an almost cataclysmic rainstorm (though it seldom rains in Athens in the summer), which flooded our basement apartment. Running out in soaking wet clothes, we knocked on neighbors' doors until one of them, Mrs. Dimitra (Kyria Dimitra), opened the door and took us in. When we told her that we were Jewish, she laughed and said that she as well as the entire neighborhood knew that. Days later the militia came to arrest us but found an empty flooded basement. We stayed with Kyria Dimitra until the liberation of Athens on October 12, 1944.

A short time after liberation, in December 1944, we were caught up in a bloody civil war between the Greek governmental army and the Communists. When everything cleared up, we returned to our family home in Veria and tried to rebuild our lives. The Veria community had been decimated; we had lost about fifty-five relatives. Many of those released with us from the Baron Hirsch camp were arrested in Athens and had been deported to Auschwitz. Of the thousands of families that were incarcerated at Baron Hirsch, we were one of only three families that eventually survived as a unit.

I believe that all our escapes are miracles. To survive, it wasn't enough to be lucky once. You had to be lucky several times. What are the odds of flipping a coin and coming up with heads several times in a row?

For a long time I was under the impression that the papers that liberated us from Baron Hirsch had been authorized by the Italian, albeit Fascist, government.

A few years ago, I read an obituary in the *Jerusalem Post* about the passing of Guelfo Zamboni in Rome at the age of ninety-seven. He was the Italian consul in Salonika in 1943. I believe that he acted on his own and made up those artificial citizenship papers. He made a list of 280 people, Zamboni's list. After the war he himself was put on a different list, the list of Righteous Gentiles at the Yad Vashem memorial to the Holocaust in Jerusalem.

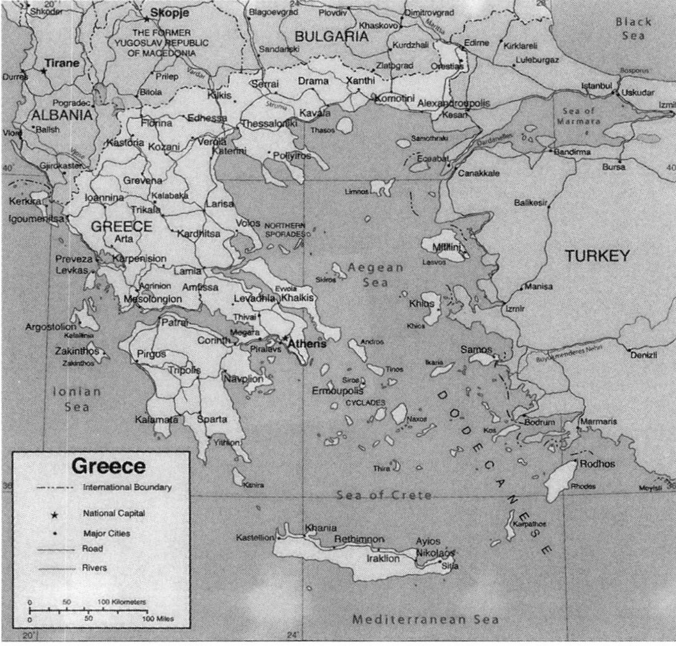

Figure 15. Map of Greece.

Figure 16. Synagogue in Veria, Greece, where Isaac Daniel and his father, Mordochai, escaped during Passover services, 1943. The only synagogue in Veria, it dates back two thousand years.

Figure 17. Isaac Daniel's entire family celebrating their first Thanksgiving in the United States, 1955. *Left to right:* Aaron, Isaac, Sarah, Mordochai, Sam, and Bella.

The Rocky Shores of Marseille: 1942

Chaya Horowitz Roth

My sister and I are holding hands
The sea rises before us
The sky looks darkly menacing
The boat to Palestine is nowhere to be seen*
We missed the boat, I fear,
And stand alone on the hard naked rock.

*The author and her sister are waiting on the rocky shores of Marseille, 1942, for a boat organized by the French Jewish Council to Palestine that would have taken them together with a group of Jewish children to Palestine.

The Train Station in Turin: March 1944

Chaya Horowitz Roth

In 1944, the German armies are growing dangerously desperate. Losing the war, they are chasing the enemy: Jews, rebels, partisans. The enclaves of Jews hiding in the mountains are reaching the point of panic. Our family decides to escape. Together we reach the Turin train station, with our guardian, Andreina. But no trains are coming, the tracks have been bombed, and we must wait.

On wooden planks and long cold benches, we wait
Gitta and I huddle together,
Andreina, our guardian from the mountains, will keep us safe
Our mother sits far away from us
I do not see her at all
The air is icy and wet
The snows are melting on the ground,
Winter remains solidly frozen
Then, black boots are strutting among the rows of wooden benches
A German soldier,
Rifle slung over his shoulder
Green uniform? Helmet?
I never look up.
I see only his rifle and boots
A child cries out:
"Mamme, Mamme, *geb mir a shtikel broit*!"*
Oh God! Whose voice do I hear?
"Be quiet little boy . . . Be quiet and still!"
"Quiet now, or forever, be still . . . "

*"Mama, Mama, give me a piece of bread!"

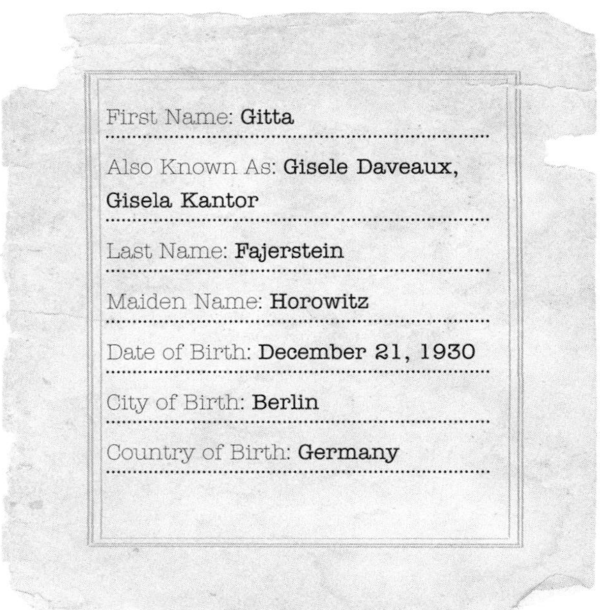
First Name: Gitta
Also Known As: Gisele Daveaux, Gisela Kantor
Last Name: Fajerstein
Maiden Name: Horowitz
Date of Birth: December 21, 1930
City of Birth: Berlin
Country of Birth: Germany

The Boot

Gitta Horowitz Fajerstein

My mother, my sister Chaya, age five, and I, age nine, had been on the run the entire war, in hiding and trudging throughout Europe, beginning with being smuggled out of Germany after the Nazis murdered our father. In December 1939, we went to Holland and then Belgium, and after many difficulties we arrived in the south of France in the spring of 1942.

On September 8, 1943, the Allied forces landed in Salerno, in southern Italy. Hoping to speed up our liberation, approximately eight hundred Jews crossed the border through the French-Italian Alps into Italy. Members of the Fourth Italian Army were also on the run; they feared that the Nazis would arrest them as traitors.

For the Jews, though helped by some of the Italian soldiers, it was an arduous journey of about three long and difficult days. Arriving across the border in the village of Valdieri, we were greeted by the Germans. The Nazis immediately set out to pick up the Jews who had escaped. Exhausted, demoralized, and unable to continue their escape, about three hundred fifty Jews were arrested, incarcerated at the Borgo San Dalmazzo Concentration Camp, and eventually sent to Auschwitz.

When our mother realized that the Germans were waiting in the valley below to round up as many Jews as possible, she made our group—consisting of Mother, Chaya, our uncle, another family of three, and me—run back into the mountains. Andreina, a good-hearted and courageous Italian woman, at great risk to herself, allowed us to stay in her *cava* (shack). It was one of the coldest and most biting winters the inhabitants had known.

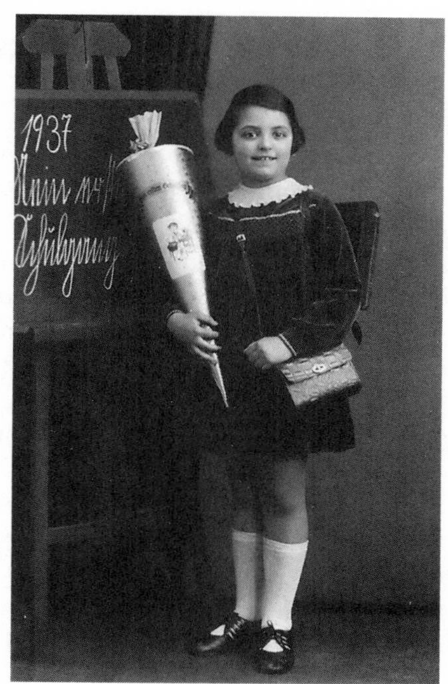

Figure 18. Gitta Horowitz's first day at school in Berlin, Germany, 1937. She holds a package filled with candy.

In early spring of 1944, the Germans stepped up their patrols in the mountains, searching for Jews, Italian deserters, and members of the Italian Resistance. It was becoming increasingly dangerous to stay there in those mountains. Our mother felt that it was again time to move to a safer place and decided that she, my sister, and I would try to get away from the mountains, travel to Turin, and from there attempt to escape to Rome, hoping to be liberated by the Allies.

We made it to Turin and waited in vain for a train. The rails, however, had been bombarded and no train arrived. Meanwhile, the Germans were patrolling the train station. Because we feared being arrested, we returned to the mountains. Upon our return, we learned that the rest of our group had moved to another mountain for safety reasons. Andreina and her daughter suggested that because I had run numerous errands from our hideout in the *cava* down to the village of Valdieri, I should go up first and alert our family and friends of our return. Wearing only a sweater, blouse, short skirt, kneesocks, and dilapidated boots, I ventured up a narrow path, walking for an hour or two. It seemed like an eternity. Suddenly the sun set, it became very dark, and the temperature dropped abruptly. I saw flickering lights in the distance, but the closer I got, the farther and farther the lights seemed to be. I continued walking, but the path became a sheet of ice; I was slipping, sliding, and terrified of falling.

On one side of me loomed the mountain and on the other side was a sheer drop into the valley below. I tried stepping on the side of the path where there were deep snowbanks. I went in knee-deep, and as I was trying to get my foot out of the snow, my foot came out without my boot. I struggled to recover my boot. I dug in the snow with my bare frozen hands and finally dug out the two halves of my boot, which had come apart. I sat down on the frozen path. Everything seemed so peaceful and quiet. Numb and afraid of falling asleep, all I wanted to do was close my eyes and just stay there. I don't know what kept me from giving up; maybe it was the thought of my mother or perhaps someone was watching over me. I don't know. I put the two halves of my boot on my lap and slowly, slowly I slid down the slippery mountain path. Besides being terrified, I don't remember anything else except the freezing cold penetrating my body. I have a deformed toe to remind me of the frostbite I suffered that night.

As I came closer to the village below, I could hear the dogs howling. I swear the dogs could smell my fear and my pounding heart. I finally got enough courage to knock on a farmhouse door. An old farmer opened the door and was kind enough to let me sleep in his stable in the warmth emanating from the cows. He even offered me some warm milk and a piece of bread. The farmer took me to a Jewish woman who was hiding with her son. I stayed with the woman and her son for three days while she had my boot repaired.

To this day, when I think about that experience, I get heart palpitations. One of many such days during the war.

PART 3

Hidden with Parents

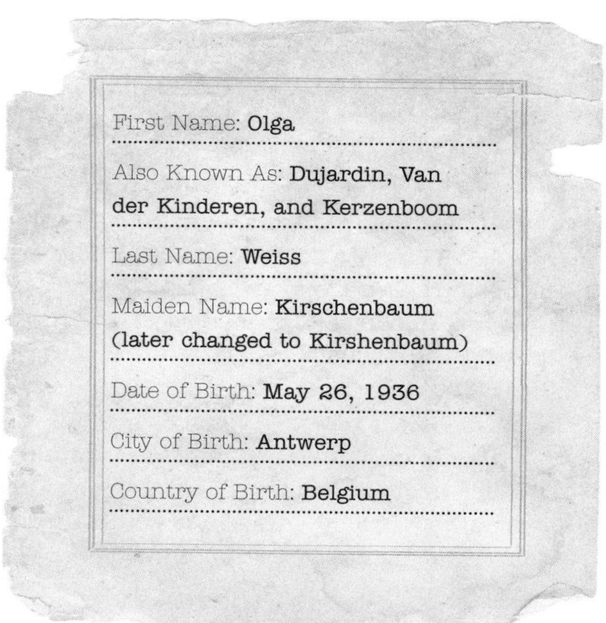
First Name: Olga

Also Known As: Dujardin, Van der Kinderen, and Kerzenboom

Last Name: Weiss

Maiden Name: Kirschenbaum (later changed to Kirshenbaum)

Date of Birth: May 26, 1936

City of Birth: Antwerp

Country of Birth: Belgium

Reminiscences of Being Hidden

Olga Kirshenbaum Weiss

I was born in 1936 in Belgium; my parents and I lived in Brussels. There were approximately ninety thousand Jews in Belgium at that time, including many refugees who had come primarily from Eastern Europe in the 1930s and later from Germany to escape Nazi oppression. Shortly after the German invasion of Belgium in May 1940, we attempted to flee to the still unoccupied northern France. Our intention was to avoid an advancing German army and return home later when conditions were calmer. On our way, our car, in a long convoy of vehicles, eventually intersected with groups of wounded French soldiers retreating from the front. They urged us to go back, and it soon became apparent that we had no other choice.

The Belgian Army resisted for eighteen days, and by the time we had returned to Brussels, the government had capitulated and gone into exile in London; it was quickly replaced by a German military administration.

The Germans began almost immediately to impose antisemitic regulations, with gradually increasing economic and social restrictions. By the end of October 1940, all Jews in Belgium were required to register in their own municipalities and to submit an inventory of their property. Jewish businesses were also compelled to post a public notice stating that their shops and buildings were owned by Jews. My parents attempted to transfer their small factory of fine leather goods to one of my father's gentile workers, but their effort failed, and soon the factory was forced to shut down.

My father, Jacques Kirschenbaum, who was born in Poland, had immigrated to Brussels in 1923. He spoke French with a pronounced Yiddish accent, and he never learned Flemish, Belgium's other language. His nose gave him a distinctly semitic appearance; his speech was animated by expressive gesturing, and his mannerisms reflected his shtetl upbringing. Because of these characteristics, he stood out conspicuously from the highly homogeneous native Belgians. In contrast, my mother, Régine Goldstein, a naturalized citizen born and raised in Belgium, had come from an upper-middle-class Jewish family, who were active in the diamond business. She spoke impeccable, Belgian-accented French, and, having lived in Antwerp, she spoke equally fluent Flemish. With her brown wavy hair and light complexion, she was indistinguishable in appearance from other native-born Belgians. She was familiar and felt at ease with the Belgian way of life and blended in easily.

In spite of the succession of ever more restrictive edicts that followed, I was still able to attend kindergarten in a public school in the fall of 1941. But before long, all Jewish children were segregated from their classmates. At first, we were isolated to one classroom, and finally we were all expelled. From then on, I no longer went to school; my parents preferred to keep me at home rather than send me to a Jewish school, out of fear of our being separated. I was only too relieved because all I wanted was to stay near them during those bewildering times.

By the winter of 1941, the Germans had instituted a *Judenrat,* the AJB: *Association des Juifs de Belgique;* its purported function was to provide for the welfare of Belgian Jews, but its actual purpose was to facilitate the work of the SS in identifying, locating, and rounding up Jews for deportation. But because the AJB was infiltrated by members of the underground Belgian Resistance, it was able to maintain, although with diminishing effectiveness, a measure of support of the Jewish community up until the time of liberation.

A few months later, the Germans also imposed curfews. Raids and roundups were sudden and random and became more frequent. Streets, stores, trains, and trams would be closed off; people were detained sometimes for hours, interrogated, and their identity papers inspected. For my mother, even going to a store to buy food became a frightening experience.

My father was caught in one of the raids while he was on his way to see a doctor. That day, he was carrying two sets of identity papers, his real ones and a set of false ones. He was painfully aware that if both sets of papers were discovered, he would be arrested instantly. He became frantic. He managed to slip away, but then he immediately sensed that he was being followed. Without quickening his pace, he crossed the street and walked into a church. Peering out through a window, he saw a German soldier waiting for him. After a long time the soldier finally gave up and left.

On another occasion, late one afternoon, my mother and I were riding a tram, which was suddenly stopped by a detachment of the Gestapo, who made us all get off and stand outside. They were searching for Resistance members, but they were unsuccessful; in anger and frustration, they began to recheck the passengers' identity papers, scrutinizing them closely in the hope of finding some irregularity. My mother and I slowly and cautiously moved backward, away from the group, toward the dense forest bordering the road, under the cover of the evening's darkness. It took us six hours to walk home. We were terrified that at any moment someone might discover us. My father, overcome with worry, had come to fear that he might never see us again.

By the spring of 1942, the German authorities made it mandatory for Jews in Belgium to wear the yellow star. However, the Belgian officials, in defiance, refused to distribute the cloth stars. That responsibility was then assigned by the Germans to the *Judenrat.* My mother cleverly sewed my star under my coat's lapel, which, when folded down, effectively concealed it. Whenever I was outside and saw a German soldier walk toward me, my heart started to beat hard until he passed me.

A short while later, summonses were issued to all Jewish males, requiring them to report to designated assembly points for work assignments. My father surmised that to obey the summons would likely have disastrous consequences. He refused to go. "If they want me, they will have to come and get me," my father told us, but it became clear to him that eventually the Germans would do exactly that, putting us in grave danger. The Resistance at that time was urging Jews not to comply with the call-up. Evidently, substantial numbers of men had failed to show up as they had been ordered, and as a result, the roundups became more frequent and more brutal. Those who followed the order were arrested and taken to the Caserne Dossin, a prison in Malines (Mechelen), a small city between Brussels and Antwerp. Malines was to become the transit site in Belgium for deportations to Auschwitz.

My parents became desperate to find some way to escape. They arranged for the three of us to be smuggled into Switzerland. Friends of ours planned to make the crossing first, then the guide would return to collect us. Anxiously, we waited in our house in the middle of the night for the guide to arrive. I remember sitting on my suitcase, with my coat on, ready to go. But the man failed to come at the expected time, and my father suspected that something had gone wrong. We quickly left the house and hid in a garage across the courtyard. A short while later I saw from the window that our guide did arrive, but he was accompanied by Gestapo agents. The guide had denounced us. We learned later that this man had also betrayed our friends and that they had been arrested at the Swiss border.

Early the next morning, without ever returning to our house, we left to find a place to hide. The place my parents selected was Rhode-Saint-Genèse, a little, quiet town in the countryside outside of Brussels. After a long, discouraging search, bypassing many signs that advertised "Apartment Available, But No Jews," we finally were able to rent a small place on a secluded street. In an effort to detract from the fact that we were Jewish, my mother explained to the landlady that I, pale and thin, needed the fresh air of the country, as had been recommended by our doctor. That was a pretext that no one, in those days, would have questioned. While we were in hiding, my mother went out only when absolutely necessary, and my father almost never left the apartment, except rarely at night, to go to a tiny garden behind the house. He remained close to the wall, shielded by trees, so as not to be seen by the neighbors. But, as a young child, I was allowed to play outside.

Our false identity papers had been obtained through contacts with the Resistance. At first, my parents decided to change our name to Dujardin, but concluded that a French name would not be convincing considering my father's poor command of the language. They then thought of the name Van der Kinderen, a legitimate Flemish name, but finally chose Kerzenboom, the Flemish translation of our German-Jewish name, Kirschenbaum, which means "cherry tree." My parents thought that would be less risky because it would be easier for me to remember to respond to a name that sounded like my real name.

In September 1942, with the permission of a kind and understanding priest, I was able to enroll in a private Catholic school, under my false name. The priest, who was the director of the school, allowed me to participate in all of the church activities, except for the rites of Communion and confession. I well remember one day, as the class was engaged in spirited singing of Christian hymns, the teacher abruptly walked up to me and ordered me to stop, while allowing the rest of the group to continue singing. At that moment, as they sang, terrifying thoughts entered my six-year-old mind: What if the teacher had discovered that I was Jewish, and as a Jew, I should not be permitted to sing Christian hymns, and what if the Gestapo was outside, waiting for the song to end, at which point they would storm into the classroom to arrest me? Then they would find my parents and arrest them. The song ended, and the teacher looked at me and said reproachfully, "Olga, you were singing so badly off-key and so loudly that I could not hear the rest of the class. From now on, please sing softer."

I, like other Jewish children in hiding, keenly sensed the peril and danger that surrounded me. By then, my grandfather and my uncle had been deported. I had seen people being arrested and being brutally pushed into cars; I heard of friends being beaten and of others having disappeared. I heard of children I knew having been given away to non-Jewish families for their own protection.

I rarely asked questions. I intuitively knew how to behave. I knew when to be quiet, what not to say, and how to avoid attracting attention. I had been given a false, non-Jewish name, and I fully realized, even at that early age, that I must never make the mistake of acknowledging my real name. I understood that being noticed and discovered could lead to catastrophic consequences for my family.

While in hiding, my greatest fear was that my parents might send me away, as so many other Jewish families had done. My mother and father, looking for a way to protect me, were considering placing me in a convent, or in an orphanage, or with peasants on an isolated farm. I pleaded with my parents to keep me. I remember telling them that I did not care what happened to me as long as I could stay with them. With deep misgivings, they finally relented. Nevertheless, the first thing I did every morning was to look anxiously into their bedroom to reassure myself that they were still there and that they had not abandoned me while I was asleep.

During that time, I experienced other deeply troubling feelings. I could not understand why my parents, who were so good to me, were being hounded and threatened at every turn. Were my parents bad people? Were they being punished for having done something wrong? Should I not respect them? Trust them? As a young child, I actually felt ashamed of my father and my mother. When I was older and I understood what our circumstances had been, I profoundly regretted my earlier thoughts. I finally recognized how badly I had misjudged my parents, and it was only then that I came to appreciate how their determination and sense of self-preservation had made it possible for all of us to survive.

While in hiding, we lived in constant dread of being discovered and captured. Ironically, the most frightful menace was our "rescuer," our landlady—a widow, Madame De Lacroix. She complained about my father's wet laundered clothes hanging to dry inside the house. Putting them outside might have created suspicion. She also complained about our using the stove's lit gas jets to warm our cold kitchen in the winter. Every complaint became a bitter argument, and every argument led to an accusation. She repeatedly threatened to denounce us to the Germans unless she was paid increasingly greater sums of money. And it would have been easy and profitable for her to turn us in: right down the street was an old mansion that had been confiscated by the Gestapo for their headquarters. Their black Citroën cars passed by our windows day and night. Whenever one of these cars slowed down in front of our house, we were thrown into a state of panic.

Finally, on September 3, 1944: the liberation! We learned that the Allied armies were approaching our town of Rhode-Saint-Genèse, and we were eager to go out and celebrate the news with neighbors, but they warned us to remain inside because retreating German soldiers were shooting their way out of the town. We waited for hours with enormous anticipation. By that evening, rumbling sounds could be heard in the distance, then shouts in the street, "Come out, they're here, the Allies are here." We all ran to the main road, and I saw our most welcome sight in four long years: massive Sherman tanks slowly, awkwardly maneuvering through the narrow street. Everyone ran to meet the Allied soldiers. People were laughing, crying, singing, dancing, throwing flowers at the soldiers, kissing them, lifting their children to them, and offering them champagne. I stood for hours on the side of the street, watching in wonder our tired, smiling liberators.

The liberation will always stand out vividly in my memory. Nothing would compare to the rejoicing, the celebration, and the emotion of that event. For me, the end of the war had come.

After the liberation, we returned to Uccle, the middle-class suburb in Brussels where we had lived before going into hiding. Our lives slowly returned to normal and I went back to school. But, even though World War II and the Holocaust had ended, the effects of the occupation remained with me for a long time. On several occasions, I was attacked by groups of boys who waited until I left school and threw stones at me, shouting "dirty Jew"; and one day, I was shocked to see a Jewish classmate being pushed into a corner and beaten by several boys. Despite the war being over, I again found myself having to hide my Jewish identity.

In school we were required to take a course on religion, or alternatively, one on ethics, for atheists I suppose; it was generally assumed that students would attend the class corresponding to their own religious beliefs. I chose Ethics, purposely avoiding the class on Judaism; the other available choice was Christianity. At the time of the Jewish High Holidays, I dreaded being seen going to the synagogue, and I was embarrassed to have to lie to the teacher about my reason for being absent during those holidays. I also refused to join Zionist youth groups or to associate with Jewish classmates, and for a long time I was reluctant to invite gentile friends to my home, especially when my father was there, as they would immediately recognize that he was a foreigner because of his thick accent. Sometimes his workers came by, and they spoke Yiddish together. When I knew my father would be home, I did not invite any friends.

Following the end of the war, displaced persons began returning from the camps. Three of my cousins came back from Auschwitz. I remember relatives and friends sitting around our dining room table, as they listened in horror to the survivors describing the atrocities they had endured in the concentration camps. My parents made me leave the room, but I sat at the top of the stairs straining to hear and not believing that people could treat other human beings so cruelly.

In Brussels, on Sunday afternoons, in the park Bois de la Cambre, Holocaust survivors, mostly from the camps, met with other survivors, including my relatives. Many of them, whose spouses and children had been murdered by the Nazis, had remarried and were starting new families. They always brought large quantities of food to the park to share with one another. Comfortable together, they told and retold their stories, confident that other survivors could fully comprehend the enormity of what they had all experienced. But I and other children who had survived the war were simply ignored. Even my mother was unwilling to respond to my questions regarding our wartime circumstances. She replied dismissively, "You were too young to remember; the war could not have left any impression on you." She was wrong: I may have been young, but I remembered the dangerous circumstances we faced during those years and especially the terror of being separated from my parents. I also promised myself that when I would have children, I would always answer their questions as best I could. And that was a promise I kept.

In 1950, when I was fourteen years old, my parents and I immigrated to the United States, moving to the northwest side of Chicago. There we changed the spelling of our name to Kirshenbaum. Moving to the United States was a difficult adjustment for my family, but to my delight, I soon found myself surrounded by large numbers of Jewish children, both at school and in the neighborhood. And, to my surprise, I came to realize that they were an integral part of the community. Walking in the street with five or six Jewish children was for me a new, exciting, and reassuring experience. And it was then I first realized that because of the war and the Holocaust, I had missed out on a childhood sustained by a Jewish environment and Jewish traditions. I also decided that when I would have children of my own, I would insist that they become knowledgeable about their history and be proud of being Jewish. And indeed all of my children and grandchildren did attend Jewish day schools. Later, I became a curator at the Spertus Museum of Judaica in Chicago, where for almost thirty years I worked with Jewish art and Jewish cultural and historical artifacts.

For me and undoubtedly for many child survivors, living through the Holocaust created unique and long-term challenges in raising our own children. I recognized that I had grown up under abnormal conditions: under constant danger of being arrested, of being abandoned, and in some cases of being mistreated by unkind strangers. Moreover, I had had relatively few ordinary childhood experiences that I could draw upon as examples of normal family life. While I was raising my children, I often thought of myself at their ages and of the wartime conditions that afflicted

Figure 19. Olga Kirschenbaum in Parc Wolvendael in the Uccle suburb of Brussels, Belgium, 1939.

Bonne Année

Chers Parents

L'année 1944 a été pour notre pays, l'année de la Libération. Je souhaite que l'année 1945 soit pour nous, l'année de la Paix.
Je vous renouvelle en plus en ce jour, mes voeux les plus sincères. bonne année, bonne

Figure 20. New Year's greeting from Olga Kirschenbaum to her parents in Brussels, Belgium, December 1944.

my upbringing. In trying to determine the proper way to raise my children, I frequently found it difficult to make decisions, and I had recurring fears of making mistakes. I was deeply conflicted, for example, about allowing them to go to a summer camp or to a college that was too far away, in my view, from Chicago. I objected to my eldest daughter's wish to live in Israel, even though I was the one who placed her in a Jewish day school that encouraged Zionism.

And above all of that, I was left with a lingering sense of disquiet. Still now, sometimes when I am traveling and especially when passing through little towns with isolated houses or farms, I cannot help thinking, "This would have been a good place to hide during the war." Often, when I see myself naked in a mirror, images flash into my mind of the naked Jewish women embracing their little children as they huddled at the edge of mass graves, awaiting their turn to be shot by a German soldier.

But then, beginning in the 1980s and the 1990s, organizations of child survivors of the Holocaust began to form throughout Europe, the United States, and Israel. I became an active member of a Chicago group of hidden children whose backgrounds had much in common with my own. I was able to share some of my deepest feelings with others whom I felt I could trust. It was only after many years of participation in our Hidden Children group that I was finally able to achieve a measure of resolution of some of the experiences I had faced during the war.

Figure 21. Olga Kirschenbaum and her parents, Régine and Jacques Kirschenbaum, at the North Sea, Belgium, 1947.

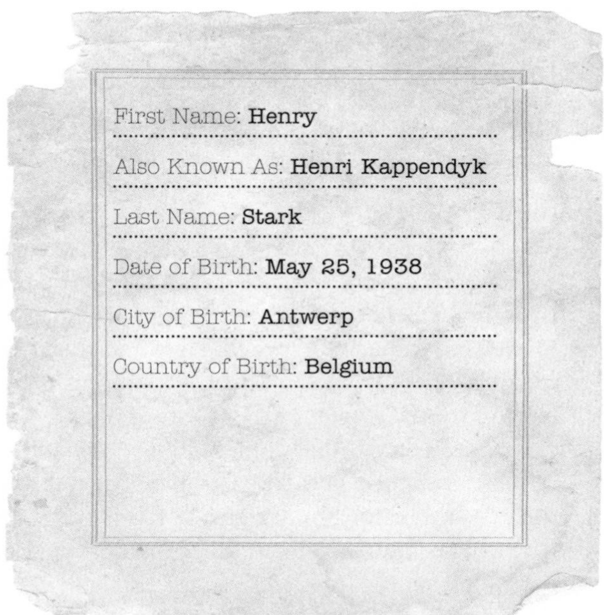

First Name: **Henry**

Also Known As: **Henri Kappendyk**

Last Name: **Stark**

Date of Birth: **May 25, 1938**

City of Birth: **Antwerp**

Country of Birth: **Belgium**

Boom 1943

Henry Stark

My mother, father, sister, and I are living on the top floor of an old apartment building on the Schelde River in the industrial town of Boom in Belgium. Carl Defuchs owns the building, and in exchange for money, he provides shelter and a minimal amount of food.

Our toilet is an oil drum. We are living there because we are hiding from the Germans who have occupied Belgium. At low tide, the mudflats between our house and the river are where we empty the oil drum, whose contents are swept away at high tide. On this particular night, large numbers of Allied warplanes are bombing the city. They are probably aiming for the large Gevaert factory that is making photographic instrumentation for the Germans. The sky is red, and the beams of dozens of searchlights are dancing across the clouds. After a while the wail of the all-clear signal goes on. The bombers are gone, but the sky is an even brighter red. It is the reflected light of all the burning buildings that have been hit. But the droning of the warplanes is gone and the spectacle, as seen from our window, is over. We have lived through one more day.

Within the year, however, Defuchs and his wife become too frightened of the risk of hiding Jews. We are forced to leave and find a new shelter.

Blood

Henry Stark

I am six years old. The Allies have recently liberated Antwerp and we are free to walk the streets. But we do so tentatively, like a patient learning to walk again after a long stay in a hospital bed. On this day my mother and I are on the tram on Avenue de Belgique, Antwerp's equivalent to Fifth Avenue in New York City or Michigan Avenue in Chicago. Here and there we see collapsed buildings, and there are many people on the street, walking in disregard of traffic rules, and the tram has to proceed slowly. I see crowds of people talking excitedly. Suddenly there is an ear-splitting crash that comes from somewhere nearby. "It is one of those pilotless bombs," someone says. The Germans are not finished yet. They have been throwing their "vengeance" bombs, the V-1 (air-breathing subsonic missiles) and the V-2 (the world's first ballistic missile) at Antwerp, London, and other places to interrupt the Allied supply line.

The tram edges forward and, sure enough, we see the dust and smoke rising from the building that's been hit. The building has been pulverized. In the midst of all of this, a British soldier is directing traffic by giving arm signals. Arm extended, and we can proceed; arm at right angle, and we must stop. His face is covered with blood. He has probably been hit by flying glass. "*Er is vervounded* (He is wounded)," I say. "*Geit er schterben*? (Will he die?)" I don't remember what my mother says. People are asking if he needs help, but he remains quiet. Maybe he doesn't understand Flemish. Nothing can distract him from his task. We wait in the tram, looking at the blood on his face, until we see the extended arm. Then the tram proceeds. I don't remember what happens next.

PART 4
Hidden with Rescuers

Coal

Henry Stark

My parents have left me in the care of a Christian family somewhere in Antwerp. To my distress, I have forgotten their names. I am maybe four, maybe five years old, and don't understand why I can't be with my mother. But I do know that there is an undefined danger all around me. I am to hide when the doorbell rings because this family doesn't want people to know that I live there.

Then it happens: the doorbell rings as we eat our dinner. I know what to do. I leave the table, make my way down the hallway, and walk down the stairs to the coal cellar. There is a mountain of coal near the narrow chute that opens to the sidewalk level. The coal will provide the heat for the coming winter. Other than the meager light that enters the chute from a streetlight, the cellar is dark. I stand next to the mountain of coal and wait for the all-clear whistle that will tell me that it is safe to come up. Time passes, maybe seconds, maybe minutes, and I grow anxious. Although I have done this several times before, I'm still not sure that the all-clear signal will come. But suddenly there is the *whit, whit, whit* from upstairs that tells me that it's OK to come up. I go up and resume my dinner, but I can still smell the coal. What is there to be so afraid of?

The Declaration

Leonie Taffel Bergman

It has been a long voyage—to America. I do not mean the eight days on the Atlantic Ocean but the long years before that led to this day.

My sister, Clara, and I were orphaned during the last year of World War II. Both our parents had been taken to Auschwitz on the final transport from Malines (Mechelen, Belgium), No. 26, July 31, 1944. Their deaths have been officially declared by the *Ministère de la Reconstruction de Belgique,* in 1947, and by the Red Cross, in an acknowledgment sent to me in 1983.

I had been hiding in several places in or near Brussels, by myself, living with different families, probably six or more, during the summer and fall of 1942, each time returning to one or both of my parents in the dark of evenings, always without knowing when or how this would take place, but going when I was told. Later that year a different home, of longer duration, was to be found for me.

In December 1942, I began a new life in a Franciscan convent in Tervuren, near Brussels. My sister, who is nearly five years younger than I, was only two at the time. She was hidden with a family who lived on a farm not far from the convent, where she remained for over three years. This family raised her as their own young child, although she does tell of harsh treatment. One event she recalls, and does not know why it happened, is that when she was sent to the basement to bring up some potatoes, someone from above pushed her down the steps, and she hurt her lip severely. She vividly remembers the surprise and the sensation, and the pain, but cannot add anything that would explain it. *Who* and *why* are still to be answered.

When Brussels was liberated by the Allies in September 1944, there was great celebration. It seemed as if everyone was out on the main streets, watching the soldiers, waving to them, finding people who hadn't been seen in a long time—being reunited with close ones. It was a time of joy. Several months later, when Germany surrendered in May 1945, the war in Europe was officially over. At last the fear could end. People could safely return, to find their loved ones; to find their homes; to find their lives. Many searched for those people important to them and hoped to have normalcy again in their lives. I, too, allowed myself to hope for what I and others anticipated would bring happiness back to us. If the time between liberation and the end of World War II had not brought any change for me, now I could expect to be claimed by someone who considered me theirs. My life was finally to be open. I could actually begin to "live" on the outside and not in hiding. I was more aware of reality than ever before. I could see how happy people were when someone freed them and took them "home." But hope disappeared for me. Nobody came looking for me. Nobody, if anybody tried, could find me. Didn't anybody care? Didn't I belong somewhere? Didn't I belong to someone? I am nine years old, and wondering: what will happen to me; what is my future?

Then I have my tenth birthday; it is the summer of 1945. I am still living in the convent. The nuns have always been nice to me. Some (maybe all) knew I was

Jewish, and they did not try to convert me. I, along with everyone in the convent, always participated in morning prayers, which took place in the chapel. This would include Communion and the taking of the sacramental wafer, given to everyone. However, because I was not Catholic I could not be included. I knew this and accepted it. But others might question why I was not participating. So Mother Superior let it be known that I was sickly and, therefore, needed to drink something when I woke up. This intake made me ineligible for the full Communion observation. In this way my Jewish identity was protected. I also participated in the choir for Christmas Mass, even dressing as an angel one year and going "on stage" with beautiful wings on my back. I liked being included in this important event, and being able to do so, openly. Since I had been in hiding with them for almost three years, I needed to go along with the rituals taking place in the convent to protect myself, as well as maintaining some sense of protection for the nuns. And, having lived there all this time, and having no other place to go and no one to claim me, I eventually accepted that I would remain in the convent and would later probably become a sister.

There were, however, friends of my parents, Helene and Joseph Kaczek, émigrés from Austria who moved to Belgium during the '30s; they had been able to go into hiding during the war years. When they returned after the war they began to look for my sister and for me. In February 1946, they were able to take my sister from her hiding home, and—with the help of the *Comité Central Israélite,* the Organization for Jewish Refugees, *Vaad Hatzala* (the American-based Rescue Committee—Belgian Section), and the "Joint," the American Jewish Joint Distribution Committee—place her in a Jewish home, where she remained until fall 1946, going to the home's campsite in the summer of 1946.

During the war, these same organizations helped to get me released from the convent. However, it was a difficult transfer, as the mother superior did not want to release me, and I did not want to leave. The convent was home. It was what I knew.

The other children went to the local parish school in town. But I couldn't go. My presence would endanger them because I "looked Jewish" and might be picked up. Therefore I spent all my days inside the convent. I knew the sisters well, as I was always with those who lived there and interacted only with them throughout the day. (Some sisters traveled into the farm areas, often near Holland, to get food for us, so they might be away for some days.) They were the ones who guided me: taught me how to knit, to cook, to clean; they were my schoolteachers as well.

They allowed me to care about others. Who else could I turn to? I didn't go "home" during vacation as some children did. I didn't have my parents coming to see me on visitors' days. The convent was my family. It was always there. I knew what to do, and I knew how I could live. I didn't always have to think how to *be* before those around me. I felt accepted.

When my leaving would be brought up, I asked myself: Where would I go? To strangers again? I did not want that. Yes, I had "housework" to do. But that life was the life I knew. It was always there. It was my "constant." It was the familiarity of the environment and the routines of living there that gave me the comfort and security that I needed.

My father's brothers lived in New York, and one of them decided to sponsor us after much urging from Mrs. Kaczek. "Did he want his brother's children to be raised in another religion?" After all, his deceased brother was an observant Jew, she reminded him.

Eventually the proper papers were arranged; the mother superior released me to the Kaczek family in March 1946, in preparation for immigration to the United States. My uncle paid $400 for our two passages to the United States; my sister and I registered our "desire . . . to immigrate to the United States" with the American Consul in Antwerp, and visas would be issued. They were issued in August 1946, and the immigration permit three months later.

Helene Kaczek placed me with the same Jewish Children's Home as my sister. Because I was in "a rather bad state of health," which I am able to remember being treated for, although I do not recall the specific ailment, the home decided to send me right away to their summer campsite in Knokke so I could recuperate. I remained there until fall 1946 and stayed in the "privileged" section at the camp, with fewer children than the other group, where my sister was. The difference that I noted was that I received one egg a week while the other group had eggs only every other week.

After the summer was over, my sister and I went back to Brussels, to the Kaczek family. They would take care of us until our visas arrived for passage to the United States. Clara and I now lived together for the first time in over four years—not since she was a two-year-old.

The American "Joint" would supervise our trip to the United States. Other children would also be going; there turned out to be about twenty of us total. Finally, the visas came; passage was arranged for the *Île de France,* leaving Cherbourg on December 4, 1946.

The Kaczek family, the friends who had facilitated our going to my uncle in New York, readied us as much as possible. Both my little sister and I always knew that our stay with the Kaczek family was temporary. From the beginning we were told that we would be going to America, to be with family, our father's brothers. All we needed to do was wait until the appropriate papers were drawn up, and our quota numbers neared. So while we felt very comfortable with Helene and Joseph and their twenty-year-old son, Henri, we were always prepared to end the life we lived with that family. A promising future was always held up for us to anticipate. During the three months we lived with them prior to departure we had received clothing, some toys, food, and much love. Here was another parting that I was experiencing—again. Everyone promised life would be good for us now. All would go smoothly; the past was over; the future would be calm. From somewhere I received a new pair of shoes, not worn by anyone yet; really brand-new.

The parting was emotional, but there was some excitement as we anticipated the voyage. The ladies in charge took me and my sister. That was a beginning for me, to spend days and nights with her on a journey. We and the other children traveled by train to France, and at some point we were taken to the port of embarkation. Everyone was emotional; both joy of the unknown and fear of the unknown seemed to alternate in our thoughts.

The crossing gave me exposure to a part of life I never imagined. The ship was very big; there were so many people. We slept in a room with several berths. Others in our group had similar arrangements. Food was plentiful, and the dining room had the vastest expanse that I would ever see. As our group entered this room, always together, and we were going to the area assigned to us, we needed to walk by a large table to our right; this table was laden with all sorts of fruits, each kind bunched together, and then touching the next variety. The table always appeared to be full, as far as our eyes could see. Of course, to our group traveling away from the deprivations we didn't even know we had endured, to see so much food on display, which we were told some people could take at will, was an unbelievable sight. Many of us couldn't name all the fruits that were on that table, but seeing this expanse impressed us.

I think the daily exposures to this sumptuous display reinforced the feeling that there had been another world existing, beyond the fearful, uncertain, and hidden world we children had come from. Many of us were too young to know the extent of the war's events, both in scope of size and vastness of destruction. And some of us (maybe many) were believing that someone from our family would eventually come forth to find us! Our thoughts were occupied by what we had experienced. We did not yet understand, much less know, what we would be experiencing. The laden table represented what might be "out there." It made me feel I still had so much to learn. If I wasn't in awe of it, I at least wondered how it came to be, and what did it mean.

While our group was not allowed to partake of this largesse, we were not envious. Our meals were served in an area on the left of the dining room, and we received sufficient food for our needs. It was enough just to be able to see the welcoming display on entering the dining room. Maybe none of us would even have dared to take anything from it, even if we were told we could do so.

After a few days on the ocean the sea got rough; the grown-ups told us that whales were trying to attack the ship with their tails, and that is why the ship was rocking so much. Many people were seasick. As the trip neared its end, activity and emotion seemed to blend, to be everywhere. People wanted to disembark, to see families, to go home. But everyone showed most excitement about seeing the Lady in the New York Harbor in just a few days' time.

People in our group were getting things together in anticipation of leaving the ship in two days. An officer from the *Île de France* came around to everyone with forms to fill out. "What should I write?" I asked him. He answered, "Well, if you have anything worth a lot of money, anything valuable, you have to write it on this paper, after your name, and sign your name on this paper."

I thought about what I had that was valuable. I couldn't leave the paper blank. Oh, I had these new shoes. I wrote that down—new leather shoes, brown, one pair. I turned in the declaration.

The day of disembarking arrived. Everyone got up early to see the Statue of Liberty. Standing on the deck, adult strangers began talking to each other and even to us children. Two different ladies, at separate times, asked me, in French, about myself. After a little while, each one gave me a dollar.

Finally we got off the ship. I would see my uncle, the one I would live with. It would be the first time I would meet him. I had dressed my best for the occasion, putting on the clothes that I thought suited me and were the nicest. I was ready.

But first I had to go through the official entry to the United States. An immigration agent came over. He had my declaration in his hand. After verifying my name, he looked at the form and at my luggage and asked, "Where are the new shoes?"

I thought about what I had written on the declaration—and then I pointed and said, "They're on my feet." He noted that on the paper, nodded, and left with a little smile. This was my welcome.

It was December 11, 1946.

Figure 22. Leonie Taffel in Brussels, Belgium, fall 1946.

ROYAUME DE BELGIQUE
MINISTERE des AFFAIRES ETRANGERES et du COMMERCE EXTERIEUR
Direction générale de la Chancellerie et du Contentieux

KONINKRIJK BELGIE
MINISTERIE van BUITENLANDSCHE ZAKEN en BUITENLANDSCHEN HANDEL
Algemeene Directie der Kanselarij en der Geschillen

Prix de la formule : 2 Frs.
Prijs van het formulier : 2 Fr.

LAISSEZ-
tenant lieu d
V.17.475
DOORGANGSBEWIJS
ter vervanging van een reispas

Le présent laissez-passer est délivré à Mademoiselle
Dit doorgangsbewijs wordt afgeleverd aan
TAFEL Lony

de nationalité apatride, née à Berlin,
van nationaliteit, geboren te
le 23. août 1935 (1)
op
résidant à Schaerbeek, rue Linné, 118
verblijvende te

titulaire de la carte d'identité N°
houder van de eenzelvigheidskaart N^r

délivrée à , le
afgeleverd te op

à l'effet de lui permettre de se rendre aux Etats-Unis d'Amérique
ten ende hem (haar) ertoe te machtigen zich naar par toutes voies libres
te begeven. accompagnée de sa sœur Taffel Clara née à Bruxelles le 14. mars 1940

Le présent titre de voyage est valable pour voir visa au verso
Deze reistitel is geldig voor

~~et pour~~ voyage.
~~*en voor*~~ *reis (reizen).*

Bruxelles, le 23. août 1946
Brussel, den

Pour le Ministre des Affaires Etrangères
et du Commerce Extérieur :
Le fonctionnaire délégué,

Voor den Minister van Buitenlandsche Zaken
en Buitenlandschen Handel :
De Afgevaardige Ambtenaar,

(1) Indiquer la profession. — Beroep aanduiden.

Imp. Lombaerts, Brux. — 200.000

Figure 23. Leonie Taffel's and her sister Clara's passports to travel to the United States, August 23, 1946.

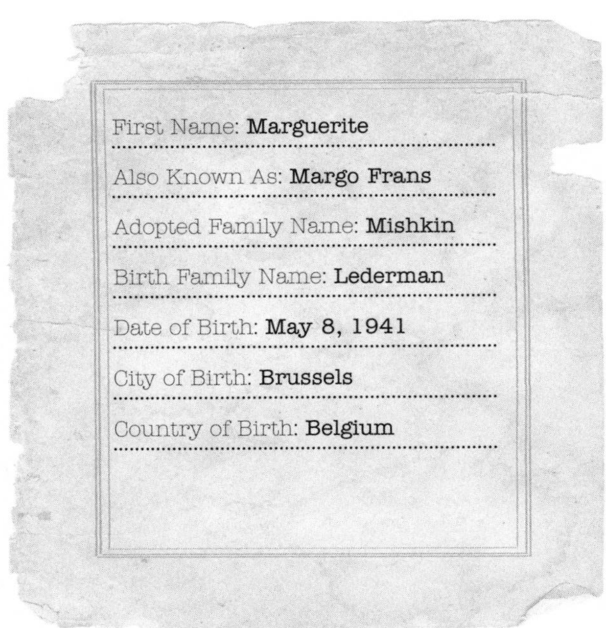
First Name: **Marguerite**
Also Known As: **Margo Frans**
Adopted Family Name: **Mishkin**
Birth Family Name: **Lederman**
Date of Birth: **May 8, 1941**
City of Birth: **Brussels**
Country of Birth: **Belgium**

Mother and Daughter—Parallel Thoughts

Marguerite Lederman Mishkin

I remember: the contour of her face
her inquisitive hazel eyes
her bright eyes filled with love
her rosy chubby cheeks
her fuzzy blond-red hair
her joyful laugh
her gleeful giggle
her shy smile
her first words
her stumbling steps
her pride in standing up
her warm little arms around me
her in my loving arms
the joy of being her mother

I don't know: her hopes and dreams
her likes and dislikes
her hobbies
her talents
her friends
her fears

her ambition
her longings
her spirit
if she got married
if she has children
if she is sad
if she is lonely
if she is happy
if she remembers me
if she survived

I was gassed.

I don't remember: her features
her hair color
her eyes
her voice
her arms around me
her smell
her feel
her walk
her smile
her laugh
her moods
her hand holding mine
being her daughter.

I know: her indomitable spirit
her unflagging courage
her unfailing love
her longing desires for me
her endless dreams for me
her selfless sacrifice
her sense of looming danger
her desperate act of trust
her defiance of danger
her clear thinking in times of peril
her determination to leave witness
her faith in a future

I survived.

I wish I could remember the past we shared.

I wish I could have seen the future we should have shared.

Figure 24. Marguerite Lederman and her mother, Rayzla Lederman, Brussels, Belgium, 1943. Courtesy United States Holocaust Memorial Museum.

Who Am I This Time?

Marguerite Lederman Mishkin

As our train pulls out of the Antwerp station, children sitting all around me are crying—it seems as if everyone is sobbing out the windows of the train except my sister Annette and me. As I clutch my doll, I look out the windows and see the faces of grown-ups, crying too, and waving at the children next to us. Why is everyone crying? I don't understand. Finally, the day has come: October 15, 1949. I am eight years old and my sister Annette is nine. Our whole Mrs. Waintraub's orphanage, at General Drubbeistraat 66 in Borgerhout, Antwerp, the place where we have lived for three and a half years, all the children and our caretakers, are starting our journey to Israel.

This is an important day, and the orphanage matrons have been talking about and waiting for it a long time. Jewish people everywhere have been waiting for this to happen for thousands of years. The matrons say that *Aliyah* means that we are returning. I don't understand the word "return." To me it means going back to Mommy. But that isn't what the matrons mean. They say it means we are going back home to Israel. But Annette and I have never been there.

I want someone to tell me what language those words—"Zionist and Youth *Aliyah*"—are. They don't sound like French words. I wish someone would tell me what those words mean. I don't know much French, and they don't sound like any Flemish words Mommy used. Anyway, the matron says that they have been preparing us for this day. I don't remember. To me all these places where Annette and I are taken are the same now. To me, it doesn't really matter anymore what the next place is. Annette and I have slept in many beds next to so many other little girls and have been told to sit at so many tables and eat whatever was just put before us. We have had so many things done to us that no one has explained before it happened that I know only one thing about this new place, whatever they call it. I know there will be no mommy and daddy there for us. Again.

We come from a place called Rumst. We lived there with a mommy and daddy we don't have anymore. Our mommy there used to take us to church to see the pretty stained glass windows and the statues of Jesus and Mary. We attended a Catholic nursery school. But we live in an orphanage now, and the matrons there say our mommy was not our real mommy.

They are happy that we are finally going to Israel. Why am I not happy? Maybe it's because I'm not Jewish, even though they tell me I am. Maybe I will be Jewish in Israel. They say Israel is a wonderful place. It is always warm there, and oranges grow on the trees. It never gets cold or snowy, and there are sunny beaches and an ocean to play in. There my skin will turn darker, and I will grow up strong, running around in the sunshine.

Of course the grown-ups say other things about Israel too, things that are harder for me to understand. They say that in Israel everyone is a Jew. Everyone. There we will be safe, and no one can ever again do to us the terrible things that happened to Jews all over Europe up till now, and especially during the last few years.

My question is, what is a Jew? I have been told that Annette and I are Jews, and that's why we are here in this orphanage instead of in a house with a mommy and daddy. I know some children live that way, and I remember that once upon a time we lived that way too. I wonder if that is why some of the children on this train are crying. Are they leaving mommies and daddies? Where are our mommy and daddy? Will we ever have a mommy and daddy again? How does that work?

I remember the woman we used to call Mommy, the woman our neighbors used to call Clementine or Mrs. Frans-van Buggenhout. She was the mommy the orphanage matrons have told us is not our real mother at all. I don't believe what they are saying. That can't be true, can it?

I have only one Mommy, the one who left us with these people who never hug us. They also tell me that I was with our first mommy until I was two years old and Annette was three. Does that make sense? I don't think this orphanage lady knows anything. It wasn't until we went to the orphanage that I was told that the mommy I remember was not my first mommy, and that she had only been Mommy from the time I was two years old until I was five. I am actually a Jew. I didn't even know what a Jew was, and I don't think I really know now.

But I do remember that mommy. As the train pulls away, I start to remember more about her. It was a long time ago, but I remember the last time I saw Mommy. Mommy, my sister Annette, and I were walking. There were lots of people on the street in Antwerp, all walking in different directions. I didn't know any of them. Both Annette and Mommy were crying. I wasn't crying because big girls don't cry. I didn't understand why Mommy and Annette were crying because they were older and bigger than I was.

We arrived at this big dark, scary-looking building. It looked as if a witch might live in the building. There were some letters on top of the door. I wondered if those letters said anything. I can't read. When Mommy looked at the letters, she cried harder.

Why would letters make Mommy cry? I asked Mommy if the letters said anything. She read, *"Home D' Enfants—Anvers"* (Children's Home—Antwerp). Why would a children's home look so scary? I thought it should be bright and cheerful like my school in Rumst. I didn't understand why that name made Mommy cry. I thought I would have fun visiting a children's home. Maybe we would play the same games I played at nursery school. Would they talk about Jesus and Mary the way they did in our nursery school? A children's home would be fun for a day.

A woman came out of the big building to greet us, and Mommy now was crying more than ever. The woman tried to take Annette's hand and mine, to lead us away from Mommy, but we wouldn't let go of Mommy's hands. Mommy was crying and asking the woman not to cut our hair.

Mommy bent down to kiss us and she told us how much she loved us, but that she had to leave us in this place. She said, "This is the hardest thing I have ever had to do." Then she walked away. If it was so hard, why did she do it? Why did she leave us in this big, cold place filled with children and matrons with stony faces so unlike

Mommy's smile? Their faces all looked blank. I just loved to see Mommy smile. Her face looked so happy. Her smile reminded me of the sunflowers that grew in our yard. Her face looked like the sun when she smiled.

Annette and I, sobbing, turned to face the woman who had pulled us away from the mother we knew and loved. She took us into another room and then another room and then another room. I don't remember anything about those rooms. They had something to do with papers and grown-ups talking about us.

Then we went into a different room. It had grown-up chairs in it, and the matron helped me sit in one. Then she put a towel around me and began to comb my hair. It began to hurt as she pulled my hair harder. "Stop! That hurts!" I cried. And then I saw the scissors. Quickly, before I could even twist away from her and climb down and run away, she began to cut my hair. Oh, my hair—I saw it falling down the towel and onto the floor. I began to kick her.

I think she called the other matron then. The other one held me in the chair, hard, while the first one finished cutting. Why did they cut my beautiful hair? I wish she had not held me so tight, so that I could run away. I knew right away I was not going to like it here. How could I when they cut my beautiful hair? Why didn't Mommy come and tell them to stop? I thought Mommy loved me. I guess no one, except Annette, loves me. Annette can't help me. I sat in that chair and thought, "No one can help me. I am on my own. Well, I'm a big girl, and I didn't cry when Mommy and Annette did. I guess I will be on my own from now on. If I ever leave this place, I'm going to grow my hair and never cut it."

Then she lifted me down with one arm and left me lying in tears on the floor while she went after my sister. I couldn't watch. When it was over, I looked at Annette. She didn't look like Annette anymore.

I didn't even recognize Annette. That couldn't be my sister. She looked like a boy. I thought, "If I didn't know this strange person, does he know who I am? I don't have a brother. I used to have a sister. But now I have no one.

"Why doesn't Mommy come back? I thought we were only going to play here and learn some more about Jesus and Mary." I thought of Mommy, gently brushing our hair into curls that morning as she did every morning, and telling us how pretty our hair was and what pretty girls we were. We were not pretty anymore. We were not us anymore, were we?

Then we were taken into a big long room with beds in it. I didn't understand. Our mommy and our home and everything I knew were suddenly gone, and I knew I would never have them again. Instead, Annette and I were going to sleep in beds in this big room with lots of other children next to us, children we did not know. What would happen if I got scared in the night, or had to go to the bathroom? I knew right away what would happen: nothing. No one would come to help us. We would be on our own in this gray and terrible place.

One of the grown-up ladies who was leading us from room to room was talking, saying something about Annette. "No!" Annette screamed. "No! My sister and I have to stay together! We have to!" I could not believe it. The lady was saying that Annette and I were to be separated. I could not stand it. I began to scream too—"No, no! My sister! My sister!" We clung tightly to each other, looking up into the face of the angry lady. She kept saying, "You are going to sleep in different rooms!" over and over, louder and louder. "Five-year-olds sleep in this room. Six-year-olds sleep in the next room. Annette will sleep in the next room. You will see each other every day! You should be grateful to be here! Be quiet!" Sobbing, we shook our heads and clutched each other more tightly.

"A little while ago I was with Mommy, and now I will never see her again. I've just lost everything else," I thought in amazement. "I will *not* lose my sister!" We stood together a long time, and finally the lady muttered something about it being time for something. And then she gave in. "All right!" she said angrily. "I will put you next to each other in this room at least for now. Come along. It is dinnertime!"

I don't remember dinnertime that night at all. But I do remember that afterward Annette and I were sent to the top of a staircase with all the other little girls. There was some kind of balcony overlooking the main hall of the orphanage, and we all stood on it looking down at the main hall. That was where all the little boys were standing. They were wearing little caps, and they bowed their heads and began to recite something in a language I had never heard before. I began to ask Annette what they were saying, but one of the matrons hushed me, whispering, "Quiet! They're saying *yizkor*!" "What's *yizkor*?" I asked.

"It is a prayer for the dead. They are praying for their parents. Be quiet!" Silently, I stood with Annette, watching, listening, and wondering. Should I pray? Was I allowed to? I knew a prayer, because Mommy had taught it to me, and the nice ladies in the long funny black dresses at nursery school had made us pray it often. But it didn't sound anything like this prayer. That one started "*Pater noster,*" which the black-dressed ladies told us meant "Our Father" in Latin. The black-dressed ladies also tried to teach us to make the sign of the cross. I practiced and practiced, but I could never make that sign. I noticed that none of the little boys were making that sign. No one here was. I did not understand.

After a while the prayer time was over, and we had to go to bed. As we got ready for bed, Annette and I said nothing to each other. With all her hair cut off, she looked so different that it was hard to remember this was still Annette, still my sister. I reached up to touch my hair again, and my hand kept going. I had hardly any hair left.

We went to bed in silence, not answering the little girls who kept wanting to talk to us until the matron shushed them and turned the lights out. I lay in bed, thinking about this morning. "This morning," I thought, "I woke up in my bed with Annette in the other bed and Mommy coming in to help us. This morning I was one Marguerite, and now I am a different Marguerite. I am a Jew. I am in a different place. I look different. Am I still Marguerite at all?" It was terrible in this cold place. Nobody knew us or cared about us. Nobody noticed us at all unless we did something wrong—and I am always doing something wrong.

A few days after we arrived, one of the other little girls asked me if I knew what tonight was. I shook my head. "Tonight," she announced, sounding like a matron, "Tonight is Shabbat. Do you know what that is?" "No," I said. "What is it?" "It means we can't do any work for a whole night and a whole day." "Oh," I said, but I did not understand. "It means," the little girl continued, "we can't do anything that is work. The matrons and the other grown-ups can't either. Make sure you don't accidentally do any, or you will be in big trouble."

That didn't seem too hard. I was too little to do any work anyway, wasn't I? That evening at supper I had forgotten our conversation about Shabbat until the little girl said to me, "There won't be any hot food tomorrow, you know." "Why not?" I asked her. "Heating up food is work. It can't be done on Shabbat." "What about this food?—It's hot." We were having soup. "That's because it was heated before the sun went down. Tomorrow we will eat cold food for breakfast and lunch. We can have hot food for supper, because the sun will set by then."

On our way back upstairs for bed, Annette and I were close to the head of the line of children. That's why I overheard the matrons when we turned the corner to go down the hallway to bed. One of them stopped very suddenly in front of the hallway light switch. "Who forgot to turn this light on?" she angrily asked the other one. "It's too dark in this hallway. One of the children will fall down and get hurt!" "What are we going to do now?" asked the other. "I don't know! If one of the children gets hurt, you and I will be responsible." It seemed very simple to me, and I wondered if the matrons didn't know how to turn on the light. "I can help!" I volunteered, and reached up, quickly turning on the switch and instantly lighting up the hallway. "What did you do that for?" the matrons yelled. "That is a sin! It's the Shabbat! Don't you know anything at all?" I began to cry. "I'm sorry!" I whimpered. "I didn't know it was wrong. Here, I'll fix it!" And I reached up to turn the light off. Then they really got angry and pulled my hand down. "Don't you know anything? Haven't you learned anything here about what it means to be a Jew?" the matrons yelled at me. The other children stared at me as if I had done something terrible, but I didn't know what it was.

One morning all of us little girls came back into the orphanage for lunch after playing outside, and there was suddenly a lot of excitement. One of us had received a package from America. I had lots of questions, and I asked anyone who would listen. Where is America? Who would send a package from there to someone in our orphanage? What was in the package? Someone told me the package was for me and that it had been sent by a group of women in America who sent packages to Jewish orphans in Europe. I ran up the stairs to the dormitory and stopped in the doorway. One of the matrons was carrying a big brown box. She had just picked it up from my bed and was carrying it over to another girl's bed, saying, "No, this box belongs to Sarah, not to Marguerite!" My heart sank, because everyone knew that Sarah was the matron's favorite. Even if the box had been sent to me, she would give it to Sarah. The matron put the box on Sarah's bed and began to open it. All the little girls stood around the box, excited to see what amazing things were coming here from the nice ladies in America.

First there were a dress and some underwear. The matron looked at these things and told Sarah sadly, "These are much too big for you. We'll have to give them to one of the older girls." Then she took out a rubber ball. It was beautiful—all pink and shiny and clean. I had never seen anything so new.

And then, from the bottom of the box, the matron took out two last things: the most beautiful doll I had ever seen, with golden hair and a darling little yellow dress and little shoes and stockings—and a letter. The matron couldn't read the letter, because it was in a different language ("English," the matron said it was); but she could read two words on the envelope. Angrily, she dropped the envelope on the bed; and all of us looked at it. It read "Marguerite Lederman." Sarah looked at me sadly, as the matron thrust the doll and the ball into my hands. I was so happy.

This was the most beautiful doll in the world, and now she was mine! I thought about what to name her, and I sat down in a corner of the dormitory with Annette and stared at the doll in my arms. "Lunchtime!" the matron yelled. "May I bring my doll?" I asked her, filled with excitement. "Of course not," the matron replied. "Just leave her here on your bed. She will still be here after lunch." And, amazingly, she was. No one—not even Sarah, not even Annette—touched my doll without my permission. She slept with me every night, and I took very good care of her.

A few days after my presents came, I was outside in the orphanage yard playing with my brand-new ball; and one of the little boys asked if he could play with it. I said no, because I had seen the boys play catch, trying to throw a ball higher and higher. Sometimes the game ended with one boy throwing a ball so high the others could not catch it and it landed on the roof of the orphanage. We called that place "Ball Heaven" because nothing ever came back from there. A ball on the roof was lost forever. The little boy who had asked to play with my ball went and told one of the matrons I had refused to share. She hurried over and took the ball from me, telling me, "You can't do that. If he wants the ball, let him play with it." I stood in the yard getting sadder and sadder as the little boy threw the ball higher and higher with one of his friends. In a few minutes it went to Ball Heaven, as I knew it would. But the doll stayed with me.

We lived in the orphanage for at least three years. So long. Memories of Mommy came to me sometimes, but I did not talk about them because I did not understand why she had left us. I remembered her saying on that terrible day that she did not want to leave us, but that someone was making her. I did not understand who or why. Sometimes I did not understand anything, and I still don't. I didn't understand why this morning we were told we would not be studying today, but that we should hurry and pack whatever we had because the long-awaited day was finally here. We are going to Israel today. Of course I brought my doll, and Annette and I walked in line with the other children. We walked a long way, several blocks at least, away from the orphanage.

We got to the train station, and I couldn't believe we were getting onto a huge train car. I found it all rather exciting until I heard the children around me beginning to cry. Now Annette and I are sitting on this train with all these crying children. It is all so strange and so sad. I thought going to Israel was going to be a good thing for us, but the other children don't think so. Why? Something must be wrong, but I don't know what it is. I begin to cry too. One of the matrons comes over to me, yelling, "Be quiet! Stop crying! You don't have anything to cry about! These children are leaving a mommy or daddy or maybe a grandma. You don't have any mommy or daddy left! You have nothing to cry about! Oh, be quiet!" I pay no attention to her and keep crying. She gives up and moves over to another child. Eventually the train begins to move. Children all around me are sobbing and waving at their crying parents through the window. I close my eyes. It helps. After a while, I open them and turn around to examine the faces of the children around me. They are quieting down, and it seems to me that they are turning to stone. Their eyes look empty, not just of tears, but of everything. I hold my doll and look out the window. Annette sits next to me, quiet as usual. The train is moving along quickly now, and the countryside is going past—fields and cows and buildings in the distance. I hear one of the matrons whisper to another, "Half an hour and we'll be out of Belgium forever. On our way to the Holy Land!" They smile at each other.

And I suppose it will be better. That is what the grown-ups say. Everyone will be a Jew, whatever that is; and no one will come to take us away ever again.

Then suddenly the train slows down and stops. I look out the window, but there is no station. Just more fields and cows. The children grow frightened. Why are we stopping? Through the window, Annette and I see two policemen coming. Quickly they climb up the train car steps and onto the train. I know right away why they are here. "Annette!" I whisper. "They're coming for you and me! I know it!"

"What?" she asks.

"The policemen? What have we done?" The two policemen hurry into the car. They are big, strong men; and they begin to speak quickly and softly to the two matrons in our car, showing them pieces of paper. The other children are completely silent, waiting to see who they are coming for. They know the policemen are coming for someone because that is how it has always been for us all. My orphanage friends have told me stories of hiding in darkness outside, watching people in uniform come and take their daddies and mommies away forever.

The matrons look almost as frightened as the children, and one of them then does what I knew she would do: she comes over to Annette and me and tells us, "Hurry up! The police are here to take you away!" I begin to scream, and Annette does too. The other children take up this cry, and the car is suddenly filled with sobbing, terrified children as Annette and I clutch at the armrests of our seats, trying to keep from being taken away again.

Of course the policemen win. Each of them carries one of us, flailing and crying, off the train as the children in the car go wild and the matrons sternly tell them to stop, to no avail. Once we are off the train and standing in the middle of a field with the two policemen, watching the train start up and leave without us, I look down at my hands—and in one hand, unbelievably, is my doll. Annette and I cling to each other, our bodies wracked with sobs, as it slowly comes to me that we are not going to Israel. We are not going to that land of sunshine and safety. We are here in the middle of a field with two strangers who do not seem to be about to kill us, but you never know.

The policemen put us into their car and begin to drive down a lane away from the railroad tracks. I don't know where we are going or who I am supposed to be this time or whether this time I will be a Jew. Or even whether I will be alive tonight. The train slowly pulls away.

Figure 25. Annette and Marguerite Lederman with Valerie Frans-van Buggenhout, their rescuer, in Rumst, Belgium, 1944. Courtesy United States Holocaust Memorial Museum.

To Annette, the Center Point

Marguerite Lederman Mishkin

When the Holocaust swirled around us,
dizzying us with disaster,
and ripping away our mother,
and ripping away our mother again,
I reached for your hand,
You reached for mine,
Two tiny hands of tiny girls,
Holding together the whole world,
For each other.

Between our hands was all the
center point
there was. I existed
to protect you, I was real
amid the unreal terror;
The pointless cruelty—miracle!—
had left this point of meaning.
Annette. Marguerite.
Marguerite. Annette.
I was I because of you.
Alone, I disappeared.
When you appeared, I was again.
We held hands and refused
To be apart, to be converted, to be blown out
like candles,
Two remaining out of millions.

Later, lied to and loaded on a ship
heading into a foggy future,
we endured.
Compliantly and calmly, as that voyage ended,
You stepped off, reached back for me, and stayed
My center point in the new place.

Suddenly we were daughters again
With a father and a mother,
a home,
a bedroom of our own.
Aunts and uncles appeared
Popping like big flowers up close

To our frightened faces.
You and I agreed to
Fit in,
Lose our French,
Be good enough to be loved,
To be kept,
This time.

Sometimes I wondered
When you would leave me.
I know how to do that, how to be
Abandoned.
Sometimes it seemed
That was all I
knew
for sure.

You never did,
Never left me in all those
drama-ridden
teenage times.
Still the center point,
Safety in the turmoil.

Then you left and married,
took a new name, walked into a new world
filled with kashruth and with babies,
with the sounds of Hebrew, of dancing, and of joy,
wearing your new last name calmly and at peace.

Alone, I found new sisters in my friends—
but never the held hand, never the center point, again.

And now, Annette, I stand in for you,
in single witness,
One last lit candle
in the chaos and the fog.

Figure 26. Annette and Marguerite Lederman in hiding in Rumst, Belgium (near Malines [Mechelen]), 1944. Courtesy United States Holocaust Memorial Museum.

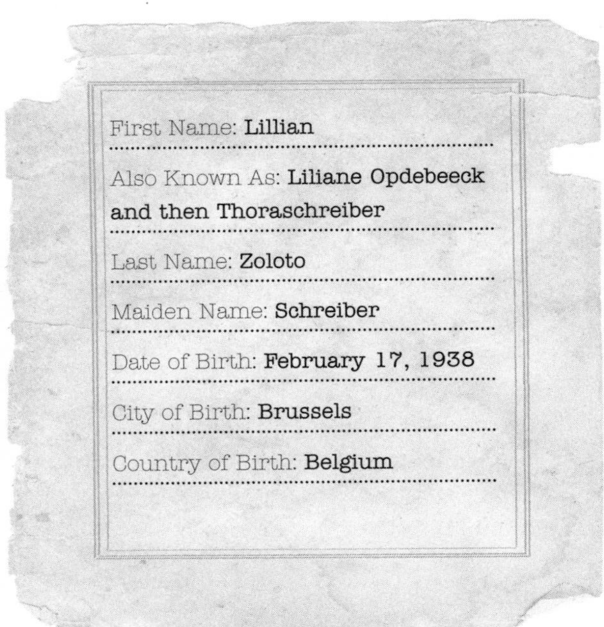
First Name: Lillian

Also Known As: Liliane Opdebeeck and then Thoraschreiber

Last Name: Zoloto

Maiden Name: Schreiber

Date of Birth: February 17, 1938

City of Birth: Brussels

Country of Birth: Belgium

A Child Remembers

Lillian Schreiber Zoloto

Early September 1942—Saint-Gilles, Brussels

I am four years old and I love my mother's hats. I parade around the apartment wearing different colored hats with veils, plumes, and feathers. My mother tells me I look very pretty.

One day she tells me I have to go sleep at Lisa and Karl's apartment and she bribes me, that day and every day after that, by letting me wear one of her hats out in the street as I leave with Lisa for the night. Lisa is my governess, and my parents trust Lisa and her husband, Karl. As a protest to the Nazi regime and its failing economy, they have left their home in Germany and settled in Brussels.

At Lisa and Karl's I sleep on a cot in the dining room, a very large room with tall windows. Through the sheer curtains, tree shadows sway and dance on the walls and ceiling of the room while Karl snores loudly in the next bedroom. The trees move and make shapes of monsters on the walls. Are they making sounds or is it Karl? I hide under the blankets, wishing for my mother and my bed.

All the hats my mother gave me remain at Lisa's apartment. Later in the war, when my parents are in hiding, they entrust their possessions for safekeeping to Lisa and Karl. They learn at the end of the war that everything was sold on the black market.

When my mother runs out of hats and bribes for me, my fear of those frightening evenings at Lisa's apartment emboldens me. I confront her, "Do you not love me? I want to stay with you always. Why do you send me away at night?"

Stunned, my mother gathers me in her arms and holds me tight. "*Ketzele,* my little kitten, I love you very much and I want us to be together all the time, but you must listen to what I tell you. There is a bad man, Hitler, who does not like people like us, and he may be very mean to us. I need to protect you because you are little. So, go with Lisa and be a good girl." The explanation may not be clear, but the danger and fear become real. I become quiet and obedient.

Late September 1942—Anderlecht, Brussels

Otto, an underground Resistance friend of Karl's, carries my black patent valise and holds my hand as he accompanies me, first by streetcar and then on foot, to the home in Anderlecht of Jean Opdebeeck, another underground Resistance fighter.

The building we enter is tall with a long, dark corridor from which we finally emerge into a courtyard with a garden patch at the end. Two smiling women, standing under an awning near a painted wooden cupboard with many drawers, fawn over me as I stand bewildered, wondering which one is the mommy of this place. One woman seems older, and I keep staring at them as they engage me. "Liliane," says the younger woman, "my little girl Christiane will soon return from her walk with her doll carriage and you can play with her." As soon as Christiane returns, she and I immediately begin to play with her many dolls while Otto arranges my stay with Josine Opdebeeck.

The following morning, the Opdebeecks tell me that I am to call them *Oncle Jean* and *Tante Josine,* as they plan to tell the neighbors that I am the child of a sick relative, and I have come to live with them. As a blond, blue-eyed child, I fit in perfectly with the family. I am also told that we are never to speak of my parents because it would be dangerous for them and for us. All of these precautions are necessary as the Opdebeecks do not know who can be trusted. With these new instructions and associated fears, I refuse to speak with anyone other than family members until many weeks later when I begin to feel more secure in my environment.

October 1942—Anderlecht, Brussels

My bedroom is very small and so is the window that is high above a dresser against the wall facing the courtyard. There is a party for Christiane's birthday, and Jean and Josine Opdebeeck, their son Jacques, and other family guests are celebrating in the courtyard. The door to my room is closed, and I have to stay in. I know not why. People are saying "*varicelle.*" I am quarantined for chicken pox. I drag a chair from near the bookcase, push it against the dresser, and climb up to see outside. Alone atop the dresser I view the party and long to be outside with the others.

A Few Weeks Later—Saint-Gilles, Brussels

Lisa, the German woman who was my governess and who now serves as a liaison between my parents and the Opdebeecks, accompanies me, Christiane, and Jacques one evening to the home of my parents. This is several weeks after I've left home, and my mother, distraught at neither having seen me nor knowing for certain that I am well cared for, has asked Lisa to bring me for a brief visit. Christiane and Jacques have begged their parents and received their permission to come along as Lisa will provide good protection.

After getting off the tram, we still have a fairly long walk to reach my parents' apartment. Suddenly, I see a German soldier in uniform coming toward us. Fear grips me as I am convinced he will know who I am and that I am not part of this family. I hold Lisa's hand very tightly, and she begins to hum a song to relax me. As the soldier passes our innocent-looking group he smiles, wishing us *Guten Abend* (good evening) in German. I am tense as we approach our destination. On the second floor of our building is a home I no longer recognize. My parents' apartment looks dismal with a single low-wattage bulb providing the only light, and the bulb hangs from a cord pulled low to avoid creating shadows on the walls above the windows. The windows have been whitewashed with paint, and the furniture is mostly gone. Two chairs in the kitchen are near the wood-burning stove. I know I don't want to be here, but my parents are happy to see me.

Just then, an unexpected sharp shrill of the doorbell stuns everyone, and I note the intense fear in everyone's eyes and face. I begin to cry softly, as I have learned to do during these strange times, and wet my underwear. I keep repeating in a low voice, "I want to go home, I want to go home." My father checks through a small unpainted corner of the front bedroom window and ascertains it is a special postal delivery. My mother instructs Lisa in an agitated voice and manner to leave immediately with us. She cannot risk the lives of the children in her apartment. I cannot remember how quickly and how we left or the return trip to Anderlecht. I discovered not too many years ago that all separations are blocked from my memory.

Many years later, Jacques, who was ten years old at the time, told me that he had contemplated jumping from the second-floor window if the Gestapo had been at the door. No further visits to my parents' apartment take place until the war's end.

Life with the Opdebeecks

I adjust happily to life with the Opdebeecks, who provide me with loving care and attention and in whose home, to the delight of this only child, I have two constant playmates. As years pass, the memory of my parents dims until eventually, when we reconnect a few years later, they are strangers to me.

Jean is a master cabinet and furniture maker. His workshop is at the rear of the courtyard, and occasionally, when we girls are allowed to visit, we gather curled wood shavings from the floor and attach them to our hair to mimic the hairstyle of Shirley Temple, a favorite child film actress.

The furniture store is at the front of the building, connected to the apartment by a double door. Josine is usually the one who rushes to tend to customers when the store doorbell summons. In the courtyard are pens for rabbits and chickens, and a rooster that bites if you come near him. We children play with the animals and keep busy while Josine is selling furniture and bric-a-brac. Books also play an important part in our lives, and I remember the thrill of receiving books for my birthdays and holidays, numbering the books, and organizing them in special order on a shelf in my bedroom. I had never been in a library and wonder if my need for order in my life prompted me to devise this system.

Each morning we walk a short distance to a Catholic church where we three children and Josine attend Mass and where I am baptized one day. Following my baptism I am required periodically to go to confession to repent for some transgressions. On those occasions, I walk into the confessional tense and hesitant as I don't know what to tell the priest who sits in the beautifully carved dark wooden booth and whose face I can discern through the metal grille. What can I possibly invent that would make sense? Shall I say I lied? Shall I say I refused to do something? I'm never quite sure what is expected of me as I can't remember anything that needs reporting. In the end there's always a string of Hail Marys to recite, and then it's over until the next time. It doesn't feel right or make sense to me, but I do love the splendor of the statues, the cavernous feel of the place, the smell of the incense, and the quiet atmosphere broken only by the tapping of shoes on the stone floor.

On Saturdays, a large tin tub with wooden handles is filled with warm water and placed in front of the coal-burning stove in the kitchen for our weekly baths. We sponge wash the rest of the week. Sunday is dedicated to spending time with relatives, and on Mondays Josine spends the day at a laundry, washing and ironing our clothes.

Food is rationed and meager, but I don't remember being hungry. I see Jean and Josine eating slowly. Sometimes they take food from their plates to add to ours as they make sure we growing children have sufficient nutrition. Photos taken at the end of the war show Jean and Josine to be very slender while we children have grown appropriately. I remember the day I received one banana in school, bringing it home, to be divided in five equal shares. On special and rare occasions a chicken or rabbit raised in the courtyard made it to our dinner table, and I remember watching a decapitated chicken running around with a headless neck. The comb of the chicken is fried in the blood of the bird to make a chewy delicacy, and the feet are boiled along with the gizzard for soup. Nothing goes to waste.

Roasting Potatoes in the Field

Jean Opdebeeck, *Oncle Jean* to me, his daughter, Christiane, and I are riding a streetcar to the outskirts of Brussels. It is a trip the three of us will make periodically to the end of the tramline to a field where Jean has planted potatoes and other vegetables. Christiane and I are overjoyed each trip with the promise of roasted potatoes and free play away from our home where adults speak in hushed tones and have worried looks on their faces. Jean builds a bonfire with branches and twigs to roast potatoes while he works in a small cabin on the field. Jean admonishes us not to touch the fire or the potatoes nor to come into the cabin. He says there is no room for us in the cabin.

When the potatoes are cooked, their skins blackened and cracked to yield the wonderful aroma of potatoes baked in an open fire, Christiane and I sit on the ground to eat while Jean carefully puts out the fire and gathers vegetables to supplement the meager provisions at home.

There really aren't many vegetables in this patch of land as time doesn't permit Jean to travel from Anderlecht to cultivate it, but it creates a decent front for Jean. Many years later I learn that Jean, involved in the Belgian Resistance, used the cabin to print propaganda leaflets that he brought back to town hidden under the vegetables he had picked. He also hid, under the cabin's floorboards, British flyers who parachuted into Belgium. Two unknowing young girls, enjoying these happy outings, created a great decoy.

1944—School and Bombings

Christiane and I begin first grade at a nearby Catholic school, and we walk to and from school, inseparable as we spend full days together either at play or school. I thrive with the tutelage of the kind nuns who find me a curious and willing student.

It is also the time that V-1s and then V-2s begin to rumble in the skies. We are told these are rockets that will suddenly stop overhead and within seconds drop to the ground. We learn to recognize their droning sound and the siren warning sound that tells us to take cover immediately under furniture or in a room away from windows. We have but a few seconds to hide and protect ourselves.

One such day, we are home from school at lunchtime when the sirens sound. The rocket seems to stop directly above us, and we scatter to our designated safe places. The building shakes and trembles as we hear a loud explosive bang, followed by a brief moment of quiet that brings us together again, each of us quite frightened, but physically intact. Then begin loud wailing sounds of ambulances and a cacophony of noise from other vehicles. When we return to school, the main street Christiane and I must cross is nearly impassable. We stand, holding hands, mesmerized and transfixed by the spectacle. We peer into cars transporting people, bloody and bandaged, from the nearby hospital that had been hit. Nobody bothers with us. I don't know how long we remained on that side of the street nor how we crossed it and got to school, but the memories of that event remain etched in my mind.

Sometimes the sirens sound at night, and *Tante Josine* and *Oncle Jean* hurriedly gather us sleepy children to take shelter in the dark cellar of the building. With only flashlights for light, we find the upstairs neighbors, all of us looking very different in our nightclothes. I remember a small, black, shiny valise containing medicines and bandages that *Tante Josine* would grab as we scurried to the cellar. Other times at *Tante Josine*'s sister's home, we would run to the backyard and crawl into a dugout protected by what looked like a mountain of sandbags. Even now, thinking of these dark hiding places and frightening times makes my heart quicken, and I attribute my fear of closed spaces to those experiences.

May 1945—War Ends—New Challenges

Announcements of the war's end are heard on the radio and then Jean's Resistance compatriots arrive, joyous and delirious, to toss us girls in the air. We all go out onto the wide street where we live to see American tanks and jeeps passing, hailed and cheered by the crowds that gather. I see people jumping on the tanks and jeeps and riding away. I wonder how they will ever find their way back.

I am sitting on someone's shoulders and soldiers are throwing things to the crowds. I catch a flat piece in a yellow wrapper, which I learn is gum and which, later in America, I recognize as Wrigley's Juicy Fruit chewing gum.

The jubilation seems endless; the throngs of people in the street stand shoulder to shoulder singing, hugging one another, jumping, and shouting, "*La guerre est finie! Vive les Americains!*" ("The war is over! Long live the Americans!") Across the street, a large black swastika has been painted on the front of a building, exposing a Nazi collaborator who has been discovered living there. A Hitlerlike mannequin burns in effigy, suspended on a wire that spans the tops of apartment houses on our street.

But the end of the war brings new challenges. Although all their possessions are lost, my parents have survived through lucky circumstances. Some of these experiences include their first-floor neighbor who convinced Germans, who were searching for Jews, that the building was vacant except for his own first-floor apartment as all the upper windows of the three-story apartment building had been whitewashed with paint. This same neighbor, carefully and sparingly, used my parents' food ration stamps to obtain food for them when they were hiding in the cellar. He could not produce many food stamps besides his own at any one time lest the shopkeepers become suspicious of his bounty.

On the few occasions when my parents were out on noncurfew hours, they carried bundles across their chests to hide the yellow stars on their jackets. If, while out, they noticed their building was under surveillance or Germans on the streets nearby, they separated and hid outside under bridges until they deemed it safe to return. If they did not manage to return before curfew, they had to spend the night under these bridges. During a period of intense roundups in their area, my parents were offered refuge in Jean Opdebeeck's workshop, where they spent one night on blankets over wood planks in the shop. I learned this after the war, as they arrived at dusk and departed after daybreak so as not to arouse the curiosity of the Opdebeecks' neighbors. My parents also carried false identity cards obtained when my mother worked as a courier for the Resistance, although these documents could not make them completely secure.

My mother's two sisters, and their families who lived in Brussels, were arrested during roundups and deported to Auschwitz, where they were killed. One young cousin survived three years of horror in the camp. Another young cousin was saved because her father was able to show proof of his service in the German Army in World War I. Thus, he saved his and his daughter's lives, but not the lives of his wife and son.

With the help of Lisa, the German governess, my parents have reestablished contact with the Opdebeeck family and are now anxious to reunite with me. I don't know these Sunday visitors, who are supposed to be my parents. If they are my parents, what is to become of *Tante Josine* and *Oncle Jean*? Everyone seems congenial, and I am feeling conflicted about what is expected of me. I have spent more than three formative years in the bosom of a loving family, and I know I don't want things to change.

The weekly visits continue. During the summer, several families including the Opdebeecks, *Tante Josine*'s sister, whose family harbored a Jewish girl during the war for a short time, my parents, and another family rent a large villa at the North Sea where we children are happy to play on the beach and swim in the sea.

Another school year passes and another summer vacation at the North Sea. These are days that I remember with great happiness, mostly unaware of the emotional tug-of-war being played out between my parents and the Opdebeecks. I am beginning to be concerned about my allegiance to each set of parents as I see shifts in their behavior and supervision of me. I hear the Opdebeecks encourage my parents to continue to reestablish themselves before I return to live with them and to let me continue to stay with the Opdebeecks in a stable home and school environment. I am conflicted about my allegiance, but I have learned through the war years to be compliant and obedient.

Late Summer 1946—Returning Home

Summer vacation is ending, and upon our return from the seaside, my mother suggests that I visit her and my father at their apartment before returning to classes. My mother's devious plan was to have me home, enroll me at a private school near their apartment, and then tell the Opdebeecks. I have no idea how this fait accompli was

Figure 27. Christiane Opdebeeck and Lillian Schreiber in the courtyard of the Opdebeeck residence in Anderlecht, a suburb of Brussels, Belgium, 1943.

Figure 28. Jacques Opdebeeck, Georges (first cousin of Jacques and Christiane Opdebeeck), Christiane Opdebeeck, and Lillian Schreiber coming home from church, Anderlecht, Belgium, May 1944—Pentecost holiday.

Figure 29. *Back row, left to right:* Joseph Thoraschreiber, biological father of Lillian Schreiber; Renée Thoraschreiber, biological mother of Lillian; Mariette Vloebergh, sister of Josine Opdebeeck; Josine Opdebeeck; and Jean Opdebeeck. *Front row:* Lillian Schreiber; André Vloebergh, son of Mariette; Régine (baby), daughter of Mariette; and Christiane Opdebeeck at Wenduine, on the North Sea in Belgium, after World War II.

received by the Opdebeecks, and because the two sets of parents became lifelong friends, I never had the courage to broach the subject.

Somehow I understand that returning home is inevitable, but I am not happy about it. To ease the transition, Jean Opdebeeck, the furniture and cabinet maker, designs and constructs a beautiful mahogany studio bed for me with open shelves for books, sliding glass doors for a curio cabinet, and an attached low cabinet at one end to store blankets and pillows. I love my private little corner in our small apartment, but I miss my Belgian family and home.

We continue to visit the Opdebeecks with regularity. I learn to take the streetcar by myself to their home. We spend birthdays and holidays together, and our lives become intertwined as families. I attend Yiddish school as my parents reeducate me in our Jewish traditions and, along the way, my pretty peach-colored rosary and cross necklace disappear.

The only way I can rebel is to not apply myself at the lycée. One day, downtown with my mother, she points to the charwoman who is cleaning the pay toilets after each use and mentions that this might be my future work if I don't apply myself at school. I had questioned many things during the past few years of separation from my parents, hiding, forming bonds with a new family, reuniting begrudgingly with my own parents, but in my eight-year-old mind, this suggestion makes complete sense. I apply myself and learn to like the new school.

June 1952

If life with my parents moves forward on an even keel after the war, it is turned upside down again for me when they decide to immigrate to America. They are sponsored by my father's sisters and brothers living in the States. Leaving the Opdebeecks and my school friends is another unwanted hurdle that brings me much sadness, and I fantasize that my parents, busy with their preparations, might accidentally leave me behind. Again, I adapt to a completely new life in a strange land. I find emotional strength in the love that was showered upon me for so long by two sets of supportive parents.

Jean Opdebeeck died in 1969, and Josine, taking her first airplane trip at age seventy, came to Chicago to visit me and my family in 1972. She would return three more times before her death in 1986, to enjoy my three children, who adored her as much as they loved my mother, their grandmother.

Yad Vashem recognized Jean and Josine Opdebeeck posthumously in 1995 for their courage and awarded them the title of "Righteous Among the Nations." Jacques and Christiane, who live in Belgium, received the medal and certificate of honor on behalf of their parents. We keep in touch, mostly on birthdays and holidays. We still share the feelings of family.

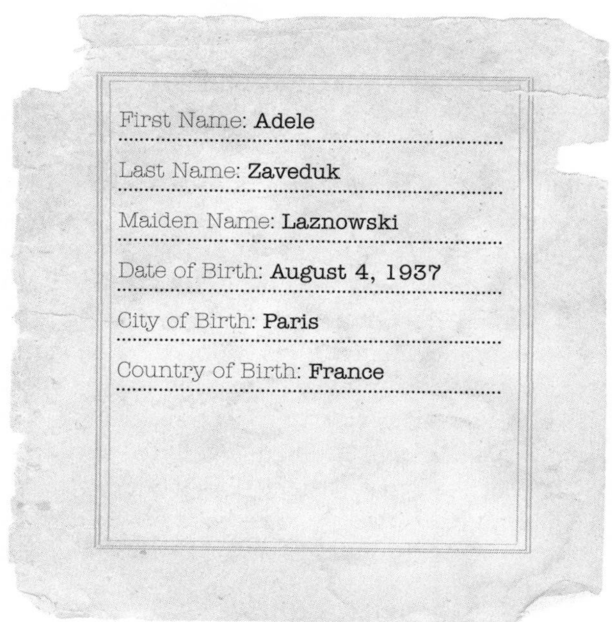
First Name: Adele
Last Name: Zaveduk
Maiden Name: Laznowski
Date of Birth: August 4, 1937
City of Birth: Paris
Country of Birth: France

Born-Again Jew

Adele Laznowski Zaveduk

Whether or not children revealed that they were Jewish could have meant the difference between life and death. This is my story.

I was born in Paris, France, in 1937, and as a little girl at the beginning of World War II, I had no recollections of being Jewish. None. Years later, after the war, I learned that my father had been a captive in Auschwitz. I didn't know that at the time. I only knew there was a war and that my father was a French soldier.

My mother never talked about religion or being Jewish to me or to my younger sister Josette, born in 1940. Perhaps she meant to protect us. I remember my mother wearing a yellow star on her coat, but I didn't understand why she tried to cover it with her purse when we were outside. Because we were under five years of age, neither Josette nor I had to wear the yellow star.

In 1942, my father was released from the French Army in North Africa and returned to Paris. Around that time, the French police were tracking and picking up all the Jewish men and sending them to Eastern Europe concentration or work camps. My father, to avoid being picked up, went into hiding and did not live with us. Several times I remember the French police, with orders to take my father, coming to our small apartment in the middle of the night, banging on the door. I was terrified. In July 1942, the French police picked up my father and then sent him to Auschwitz at the beginning of August. My mother, through an underground agency that helped find hiding places for Jewish children, was able to place my sister and me with a Catholic family in the countryside, in Brou, a small village near Chartres.

My mother left Josette and me with Madame Moulard, a widow, who with her daughter and her daughter's three young children lived in a small two-room apartment above an old vacant store. There was a small kitchen, without running water. The bathroom and a water tap were downstairs in the vacant store. We had to go outside and then enter the store. At night it was scary for a little girl because the store was dark without any electricity. I also had a chamber pot under the bed for immediate necessities at night.

As a mother, I now realize how difficult it must have been for my mother to give up her children. But she knew that the Nazis were rounding up Jews and that women with children were shipped immediately to death camps.

After leaving my sister and me with Madame Moulard, she tried to find work in the neighboring farms to hide and be close to us. When I was an adult my mother told me that Madame Moulard denounced her to the police, who found her and forced her back to Paris on the same day. She never had a chance to say good-bye to us, no hugs, and no kisses; we were being left alone. After returning to Paris she was picked up in September 1942, along with many other Jews in another roundup and was sent to Drancy, a detention camp on the outskirts of Paris, and from there to Auschwitz.

As I look back, our mother's decision to hide us with a Catholic family saved our lives, but at that time we felt abandoned, left alone with strangers. We cried a lot and looked for her, but what can two little girls do when they feel abandoned? Madame Moulard told us that this is what happens to bad people. I always wondered who were the bad people? Was it us? Was it my mother?

Madame Moulard treated us no better or worse than she treated her own family. She had a humble household. The war was going on and there was little food and few basic necessities. In the summer we went barefoot, and in the winter we wore wooden clogs that we wrapped with old newspapers tied with a string around our feet to keep them warm. When she and her daughter drank, they hit all of us kids, including their own, for no reason. There was no warmth, no kindness, nor love. She was a no-nonsense woman. She did share food, clothing, and shelter with us; but most of all she shared her Catholic religion. We lived in a two-room house where I saw a crucifix on the wall of each room along with pictures of the Virgin Mary, Baby Jesus, and several saints, whose names I have forgotten.

The small Catholic church, the only one in town, was two blocks away from Madame Moulard's home. Like all the children in her family and the surrounding community, we attended the small grammar school in Brou, visited the church daily, and went to Mass every Sunday and holidays. Josette and I were like typical French Catholic girls living in a rural town. Reading my catechism presented no conflict because I had no memories of any other religion. In church we learned that the Jews killed Jesus, and they were bad people.

During the time we were with Madame Moulard, a boy named Joseph came to live with us. In 1990, on my first trip back to Brou after the war, I learned he was Jewish. Moulard's three grandchildren, Josette, Joseph, and I slept in one bed. One day we were all in bed sick with chicken pox when I heard heavy footsteps coming up the stairs to the bedroom. Madame Moulard rushed in and grabbed Josette, Joseph, and me out of bed and pushed us under the bed. Frightened, we were hugging each other and trying not to make any noise that would attract attention. Three SS officers marched into the bedroom and asked for the *Judenkinder,* Jewish children. When they saw the sick children covered with pockmarks in bed, they left immediately. That night I prayed that the entire German Army would catch chicken pox. Because I didn't know I was Jewish, this entire incident was strange to me because, after all, I was a Catholic girl. Someone must have denounced us, but Madame Moulard never discovered the culprit.

Germans were searching for Jews everywhere, even in the school, where they would ask teachers for any *Judenkinder.* I remember one day when my teacher heard the Germans coming to our classroom, she signaled some of us to play in the fields outside. She knew who the Jewish children were in her classroom. She told us to stay outside until she called us to return after the Germans left. Our teacher defied the Germans and told them there were no Jews in her classroom. In retrospect, I do not know how she knew we were Jewish. At that time I still thought I was Catholic and the Germans were doing this because we were strangers, not from this town.

Almost four years later in 1945, our parents, who survived, were liberated from the concentration camps and returned to Paris. Jewish agencies helped reunite us with our parents and once again we became a family. I, however, experienced emotional problems. The most important one was that I doubted that those "people" who had taken us away from the Moulards' home were our real parents. Josette and I had no memories of them as being our parents. For us, they were strangers who took us away from the family and home we thought was ours. After all, I was five years old, and Josette two, when our mother left us with Madame Moulard. We lived now with a couple who to us were strangers. They looked thin, and their expressions were sad. When our parents returned and took us back, I was an eight-year-old girl, who thought I was Catholic, now living with a Jewish mother and father who were not religious. Unlike Madame Moulard's home filled with religious objects and church teachings, I only remember an occasional white tablecloth and a switch from our routine meal to a chicken dinner. When I questioned the significance of the more festive meal, my mother said it was a Jewish holiday, but she didn't explain its meaning to us.

To further complicate our lives, because we were raised as Catholics, we had been taught that Jews killed Jesus Christ. We did not know how to feel connected to the Jewish couple with whom we were living and who said they were our parents. I wanted to go to church on Sundays, which my mother would not allow. She said, "Jewish children do not go to church." At school, during recess, I would ask my friends to teach me what they had learned that Sunday in church. I dreamed about my first communion. I continued to bring crosses home and hid them, but my mother always found them and threw them away. I knew I was confused and angry with this mother who had abandoned us. I missed what had been my consolation in time of need, "the love for Jesus and the church." It was some time before I could think about what my parents' reaction to our Catholic training must have been, especially after the price they had paid for being Jews.

Going forward, a few years later, Josette and I accepted that these were our parents who had returned to claim us. They were kind and gentle to us, but the normal, loving emotional ties between mother and daughters did not exist for me or my sister. I remember Josette saying to me years later that our young sister Silvia, born years after the war, had a mother and that we did not. She said to me, "Adele, you are my mother." To this day it is difficult for me to trust anyone or sometimes show love or affection. To compensate for this lack in me, I shower my loved ones with kindness and understanding. The image of our painful separation as children still colors my thoughts. In retrospect, I was afraid to show affection by hugging and kissing my children. I wanted to spare them if some day we were separated, as I was from my mother. It took a long time, but I was able to correct this later.

Neither one of our "new" parents practiced Judaism, so nothing replaced Catholicism in my life. They occasionally celebrated the Jewish holidays, but they neither taught us about Judaism nor explained the holidays' meaning. I had no Jewish friends or relatives in Paris; they all had disappeared during the war. My parents, Josette, and I were the only survivors of what once was a large family.

My mother had two brothers and a sister who had immigrated to Argentina long before the war. As a result, in 1950, my parents decided to move to Buenos Aires, Argentina, to join them. Our family now included a third child, a little brother, born after the war. My father died from a heart attack before we were able to leave. My mother took her two daughters and young son and left France

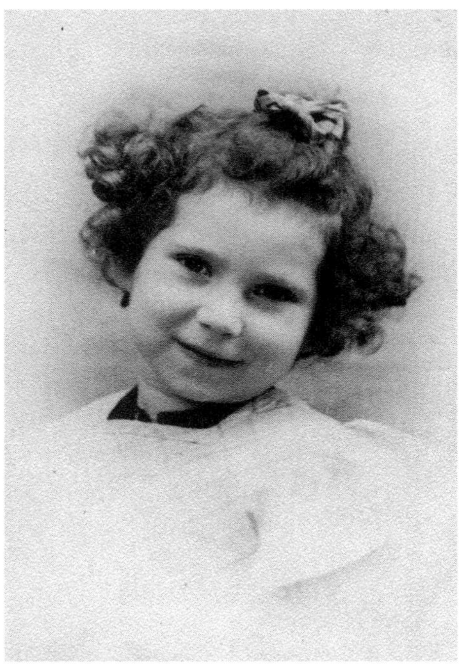

Figure 30. Adele Laznowski,
Paris, France, 1940.

Figure 31. Adele Laznowski standing in front of the house in Brou, France, where she and her sister, Josette, were hidden from 1942 to 1945.

Figure 32. Adele Laznowski and her sister, Josette, Paris, France, 1948.

forever. The Buenos Aires Jewish community was my first introduction to Judaism. I enjoyed it, but never felt part of that community.

I was seventeen when my mother remarried. My stepfather was a religious Jew. The focal point of his life was observing Jewish laws and customs. Suddenly, I found myself living in a religious kosher home. My life went from a strict Catholic upbringing to a marginally Jewish home, and finally to a strictly observant Jewish home. I had great difficulty with the changes, like separate dishes for milk and meat and observing Shabbat. I was seventeen and Josette was fifteen. We were used to going out with friends. We had no idea what Shabbat meant. Sometimes I purposely mixed up the dishes. I had been raised, however, not to challenge but rather to accept. I started to learn a lot about Judaism, more as a sign of respect for my mother than as a believer. When I was a teenager in Buenos Aires, all my friends were Jews. I went to my stepfather's synagogue on the holidays. It was Orthodox and because I was unfamiliar with the customs, I did not feel comfortable when I visited him there.

Also causing confusion, unlike Jewish teenagers, the greater society of Catholic girls were unable to visit a friend alone without a chaperone. Catholic girls would reproach me because I could go out alone, implying that they were good and I was bad. Because most people living in Buenos Aires belonged to the church, every activity related to religious holidays and the church. As a Jew I felt left out. I was excluded from their life.

Argentina is a Catholic country. The Jews had never been fully accepted into the larger society, nor did they feel part of the state. There was freedom of religion, and there was a very active Jewish community. However, antisemitism was widespread. I had to live with it every day. What I had accepted as a "Catholic" child living in France had seemed normal to me, but now had become unbearable. From time to time, graffiti would appear on the walls that read in Spanish, "*haga patria, mate judios,*" which means, "be patriotic, kill Jews." I heard people saying, "Jews are rich; Jews are Christ killers."

I met Ben when I was seventeen years old. We were married two and a half years later. When our first son, Victor, was four years old, I decided, with Ben's support, that Argentina was not the place to raise our child. My sister, however, became a lawyer, married a lawyer, and remains in Argentina. Their careers are not transferable to the United States. Despite the distance, we see each other often.

In 1963, we left Argentina for the United States and settled in Oak Park, Illinois, where our second son, Mitchell, was born. In 1971, we moved to the Chicago suburb of Northbrook and joined Congregation Beth Shalom. I felt comfortable and was accepted by the congregation. Soon I was asked to take important positions in the synagogue. Becoming involved hastened my integration into the community. Something had taken hold of me, a rebirth of sorts, because now I finally feel at one with the Jewish community.

Today I am a woman who has lived in the dark days of the Holocaust and survived. I have raised my children to understand and love their heritage. I have become a "born-again Jew."

Taste of Liberation

Adele Laznowski Zaveduk

It was late summer of 1944, when I was seven and my sister Josette was five, in France. The American troops were liberating France, one town after another. They came to our little village of Brou, about seventy-five miles west of Paris. It was a joyous day for everyone, and their happiness was contagious. I was excited. I knew I wouldn't have to be afraid of the Germans anymore. I was able to run around, jump, scream, and sing without anyone telling me to stop. There was a large convoy of trucks and huge tanks slowly rolling down our narrow streets.

All the villagers were laughing, singing, crying, waving, and hugging one another. The convoy stopped and we children surrounded the big, tall tanks. American soldiers stood on top of them, waving, smiling, and talking to us in English, which we did not understand, while we were jumping around and shouting, "*Liberté*" (Freedom) and "*Mort aux Boches*" (Death to the Germans). What chaos! They threw sweets at us. Every child was trying to get some. My sister Josette was lucky. She was able to grab a roll of Life Savers. She savored them, and even today the sight of those candies makes her smile.

I was not as lucky. I grabbed a little yellow box of Chiclets gum, which was unknown in Europe. What a pretty yellow box. I opened it and put the little white tablet in my mouth. It tasted horrible and stuck to my teeth and gums. I threw the candies out and kept the yellow box. It was the only thing that really belonged to me. It made me happy to own something that no other child had. For one year it was my little treasure.

When my father was liberated from Auschwitz, he came looking for Josette and me and took us back to Paris, where he temporarily left us in an orphanage because he didn't have a place of his own yet. I don't remember the name or location of the orphanage, but I believe it was a secular one because there were no nuns or priests running it. We were scared. We did not know this thin, sad-looking man who claimed he was our father. We lost the sense of security we had living with Madame Moulard. In 1942, my mother, with an underground agency's help, had taken us to live with her and keep us out of danger. She was the only family we knew.

At our arrival at the orphanage, my sister and I were separated because of our age difference, which meant we went to different classes daily and stayed in different dormitories. Due to the regimentation, we were unable to see each other during the week. I also missed being outdoors in the country with Madame Moulard. From then on Josette and I saw each other only on Sundays because that is when our dad came to see us. The orphanage gave us new clothes and disposed of our old ones. They also took my little empty yellow box. That day I lost my little treasure forever. It was taken away from me.

Recently I told this Chiclets box story to my seven-year-old granddaughter. She bought a little box of Chiclets, made a card, and gave it to me so I would have my little treasure again.

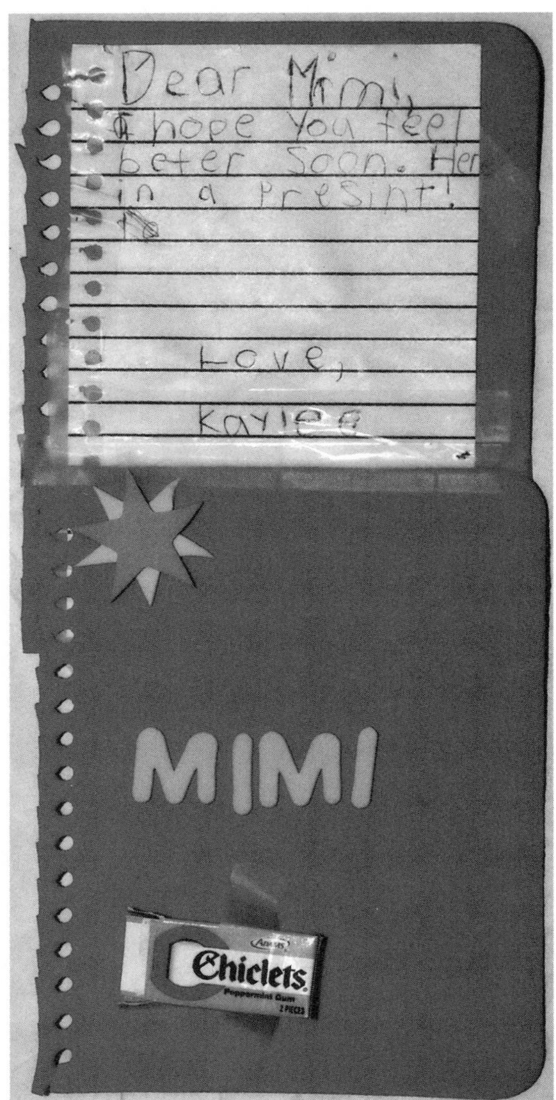

Figure 33. Card from Adele Laznowski Zaveduk's granddaughter after she learned that the orphanage took away Adele's yellow Chiclets box; made in 2006.

Happiness and Sadness

Adele Laznowski Zaveduk

What a happy, perfect summer day it was. The townspeople were overwhelmed with joy. Today we were free from the Germans who were occupying our town, thanks to the American troops, who were liberating France one town after another. You could feel the happiness everywhere; everyone was smiling, crying from joy and sadness. We, the children, were overexcited, running around, eating the candies that the American soldiers had given us, not fully understanding the importance of that day. I was thrilled with my little empty Chiclets box and could not wait until the evening for the upcoming big celebration. At sunset, we joined everybody else at the village square across from the town hall and waited for the big bonfire, music, and dancing. There were a lot of tears again. It was very noisy and then silence. That was strange and did not fit with the ongoing festivities. Everyone was searching for the reason. We children did not know where to look.

Down one of the streets coming toward the square were a group of women marching slowly toward us—some were crying, some cursing, some in silence, all with their heads bent—and beyond them were some men pushing and forcing them forward. We didn't understand the sudden change of mood, and then we noticed that all of them had shaved heads, and when they passed by us I saw that on the back of the skull there was a swastika painted with black tar. What a horror, especially for an eight-year-old girl to see. It hurt just to look and listen to them.

I tried to ask what was happening and why. The answer was that "they are bad persons" or "they are bad women." In my mind I could not imagine such a punishment. They were pushed away and left the town in shame. Those Frenchmen had taken justice in their own hands; they felt that they had the right to punish everyone that had collaborated with the enemies, done business, or were friendly with them. Later I learned that the fate of the men that were collaborators was worse: they had disappeared, presumably killed for revenge. That night I remembered all that excitement, asking myself why the same statement, "She is a bad person," had been said to me by Madame Moulard when my mother had left me with my sister in Brou three years earlier. I still wonder: who or what is a bad person in the eyes of a child?

Since then, any bonfire makes me uncomfortable.

First Name: Nicole
Last Name: Terry
Also Known As: Nicole Dejan
Maiden Name: Dreyfus
Date of Birth: September 5, 1934
City of Birth: Strasbourg
Country of Birth: France

The Borrowed Saint

Nicole Dreyfus Terry

Hiding, in a Catholic School, Égletons, France, 1944

When the war began, on September 3, 1939, I had just turned five and my sister, Simone, was a two-and-a-half-month-old beautiful infant. We lived as a family with our father (Papa), mother (Maman), my sister, and me, Nicole, in Paris.

My memories of the war are few, but the ones I have are vivid. In 1940, with the surrender of France to the armies of the Third Reich, my immediate family along with my cousins, uncles, aunts, and grandparents became refugees and retreated to Brive-la-Gaillarde, a small town in central France. Brive was in Vichy France (*La Zone Libre*), the region not occupied by the Germans. We lived in this area, moving periodically from one rented place to another. We children had much free time with little adult supervision. Our minds were full of imagination; we made up many games, such as climbing on the back stair of a parked bus, running over the *imperiale* (luggage rack), and sliding down the front of the bus as fast as we could. Around the corner was a lumberyard. We used to sneak in and build a house by stacking boards, until the house collapsed on me, little Nicole. Ouch. That entire week I had to pretend that my back did not hurt. It was a good thing that we only washed our whole body once a week, so Maman did not see the bruises all over my body.

Papa, Maman, and all the adults hid their fears of being arrested by the Nazis from us children. They were so good at it, but at night I could hear them whisper and listen to the old radio. I remember "*les Français parlent aux Français*" (the French are speaking to the French) and the boom-boom-boom sound of the English clandestine BBC broadcast.

The happy period for us children ended in early 1944, when the protection afforded Jews of French nationality came to an end. (Our family traced its French origins to the eighteenth century.) The Nazis began rounding up the French Jews for deportation to the death camps. This was when my parents made the heart-breaking decision to split up our little family and send Simone and me away. They knew that even with our false identity cards that described us as the Christian family "Dejan" (our real name was Dreyfus), should the Gestapo stop the four of us, they would not easily be fooled by our name. They could check if my father was circumcised, after which we could no longer pretend to be Christians. The four of us would then be slated for extermination.

To be safe, they sent Simone and me (I was already nine) to a Catholic boarding school, École Sainte-Jeanne-d'Arc, in a village called Égletons, about thirty miles northeast of Brive. There were about thirty girls in the school; twenty were Catholics from the surrounding villages, and I later learned that ten of us were Jewish hidden children. Papa and Maman hid in the mountains of Auvergne, some one hundred miles east of Brive. Madame Brandy, our pretend godmother, a good woman and Catholic neighbor from Brive, escorted Simone and me on the train to the school in Égletons. The bridges and train tracks would later be blown up by the *Maquis*, the French partisans. Our train was probably one of the last to come through. All I remember about the trip was having an annoying piece of charcoal in my eye.

We stayed at the convent about six months until liberation. I have some fond memories of this time in Égletons: holding the hands of the mother superior and Simone as she showed us her collection of butterflies—so many shapes, so many colors. Mother Superior taught everything, but she was best at teaching math. I loved the excitement of finding the answers to the math questions, especially the ones dealing with how fast will water from a faucet fill up a tub, or when will two trains leaving from different stations and at different speeds arrive at their destinations?

Mother Superior and the young nun Marie Aimée hid us Jewish children. I did not know until long after the war that they were risking their lives to save us. Every day they took all the children for long walks. We crossed the local bridge over the railroad tracks. I could see that the rails were still rusty, which meant that no trains were coming through. I knew that as long as the trains did not come to Égletons, my parents would not be coming either. We missed our parents, Simone especially. The loving nuns and I took good care of her, but she wanted her Maman and her Papa.

One day, as I was missing my parents more than usual, I went to the school's little white chapel, knelt on the prie-dieu, the special kneeling chair, and started praying to the statue of Sainte Thérèse de l'Enfant Jésus. How well I remember her. She was beautiful in her white long dress, her sky-blue cape, and in her clasped hands always holding a bouquet of fresh flowers. Is this why I love flowers so much now? I prayed, "Please Sainte Thérèse," I said, "make Papa and Maman come and take us home now, it has been so long." I must have been there for a while when suddenly I felt a strong hand on my left shoulder and heard the soft and powerful voice of Mother Superior, Mère Elisabeth de la Trinité.

To this day, I can hear her words: "*Ma petite Nicole, je te prête cette sainte pendant que tu es chez nous, mais n'oublies pas que tu es une petite fille juive, et que des que tu retrouveras tes parents, tu devras oublier cette sainte.*" ("My little Nicole, I lend you this saint, while you are here with us, but do not forget that you are a little Jewish girl, and as soon as you are back with your parents, you must forget this saint.")

This was the first time I was told that I was Jewish. My parents never mentioned that we were Jewish at home, even when Maman was getting us ready to go to the convent.

Figure 34. Nicole Dreyfus with her parents, Irma and Armand Dreyfus, and baby sister, Simone, Paris, France, September 1939.

Figure 35. Nicole Dreyfus and her sister Simone at the convent in Égletons, France, September 1944.

Armand Can Do Anything

Nicole Dreyfus Terry

Everybody knew that my father, Armand, could do anything. We knew that wherever we would be, my father would always be there for us, especially when my sister, Simone, and I were in hiding, separated from our parents for months.

My papa's bicycles were never new. They did not have ten speeds, only one, when it worked. They never had new tires, only retreads, and used inner tubes that Papa constantly needed to repair.

Chambois 1940

In May 1940, the Germans had invaded France and were approaching Paris. My father, stationed in central France at the Bourganeuf army base, contacted my mother and instructed her to leave Paris "immediately." So she did. We piled into our Citroën, my Great Aunt Meme, my nine-year-old cousin Claude, nine-month-old Simone, and I, plus the baby bed, blankets, pail of wet diapers, little *petit pot* (baby potty), pillows, food, and clothing. As we passed the crowds of walking civilians, we were grateful not to have to walk carrying all these items. The roads were packed. We moved slowly. It was a horrible exodus scene.

The main problem for my courageous mother was that she barely knew how to drive, not even how to drive in reverse. But for me, only six years of age, my main fear was caused by my cousin Claude, who on purpose kept murmuring, "*Il y a des loups*" (There are wolves). Not only was I squeezed into the backseat, but now I had to keep my feet up so I would not be bitten by wolves.

One night we slept in a barn. The next morning Claude heard clanking noises. There were tanks passing. The Germans were now in front of us. Maman realized that we had to stop fleeing. We stopped going east. Claude told me later she had to ask a German soldier to turn the car around. Maman found lodging for all of us in a house in the small Normandy town of Chambois; we stayed there about a month.

On August 5, 1940, Claude and I, sitting on the stoop in front of the house, saw a soldier in a French uniform riding a bicycle toward us. It was Papa. How excited we were. We hugged him and ran into the house shouting, "*Papa est revenu!*" (Papa's returned!). He had "borrowed" a bicycle at the Caen train station and ridden the forty-one miles to Chambois to reach us. He knew where to find us from a telegram Uncle Paul, Claude's father, who already was in central France, had sent to Papa. Uncle Paul's telegram said, "Good news from Chambois. Irma and children are there." Irma was my *maman* (mother).

On August 6, between noon and seven, Papa loaded the bicycle in the Citroën and returned it to the Caen train station. On August 9, Papa took the wheel of the Citroën and drove us all back to Paris. A few days later we left Paris. The German authorities had requisitioned our car. We took a train to the Loire River that divided the occupied from the unoccupied zone. A Christian man that we knew smuggled us into the unoccupied zone. From there we took a train to Brive.

Brive-la-Gaillarde, 1943

Papa, Maman, Simone, our extended family, and I were refugees in Brive, central France. The food ration tickets we had were not enough to feed us. Papa rode his bicycle, this time his own, to surrounding villages to get food. One time he took me along, and I sat on the back carrier. As we rode back to town, with me sitting on a big sack of flour holding onto my father, I felt his back stiffen, and he was suddenly soaked with perspiration. We had been stopped by a gendarme who demanded to see Papa's identification card, where the word *juif* (Jew) was stamped. All I remember was tension. Although Papa showed the gendarme his identification card, nothing happened. He let us go. I trusted Papa. "Armand can do anything."

Égletons, August 27, 1944

My sister, Simone, and I were hiding in a Catholic boarding school in Égletons, central France. We had been there for a few months. My parents were hiding about twenty-five miles from where we were hidden. It was a dry, rocky, poor area, sparsely populated by four small farms. They had a tiny house with no electricity, running water, gas, or toilet facilities in the middle of those farms. They cooked on an open fire. My parents stayed in that location for about a year. All they heard on the radio was that Égletons was bombarded and that the inhabitants had fled to the country. Our parents had no way of knowing if we were dead or alive.

On the hot afternoon of August 27, 1944, Papa appeared at the convent on his bicycle. He had ridden from Lacave, where my parents had been hiding, to Égletons, on a narrow, poorly paved mountainous stretch. I still have his "pass" allowing him to travel between Lacave and Égletons, valid until September 6, 1944. When he reached us, he was hot, exhausted, with sweat dripping from his nose. He had sores all over his buttocks, and he almost fell off his bicycle. I remember the feeling of relief when I saw him, but I had never doubted that we would see our parents again; "Papa can do anything." How comforting his hugs were for me, but for my sister it was different. When he sat on Simone's bed, she screamed, "Papa is messing up my bed!" She was proud of being able to make her own bed like a soldier.

I was so happy that I gave Papa my most precious treasure, a brass bullet I had found in the courtyard. It was probably left from the fierce battle at Égletons. I did not understand why Papa grabbed the bullet from my hand without even saying thank you. Instead, he ran outside and "broke" my gift.

We were later reunited with both my parents, but surprisingly I have no memory of this. I do remember every evening from 1939, during which Maman helped me with my prayers. Sometimes it ended with "Please God make Papa come home soon." Sometimes it ended with "Please God make Papa never go away." And it worked.

After the war my family remained in France. I went to Israel, where I met an American whom I married. I was the only one in my family who left France to live in the United States. My sister married and remained in France.

When Simone passed away in France, she left two young children, ten and twelve years old. Life became difficult for them To this day they know that wherever I, Nicole, am, close or far, I am always there for them.

Merci, Papa.

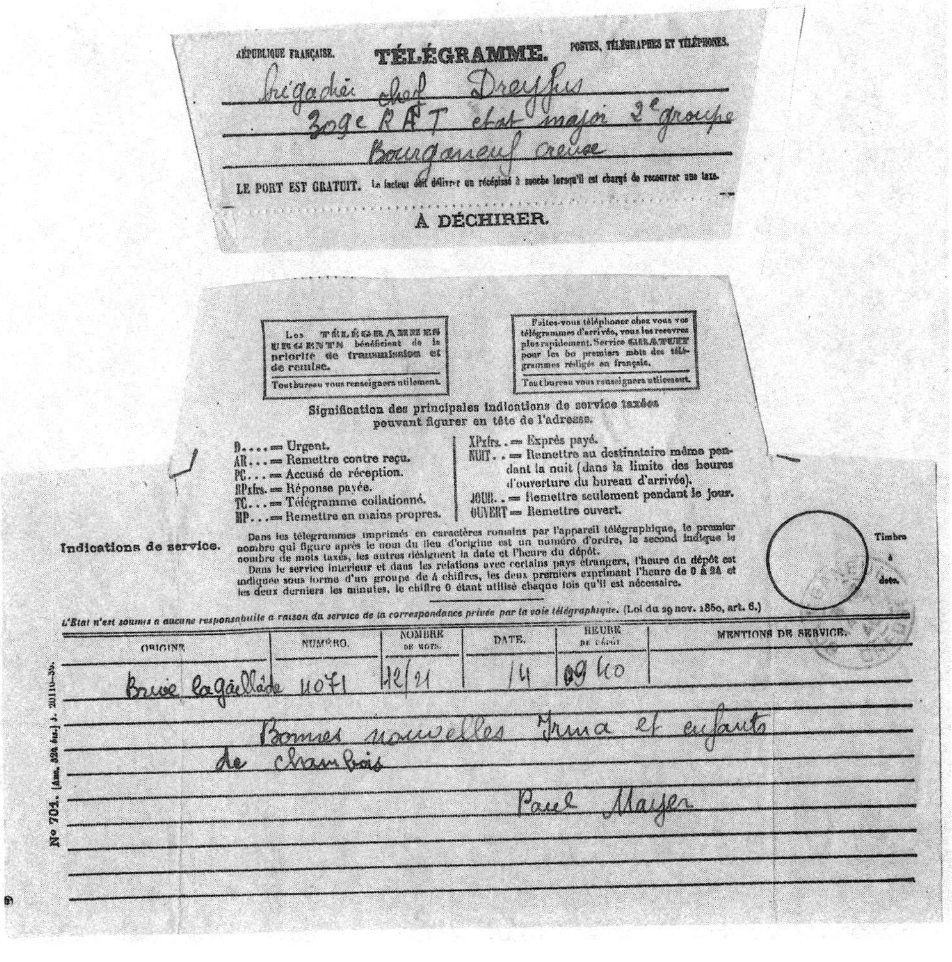

RÉPUBLIQUE FRANÇAISE. TÉLÉGRAMME. POSTES, TÉLÉGRAPHES ET TÉLÉPHONES.

Brigadier chef Dreyfus
309e RAT état major 2e groupe
Bourganeuf creuse

LE PORT EST GRATUIT.

À DÉCHIRER.

Brive lagaillarde 1071 12/11 14 09 40

Bonnes nouvelles Irma et enfants de Chambois

Paul Mayer

Figure 36. Telegram from Nicole Dreyfus's uncle to her father, who was in the French Army, informing him that his wife and children had arrived in Chambois, France, 1940.

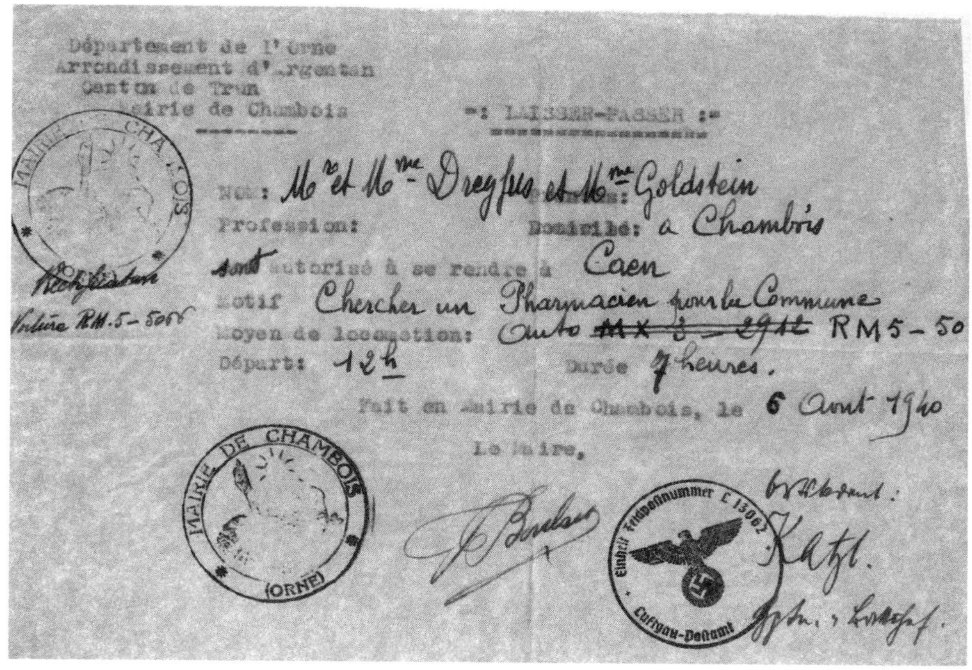

Département de l'Orne
Arrondissement d'Argentan
Canton de Trun
Mairie de Chambois

-: LAISSER-PASSER :-

Nom: Mr et Mme Dreyfus et Mme Goldstein Prénoms:
Profession: Domicilié: à Chambois
sont autorisé à se rendre à Caen
Motif Chercher un Pharmacien pour la Commune
Moyen de locomotion: Auto RM5-50
Départ: 12h Durée 7 heures.

Fait en Mairie de Chambois, le 6 Aout 1940

Le Maire,

Figure 37. Pass used by Nicole Dreyfus's father, on August 6, 1940.

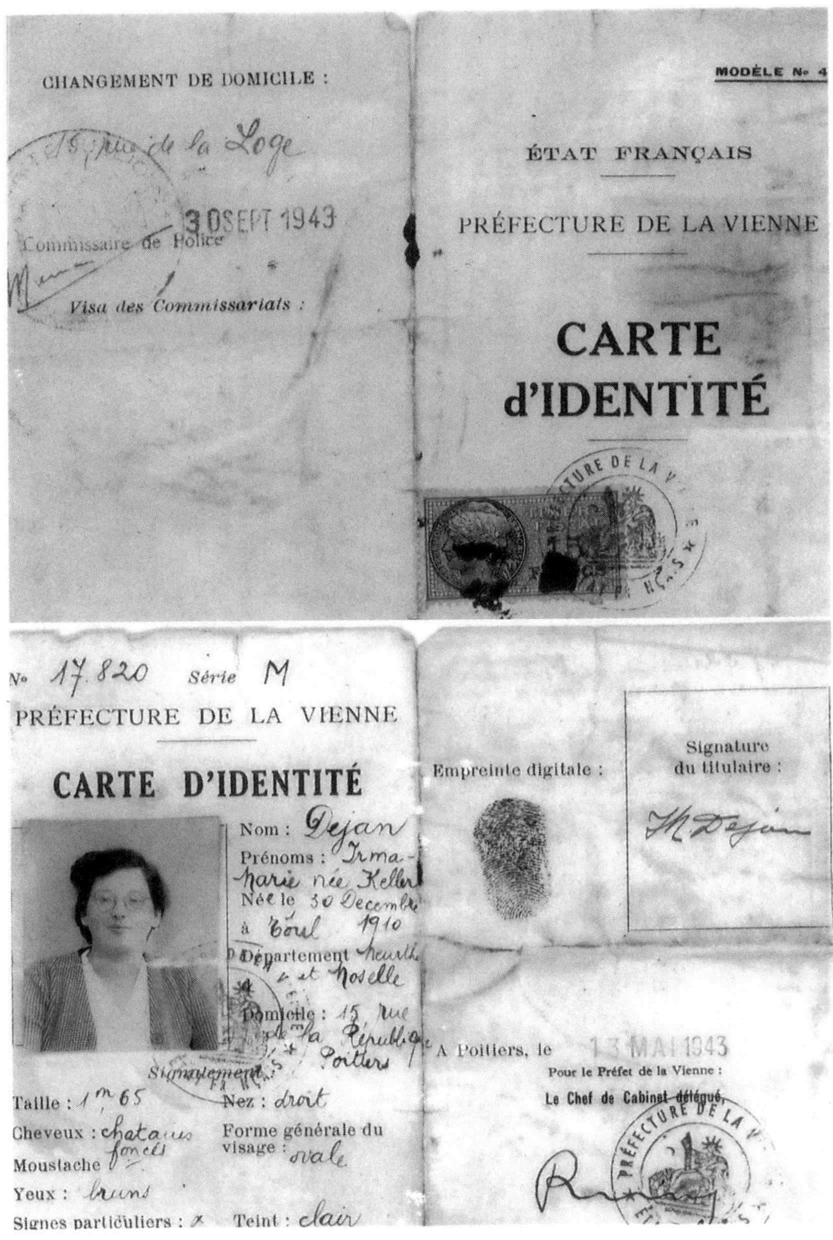

CHANGEMENT DE DOMICILE :

16, rue de la Loge

30 SEPT 1943

Commissaire de Police

Visa des Commissariats :

MODÈLE No 4

ÉTAT FRANÇAIS

PRÉFECTURE DE LA VIENNE

CARTE d'IDENTITÉ

No 17.820 Série M

PRÉFECTURE DE LA VIENNE

CARTE D'IDENTITÉ

Nom : Dejan

Prénoms : Irma-Marie née Keller

Née le 30 Decembre 1910

à Toul

Département Meurthe et Moselle

Domicile : 15 rue de la République Poitiers

Signalement

Taille : 1m65

Cheveux : chatains foncés

Moustache —

Yeux : bruns

Signes particuliers : x

Nez : droit

Forme générale du visage : ovale

Teint : clair

Empreinte digitale :

Signature du titulaire : M Dejan

A Poitiers, le 13 MAI 1943

Pour le Préfet de la Vienne :

Le Chef de Cabinet délégué,

Figure 38. Nicole Dreyfus's mother's false identification papers with the name Dejan, May 1943.

Long Live Liberated Alsace, a Child's Vindication

Nicole Dreyfus Terry

In southern France, during the bitter cold winter of 1942–43, I was in second grade at the *École de jeunes filles* (school for girls). My parents, my little sister, Simone, and I were refugees from Paris, in the small town of Brive-la-Gaillarde, in the Vichy Free Zone.

I was a shy, seven-year-old little girl, never sitting in the front or in the back, but in the middle row, probably not to be noticed. One day in class, I must have done something wrong, as the teacher punished me and sent me to the back of the room. My punishment had nothing to do with being Jewish or foreign to this community. Sitting there next to a massive black coal-burning stove, the only source of heat during the winter, was a pupil who seemed to be constantly punished. She was bundled in an oversize, old gray coat and a triangle hand-knit scarf. I remember whispering to her, "It is nice and warm back here."

She replied, "Now you know why I always misbehave; I want to sit here, close to the stove to keep warm."

Because of the severe cold and poor nutrition, my toes and fingers were frostbitten. When I came home from school, Maman squeezed my icy little hands in her soft and deep armpits, because I was so cold. Her armpits were warm, but my fingers stung a lot. I never told her how much it burned. Maman was happy to share her warmth.

In the class, I was among five Jewish refugees from the north. Because we were in the Free Zone, we lived in the open and did not have to hide. However, we were different from the other girls. We all had darker hair and did not speak with the thick French southern accent. To the teacher we were refugees, although I do not believe she knew we were Jewish.

All the children in the class had lice. Maman had killed all the lice in my hair, not an easy job. She soaked my hair with a solution of naphtha and vinegar, then wrapped my hair in a cloth rag, night after night. I remember the awful smelling odor, and how the fumes burned my eyes and Maman's eyes as well.

One day in class, our teacher, Madame Kussack, a tall, severe-looking woman with a pointy nose, started walking between the rows of wooden benches, stopping by each student to examine her hair. When my turn came, she lifted my black curls, walked away, then came back and inspected my locks again. Later, at recess, in the bleak and gray courtyard, something made me turn around: I saw Madame Kussack talking to the other teachers and pointing at me; she touched her head. Of course, I knew that she was talking about me and my lice. I felt so humiliated, I wanted to sink into the ground.

I came home crying and told Maman that Madame Kussack had embarrassed me and how hurt I was. Maman consoled me and swore that I did not have lice but that the dead eggs were still sticking to my hair—very visible in my beautiful black hair. Consoled by Maman, I returned to class the next day.

Although this experience crushed me, I soon began to worry about more immediate frightening events. Around the beginning of 1944, Brive, which was now in the Occupied Zone, became too dangerous for us. Our families left and went into hiding in the village of Canteloube in the hills twenty-five miles away. June 6, 1944, was D-day. In August 1944, the south of France was liberated. We came out of hiding and returned to live in Brive for a few months until train transportation was restored. In March 1945, we returned to Paris before the June 8, 1945, armistice.

This was the first time I finally wore a dress made for me and did not have to wear my boy cousin Claude's outfits. Allied troops had landed in the region. Papa proudly brought home pieces of parachutes he had found in a field nearby; my resourceful Grandmère made a dress just for me. This was a happy moment.

In Brive I returned home to the same school, of course in a different class. The war was almost over and most of France had been liberated except for Alsace, a province on the German border. Before the war, Papa, Maman, Simone, and I lived in Paris. The rest of our family lived in Alsace and, like us, became refugees in Brive. The four of us had spent much time in Alsace, so the Alsatian culture, costumes, and songs were part of my upbringing. I could even speak the Alsatian language. Our family traces its roots in Alsace to 1775.

When I went back to school in Brive I was nine years old. On February 19, 1945, the teacher gave us a *composition de dessin* (art drawing assignment). The theme was *Vive L'Alsace Libérée* (Long Live Liberated Alsace). What a gift this assignment was for me. My head was buzzing with excitement as I drew feverishly on my sheet of paper with my green, red, blue, and black pencils.

In northeast France, on the border of Germany, rich in natural resources—coal, iron, and oil—and with an ideal climate for the culture of grapes, Alsace produces

Figure 39. Classroom in Brive-la-Gaillarde, France, where one teacher first insulted and another later praised Nicole Dreyfus, 1942–43. Nicole is standing in the third row, *third from right,* with two big buttons on her coat.

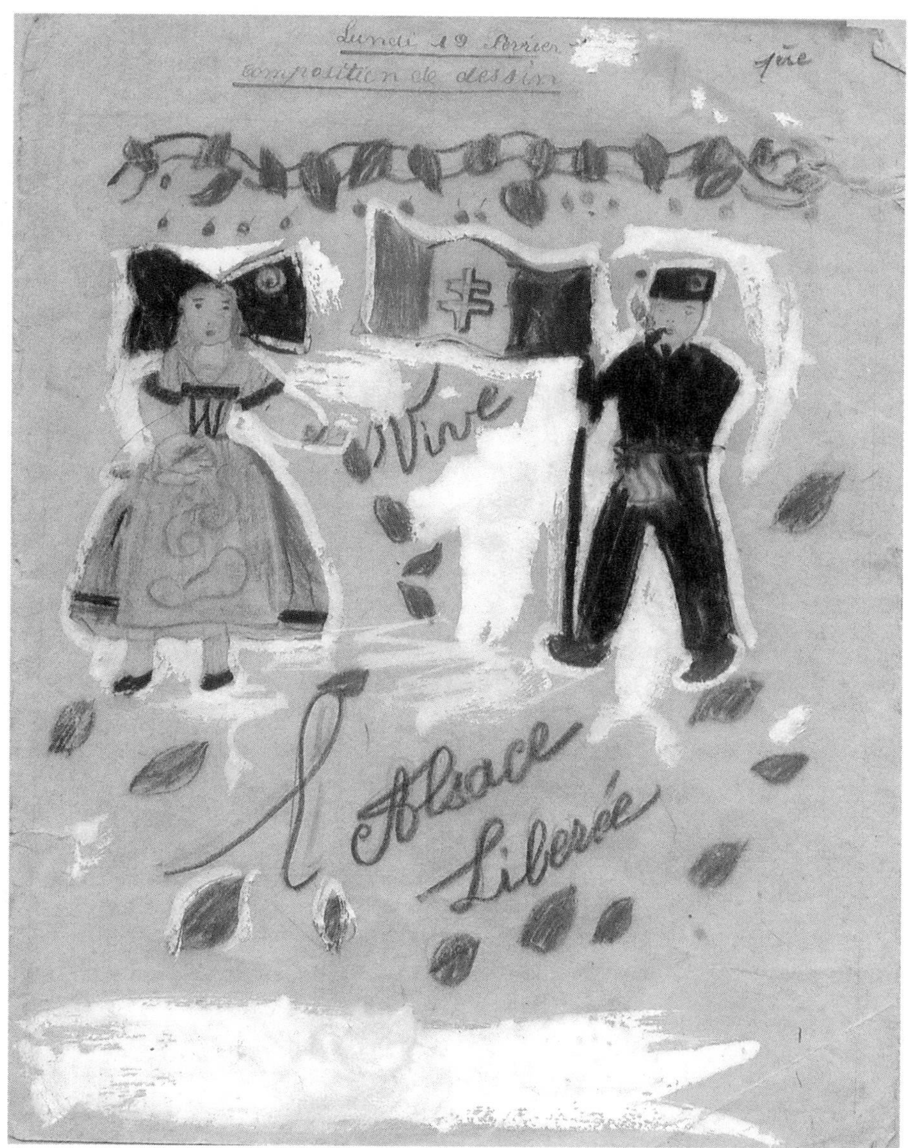

Figure 40. Nicole Dreyfus's artwork that was judged best in her class in Brive-la-Gaillarde, February 19, 1945.

some of the best white wine in the world. Because of its strategic location along the Rhine River, the border between France and Germany, Alsace had been the center of continuous disputes between the two countries.

France was about to regain sovereignty over Alsace. Everyone in France was waiting for Alsace's liberation. On November 23, 1944, French forces liberated Alsace, including its capital, Strasbourg.

A few days later the teacher walked in the classroom holding our graded drawing assignments in her hand. I remember how anxious I was to hear the results. The teacher came next to me, then turned to the class and said, "This little foreigner (apparently to her all who were not local people were foreigners) has the best grade. She is *première* (first place, or has an A+) in this art project, far ahead of every one of you." She held my drawing high so the whole class could see all the details, the French flag bearing the Cross of Lorraine, the Free French emblem, two children in the Alsatian costume, the boy dressed in black with a little matching round hat, the girl wearing an oversize black taffeta bow hairpiece, and written in large letters across the drawing, *Vive L'Alsace Libérée.*

This time the teacher was pointing at me with a smile. My painful humiliation of the winter of 1942 gave way to pride. My heart was filled with joy.

Thank you, Papa, for keeping everything, as I still have the art composition. I love to share it with my children and eight grandchildren.

Vive L'Alsace Libérée

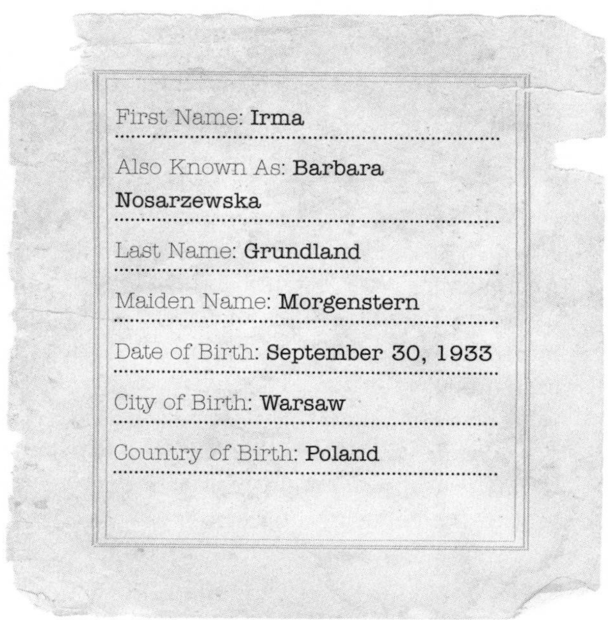
First Name: **Irma**

Also Known As: **Barbara Nosarzewska**

Last Name: **Grundland**

Maiden Name: **Morgenstern**

Date of Birth: **September 30, 1933**

City of Birth: **Warsaw**

Country of Birth: **Poland**

The Warsaw Ghetto: The Last Night with My Parents

Irma Morgenstern Grundland

I am a child survivor of the Holocaust.

I was born in the beautiful city of Warsaw, Poland, in 1935. When I was five, my parents and I were sent to the Warsaw Ghetto under German soldiers' guard. The Nazis allowed us to take only a knapsack on our shoulders and the clothing we were wearing. At first we lived at 7 Ceglana Street: then the Gestapo moved us to a one-room apartment on Szczęśliwa Street.

Many of the people in the ghetto died of hunger, typhoid fever, and other diseases. Even today, so many years later, I can still see the dead bodies of children and other people lying in the street in front of me, while people passed by and covered the bodies with newspapers.

Occasionally, I smuggled food, which was forbidden, from outside the ghetto. I squeezed through a small opening under the ghetto's barbed-wire wall. Once outside, I held a piece of jewelry in my hand and asked the Polish people selling food if they had a loaf of bread in exchange for the jewelry. Once I got some food, I crawled back under the barbed-wire fence and returned home. I had stayed outside the ghetto only about fifteen or twenty minutes to avoid detection. Many children were killed while smuggling food. At home the only other time I had something to eat was when my parents on their way home from work were able to bring me soup that was made from beets and old black bread soaked in water for our main meal.

In our apartment I was terrified, especially when I heard German soldiers' voices on the staircase or on the street; I would hide under the bed, thinking in my childish mind that I was in a safe place and that the Germans would not find me. Many children were taken from their apartments and either shot on the spot or sent to concentration camps.

My parents were sent to a forced labor shop called Oxaco. I am spelling the shop's name as it sounded to me. My mother was taught how to sew uniforms, while my father sewed on buttons and snaps. They worked from dawn until sundown. The white uniforms that they made in the shop were worn by the German Army during the winter. I and the other children were not allowed in the shop where my parents worked. If a child was caught, death was the punishment. Every morning we kissed, hugged, and cried because we did not know if we would see each other again.

There were days when my parents smuggled me with them to work. I remember once the Germans called everybody from the shop to stand in line for a selection. The healthy-looking ones were spared and sent back to work. The others were sent to the concentration camps. My petrified mother hid me in a pile of white uniforms and put a sleeve in my mouth so that I would not be heard if I cried. After the selection my mother ran to the pile of uniforms to see if I was dead or alive.

I remember when I had whooping cough, I hid with my grandmother at the cemetery on Gesia Street in an underground bunker. I stayed with her for a time, but I was lonely and wanted to go back to the ghetto to be with my parents. My grandmother arranged for me to return to my parents. Many other people were hiding in the same bunker. The Germans discovered them with hunting dogs. A few days after I left, she was murdered in the bunker. I thanked God and was grateful that I had been spared from that raid, but I cried for my grandmother and the others who were killed that day.

The conditions in the ghetto deteriorated from day to day. Because I was so young, I thought life was always like this. More people were shot daily, and more bodies were lying in the streets. My grandfather was shot in front of the house where he lived. My aunt fell to her death when a Nazi soldier pushed her from the third-floor window. Her only son, Lusio, two years older than I, stayed with us.

Lusio was tall and thin. He had brownish-red hair and light eyes. Whenever we heard German voices nearby, we rushed to hide under the bed and stayed there a long time, waiting until it was quiet again. We had nothing to play or write with. Our only entertainment was running around chairs.

My parents met a Jewish man from the city of Baranowicze, who was visiting neighbors. He said that his name was Staszek Laskowski. No one knew that he was a Jew. He looked like a filthy peasant wearing dirty clothing and tall boots. Blond, blue-eyed, with a long curly mustache, he actually was a dentist, and his real name was Mosze Antopolski, my savior. He had Christian friends in Warsaw, and he asked my parents if they would consider giving me away to a Polish policeman named Pietruszka whom they would have to pay. It was extremely difficult for my parents to decide to part with me, but finally they did. Only now can I imagine what went through their minds. Mosze Antopolski, responsible for saving me, now lives in Petah Tikva, Israel. I was sad that my cousin, Lusio, could not join me when I escaped. Lusio was circumcised. In Poland only the Jewish boys were circumcised.

Because Antopolski could not find a safe hiding place for him, he was sent with my parents to Treblinka, where they were all murdered.

My parents worked hard to prepare me for my departure. Mother taught me all the Christian prayers from a catechism that Pietruszka brought her. I carried it with me throughout the war. That prayer book is the only object I have of my dear mother. I can feel her fingers when I touch that prayer book. I remember her testing me on my knowledge of the catechism so that I would be able to answer any questions with ease, if the Germans caught me.

The Polish policeman bought a birth certificate for me from the church. My parents told me that my new name would be Barbara Nosarzewska, but they wanted me to remember that after the war my name would again be Irma Morgenstern. They wanted me to always remember that I was Jewish and instructed me that after the war I was to return to Warsaw to 4 Sienkiewicza Street, my grandparents' property, to see if anyone in our family had survived.

The last night before my departure we were sitting, huddled together, hugging and crying. My mother washed me and cut my fingernails, and my father cut my toenails. They were hugging and kissing me all night. My mother gave me her picture, but my father did not give me his. He probably was afraid to be recognized as a Jew. As long as I live, I will never forget that night.

The following night, on February 27, 1943, when I was seven years old, my parents put a stepladder against the brick wall covered with shards of glass and barbed wire on the top. We kissed good-bye for the last time. I climbed to the top of the wall, looked at my parents for the last time, and jumped to the Aryan side of the city.

German soldiers were shooting at me from both sides, but I ran as fast as I could to the third floor of the building, where Mr. Pietruszka waited for me. He gave me my new birth certificate, and from that moment on I became Barbara Nosarzewska. We left the building and took the trolley to his apartment in the Grochów suburb.

Mr. Pietruszka had a wife and three daughters. All of them were blond and had blue eyes. I did not look like them; I had dark brown hair and sad brown eyes. At first I played with the Pietruszkas' little girls outside. After a short while the neighbors began to talk about me. The Pietruszkas learned that the neighbors were gossiping about their hiding a Jewish child. To be caught hiding a Jew was an automatic death sentence for their entire family and me. Mr. Pietruszka divided a closet and made a hiding place, where I spent about six uncomfortable weeks. The closet was long and dark. Clothes were hanging in the closet. I sat on the floor. Because there was no light, I could not tell what time it was. They brought me food and put a chamber pot in the closet to take care of my biological needs. Sometimes at night they took me to the kitchen to sleep.

Mr. Pietruszka went to the ghetto to visit my parents but found that the building where we lived was empty. Someone told him that all the Jews were taken to Treblinka Concentration Camp. No one in my family survived. I had become an orphan. I cried for many days and nights. I used to wake up in the middle of the night and wonder: Who am I? My name is Barbara Nosarzewska, but I am really Irma Morgenstern.

On a spring day in 1943, I saw a very red sky and I asked Mr. Pietruszka where the fires were coming from. He told me that it was the Warsaw Ghetto uprising. We saw the fires illuminate the sky for days.

Continuing to fear for the safety of his family, Mr. Pietruszka got in touch with his cousin, Viesia Pietruszka, a Christian who lived in Boryczowka, Ukraine, a tiny village. She took me in and cared for me like a mother. When the Russians first occupied this area, because her family was wealthy, they had sent her entire family to Siberia, where they were killed. After what I had been through, I needed a lot of love, and she was able to give that to me. I soon began to call her Aunt.

After the war in January 1946, when I was ten years old, Pietruszka went to 4 Sienkiewicza to determine whether anyone from my family survived. He learned from the concierge that Emilja Goldstein, a distant cousin of my paternal grandfather, survived. Emilja also had been told to return to this property after the war to learn whether anyone from our family survived. She was old, wore thick glasses, and agreed to take care of me. Pietruszka arranged a visit with my Aunt Viesia and Emilja.

My aunt was sweet, warm, and always full of hugs and kisses. Emilja, whom I never saw before, wanted to take me to Warsaw forever. When I heard this, I lay down on the floor and started to cry. It took a long time to calm me down. From 1943 to 1946, I lived in a loving environment with my aunt. To calm me down, Aunt Viesia promised that I could return to her anytime, if Emilja did not treat me well. After her promise, I went with Emilja to Warsaw. Perhaps because traveling was so expensive and difficult, I did not see my aunt again, but I did correspond with her.

Emilja and I lived at 4 Sienkiewicza in one room. I was lonely for a long time. Emilja sent me to school, where I made friends and life became rosier. Unlike my aunt, Emilja was not a warm person. I needed a lot of love, which she was unable to give. We sent packages of clothing, tea, cookies, and candies to Aunt Viesia. She liked them a lot. While I was still in Warsaw, I learned that she had died. I will never forget her; she was like a second mother to me. I wish I could hug her today.

Figure 41. Irma Morgenstern in Poland, 1946.

Figure 42. School picture of Irma Morgenstern, *second from left in the back row,* when she was living with her cousin Emilja in Warsaw, Poland, 1948.

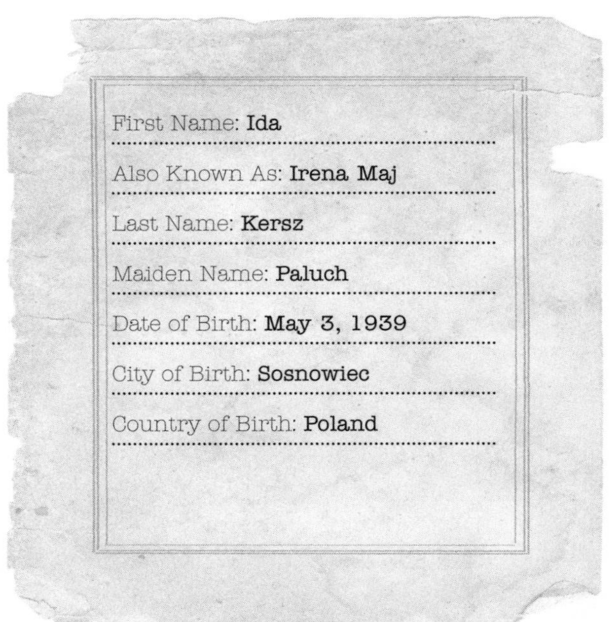

First Name: Ida
Also Known As: Irena Maj
Last Name: Kersz
Maiden Name: Paluch
Date of Birth: May 3, 1939
City of Birth: Sosnowiec
Country of Birth: Poland

The Christmas Gift

Ida Paluch Kersz

Ever since it happened, I continue to see this scene over and over. As I grew older, it has seemed like a nightmare. Within a few months of the outbreak of World War II in Poland, the Nazis had begun herding Jewish people from Sosnowiec to the nearby Środula Ghetto, later selecting them for either slave labor or extermination. Sosnowiec, in south-central Poland, is near the larger city of Katowice.

In August 1942, when I was three-and-one-half years old, we were in a selection line. The Germans ordered the children separated from their families. I remember seeing a crowd of people screaming and running in different directions. It seemed that our mother, Ester Wajntraub, was ahead of the crowd. My older sister, Genia, born in 1931, my twin brother Adam, and I were running behind her. Then, Mother ran into a building entrance; to the left was a wooden staircase. She ran to the second floor and opened a door, thinking that it was a room with a window. It was a closet; she turned away to run up another set of stairs, climbed through a window, and disappeared. Sometime later, I saw her lifeless body lying on the ground. My mother's suicide confused the Gestapo and ruined their plan. Fearing rioting from the crowds, they stopped the selection for the day.

My father, Chajm Lejzor Paluch, who was born in Żarnowiec in 1904, had left for the big city of Sosnowiec looking for work, mainly as an apprentice tailor. The first years of the apprenticeship consisted primarily of household chores. My mother came from Szczekociny. She was part of a large family of eight sisters and five brothers. After my parents were married, they lived in a suburb of Sosnowiec, Pogoń. The neighboring cities were densely populated with Jewish people.

In 1938, when my mother was pregnant with me, my parents paid no attention to the dark clouds gathering over Europe, nor the Nazi blanket, red for blood, white for death, black for hopelessness, nor the swastikas' deadly blades—otherwise, they would not have had any more children. They already had Genia, our older sister. As I was later informed, I was born a twin, shortly after my brother, Adam.

We were born in the coal-mining city of Sosnowiec, Poland, on May 3, 1939, the anniversary of the Polish Constitution. As I learned later, Mother did not know that she was carrying triplets or twins. Sometime during the pregnancy, she lost one of the babies. A few weeks later, she felt movement in her belly and the doctor confirmed her suspicion that she was still pregnant. At no time prior to delivery did she suspect that she was carrying twins. When the time for delivery came, my brother Adam was born first, healthy and noisy. I was born five minutes later as a "blue baby": lifeless. The doctor, who delivered us in the hospital, asked Mother if she wished to save the baby girl. My mother cried hysterically and pleaded with him to save me.

On September 1, 1939, four months after my brother and I were born, World War II broke out. Father enlisted in the Polish Army to defend our country. Mother never saw him again. She was left on her own with three children; two infants, still dependent on their mother's milk. In 1942, the Nazis moved about twenty-eight thousand Jews from surrounding towns into the open Sosnowiec Ghetto that had no barbed wire enclosing it, and later into the smaller Środula Ghetto surrounded by barbed wire. Mother had been running a children's clothing store that my parents had owned, while my ten-year-old sister Genia took care of us. Mother, her sister Rose, and her children were together when our mother committed suicide and people were running into hiding. This break in the Gestapo activity gave my Aunt Rose the opportunity to snatch us away and lead us quietly from the horrible sight of my mother's death to her own hiding place in the Środula Ghetto. Due to the trauma of seeing my mother's death, I do not remember anything about the hiding place.

A few weeks later, Wilhelm Maj, a produce supplier to my aunt's fruit store, came from Częstochowa looking for her. The neighbors told him that she was living in the Środula Ghetto. He stood at the barbed wire surrounding the ghetto, as I was walking with my aunt. Wilhelm Maj asked my aunt who I was and she told him, "This is the child of my sister who committed suicide, and she is one mouth too many to feed." Wilhelm offered to take me with him on the condition that I would always remain with him. There were no other options. As darkness approached, Aunt Rose handed me to the man over the barbed wire, and he took me home to his wife in Częstochowa. The city's name has a special meaning for me. In Polish it translates to *OFTEN HIDES*. It was the last time I saw my family.

It was Christmas Eve of 1942, and as Wilhelm introduced me to his wife, he said, "Here is your Christmas gift!" She embraced me and immediately accepted me as her own child, even though she was three months pregnant, and was aware that death was the punishment for hiding Jews. They told me to call them Mom and Dad. We lived in a two-family small house with a tiny backyard. I woke up that night and saw the couple decorating a Christmas tree. The next morning, I called them Mom and Dad. Wilhelm was dressed in a Santa Claus suit, but he did not fool me, I still called him Daddy. About twenty years ago when I invited my Polish mother Jozefa to my home in Skokie, Illinois, she told me that when I first arrived in her home, I was miserable. I couldn't stop crying for almost a month. I wanted to see and be with Genia and Adam. Finally, my new parents' affection and kindness won me over.

I remember being dressed in a long dress and being in a huge church. The smell of the incense was intoxicating and new to me; someone splashed water on my head. The priest was talking in a strange language. After that, I was called Irena Maj with a new Christian birth certificate dated January 4, 1942. My new parents told their priest that I was their own illegitimate child and that they had hidden me in a village until they were married. I had a new family. My adoptive mother's name was Jozefa Maj, maiden name Domanska. I climbed on their laps, I rode on a bicycle, and I played with children in the backyard. My parents loved and cared for me.

During the winter of 1943, Daddy earned a living by going on the road with a horse and wagon to the neighboring towns and villages selling cigarettes and vodka. He traveled with two companions: Franciszek and Leon Mlek. On February 11, 1943, they went to the village of Odorz. The wagon was loaded with illegal merchandise, tobacco, vodka, and produce. That was all Jozefa knew. On that day the Gestapo arrested and executed them on the spot. Witnesses told Jozefa that before her husband was shot, he loudly expressed concern for his beloved daughter Irena. Recently I discovered why they were shot: they were smuggling ammunition for the Polish Underground A. K.—*Armia Krajowa*—and for the partisans in the forests.

I remember the cold snowy day when Wilhelm's body was brought home. The horses were nervous and wanted to go to the ditch to avoid the slippery road. Grandma, Mother, and I were sitting in the wagon, petrified and screaming hysterically because Grandpa, drunk, was whipping the horses mercilessly. Father and his companions were buried in the Częstochowa cemetery next to each other. After the war, Grandpa built a big family monument with a porcelain picture of the young father and a poem below it that read, "*Śpij tatusiu ukochany już się nigdy nie zobaczysz ze swoimi córeczkami*"—"Sleep beloved Father, you won't see your daughters ever again."

Upon learning of Wilhelm's death, we were all crying. From then on Mother and Grandma always wore black clothing and hats with a black veil covering their faces. I wore a black band on my coat's sleeve. I missed him. Once again I felt abandoned, afraid, and sad. Everyone, including me, blamed the Germans for his death. No one laughed anymore. A few months later, Jozefa delivered a baby girl, whom she named Wilusia after her deceased husband, Wilhelm.

Jozefa had married Wilhelm, her high school sweetheart, without his parents' blessings. Jozefa was a poor widow dressmaker's daughter. Wilhelm's father, my Polish paternal grandfather, was an officer in the czar's army before the Russian Revolution. Later when the Communists came to power, his family took refuge in Poland. Wilhelm's family looked down on Jozefa and disowned Wilhelm after learning he had eloped and his wife was from a humble background. He was their only son and heir to their wealth, which they were able to bring to Poland after escaping from the new Communist regime and settling in Częstochowa.

Grandpa Maj, a wealthy man, had a warehouse storing coal to sell to neighbors for the harsh winters. Grandpa also had a taxi service, taking people to the town in a horse and carriage. I remember that he had a special black funeral carriage to take the dead to the cemetery; however, only a horse and simple wooden wagon took my father to the cemetery for burial. Another white carriage with white leather seats was used for weddings. When a carriage was in use, it was usually decorated with flowers, white ribbons, and greenery. In addition, Grandpa Maj owned a billiard room with a restaurant, and a *magiel* (mangle), which pressed linens with large wooden rolling pins.

After his son's marriage to Jozefa, Grandpa, with all his money, never gave Wilhelm a job in his businesses. After the loss of his only son, Grandpa became an alcoholic and threatened all of us with his violent behavior. He frequently cursed his wife, also named Jozefa, called her names, and said things like *kurwa twoja mać* (your mother was a whore). He kicked her legs; after a while the wounds did not heal. Grandpa never reconciled with his son. After Wilhelm's death, when Wilusia was born, and I was four, Grandpa allowed us to move in with him because Mother had no income.

Hell started for us. Because Grandpa was in a constant rage, he tore the apartment apart, broke dishes in the china cabinet, broke furniture, and threw the pieces at us, while shouting explicit swear words. He chased me with a whip made of a rabbit's foot and long strips of leather. Every time he hit any of us he shouted, "Now you know who is the boss; I, Władysław Maj." Sometimes I hid in their grandfather clock that had a cabinet large enough for my body to fit. I sat down with my knees under my chin. I shook and prayed to God to save us from harm inflicted by the drunken Grandpa. Many times on cold winter nights, we ran out in the yard in our nightgowns, just to get away from this wild, uncontrollable man. Day after day he got up in the morning, half-asleep and still in his underwear, he went across the street to buy alcohol. He drank until he exhausted himself from screaming and chasing everyone around.

The nightmare finally ended when Grandpa passed out in his bed, usually in a pool of his own urine. Grandpa fed alcohol to his horses, the German shepherd, and even poured it into the canaries' water container. The neighbors heard his screams, but no one wanted to get involved. The only safe place was Wilusia's crib; he left her alone. Right then I decided that I would never drink alcohol or beat my children when I grew up. Grandpa's alcoholic rages lasted from the time I was four until I was seven when my Jewish father came to claim me. My mother, in desperation, also started to drink to cope with the horrible situation we were in and tried to stay sane, despite the struggle of everyday survival.

To earn our living and to get away from Grandfather, my mother took me on trains with her to sell merchandise that we carried in suitcases. My presence helped her sell because people had more compassion for a woman with a small child. We sold tobacco, cigarettes, and vodka. I learned how to fold the tobacco in tissue paper and seal it with my spit. When the supply of vodka ended, Jozefa and I collected old alcohol bottles off Częstochowa streets. Jozefa washed them, filled them with vodka, and then she made a brown wax seal on top of the cork pressing it with a *grosz,* a small coin, to make it look authentic. When we ran out of real vodka, we filled the bottles with half water and half alcohol, passing it off as 100 percent alcohol. For this reason, we often changed the routes on the trains, avoiding recognition.

The trains were always crowded with people. At every train station, the Gestapo, accompanied by ferocious German shepherds, looked for suspicious people, mainly Jews or contraband smugglers. On one of our escapades, Mother and I were separated when she stepped off the train first. I did not make it on time because the train was moving and the doors closed. I started to cry louder and louder until the conductor came and took me home with him at the end of the trip. I remember crying, screaming, and not wanting to eat or talk to anyone. As Mother later told me, she noticed my absence immediately and went to the train manager's office begging him to look for me. She came across a sympathetic person because the next day we were reunited. We were thankful to the people who helped us find each other. Mother gave away free cigarettes to everyone in the train manager's office.

Often when we traveled by train we slept in different cities. It was typical for people who lived close to train stations to house travelers for the night. Mostly I slept on the floor with other children lined up like sardines, head to feet to head, and so on. I remember the little striped booths where German soldiers guarded the cities. Occasionally they stopped people to show their documents. Most of the time the Gestapo kept German shepherds, who barked and showed their teeth.

One unlucky trip took us to the Gestapo headquarters in Częstochowa. When we came home on the train, the Gestapo was looking through people's luggage, pointing to the ones they wanted opened. They pointed at our suitcase. I volunteered to open it, while Mother pretended not to be interested. However, when they opened it, they discovered cigarettes; we were arrested and taken to headquarters. They sent Mother and me to two different rooms for interrogation.

Screaming uncontrollably, I found myself sitting across from a uniformed Gestapo man sitting behind his desk. I was afraid that we would be killed because I knew that is what the Gestapo did. Many times I saw them shooting people in the street, and I knew the Germans killed my father. Scared without my mother, I looked around the room. On his desk, I saw family pictures. He stared at me for a while and then picked up the telephone and spoke in German to someone. The next thing I remember was meeting Mother in the hallway. The Nazi gave us back the suitcase with a warning in broken Polish. "Don't do this again. I have a little daughter like you, but someone else won't be as generous as I am. So don't let us see you again." We could not adhere to his warning. How else would we survive?

Life was full of dark secrets, dark skies, and dark apartments. At night, we were awakened by loud sounding sirens, warning the city population of an imminent air raid. We had to run to the basement for cover. Our only light came from a dim, smelly kerosene lamp. We needed to cover the windows at night with dark blankets.

We were hungry. Mother started to sell her furniture, clothing, and jewelry. She invented a flour soup that we called "white borscht." She made it with a cup of water and a spoon of dark flour left for a day or so to get sour. Sometimes she would cook it on the stove when there was coal. Otherwise, we ate it cold. Mother was always fair about dividing the food and bread between her daughter and me. Because I had holes in my shoes, in the winter Mother wrapped paper around my feet to keep them as warm and dry as possible.

I remember being sick quite often during that time, although I never was seen by a doctor. When I had whooping cough, Mother ran to the neighbors in a panic because I was choking and blood was pouring out of my nose. She bundled me up and put me in the small garden surrounding the front of our building to get some sunshine and color in my cheeks.

The longer the war went on, the hungrier we were. We went through the neighbors' garbage looking for potato peels to cook. When there was no food Mother could only say to us, "Go to sleep, and maybe you will forget that you are hungry." However, to sleep through the night was impossible. The bedbugs kept us awake, and sometimes, we could not stand it anymore, so in the middle of the night we would shake the mattresses and pour hot water on the bugs to kill them. I will never forget the foul smell of the dead bedbugs. Even today, I start itching just thinking about it. The lice bit us day and night. They were in my hair and in my clothing. Our favorite time together as a family was to look for lice in one another's hair. I learned to kill them between my nails. I also learned to remove their eggs from my hair by squeezing each hair between my nails and pulling them down.

Often Mother and I had visited her girlfriend who lived across from the fire station where Mother had a firefighter boyfriend who beat me when she was not around. From her friend's top-floor window, we watched the firefighters exercise, climbing tall ladders and scaling ropes. Sometimes they practiced marches, playing their tubas and other musical instruments. On holidays, they marched in the middle of the city, and we children followed them as far as we could.

But one visit to Mother's friend still haunts me. I stood in the building entrance and heard popping-like noises. People were running in all directions, many falling on top of one another. Then I saw a carriage and plain wagons with horses loaded with the bodies piled high. Mother came down and grabbed me in her arms and went back to her friend upstairs. She held me tight and whispered repeatedly, "Thank you God for sparing Irena." Only recently, I learned that we were in the forbidden part of the Częstochowa Ghetto, where half the street was still populated by Polish residents and the other was restricted to the Jews. What I had witnessed was a daily massacre of the Jews brought to Częstochowa by train.

On Sunday mornings, we usually went to Jasna Gora, a famous fortress and monastery, for a Mass. At the end of the third boulevard, we walked up the hill where a stone wall surrounded the church. Below, there was a deep depression in the ground covered with trees, bushes, and grass. This represented "the way of the cross" and final statue of Jesus Christ where he was hanged on the cross that he had carried. We usually came to the unveiling of the Black Madonna's icon and stayed through the Mass until it was covered again. It was always crowded. I saw people punishing themselves by crawling on all fours, and later sprawled out on the stones in front of the altar crying and asking God to forgive their sins. Mother explained to me why they did this and said the real sinners were those killing the innocent, not the people crawling alongside us.

As we walked to Jasna Gora, I saw a German soldier, and he smiled at me. I stuck out my tongue. He shook his finger disapprovingly at me. Mother, behind me, watched in horror. When she caught up with me, she asked, "Irena, why did you do that?" I said, "Because he killed my daddy!" Any uniformed man symbolized the enemy to me.

In Grandpa's apartment across the hallway from us lived a family of five. The parents kept a low profile during the war because the father, a university professor, was in as much danger as if he had been a Jew. The Nazis were out to destroy the Polish intellectuals so that the Polish masses would be kept in the dark.

The professor's twelve-year-old daughter, Aldona, was a Jew hater. Like my Grandpa, she repeated the stories about the Jews catching Polish children, killing them, and using their blood to make matzos for their Passover holiday. Other children told me this story, and like many, I acquired a hatred and fear of Jews. I was also afraid of ghost horror stories that were a favorite subject among the adults who lived in our building. The ghost tales kept me up at night and scared me. When in bed, I covered my head with a blanket, leaving only a small hole for my nose. I was afraid that the ghosts' cold hands would reach for me in the darkness of the night.

One day when I visited Aldona and no one was home, I noticed an open jewelry box. I wanted this treasure. Suddenly, I felt uneasy. I had been told that people who steal were punished after they died by going to hell, a place deep under the ever-burning ground where sinners burned for eternity, with the devil himself in charge. During the holiday *Ostatki,* similar to Halloween, many wore red or black devils' costumes with masks, horns, and tails, and carried large pitchforks. It was also popular during *Ostatki* to dress as an Orthodox Jew. The Poles wore long, dark coats, a black hat, and glued-on mustaches, beards, and strips of hair hanging by their ears.

When I told my mother about my fear of hell, the devil, *Ostatki,* and Jews, Mother was indignant about what these people did and said. She never participated in anti-Jewish gossip. She wanted her daughters to be God-fearing people who would love their neighbor as themselves. She never passed a beggar without giving him some money or bread. She taught us to be courteous to strangers, respect elders, be polite to all, and thank people for favors.

She made me stand next to her and pointed out how small I was. Then she told me the minute I reached her shoulder, I would be a grown-up girl. She always praised my helpfulness and my being an excellent sister to Wilusia, whom I often carried in my arms to protect her. Mother bragged how good-natured I was, how she could wake me up at any moment. I did not complain or cry and was ready to travel.

The Red Army liberated us on January 17, 1945. My own father returned from Russia in 1947. To reclaim me, he sold my maternal grandparents' property and went to various Jewish organizations that were involved in finding Jewish hidden children and asked them for monetary help. Only after a big fight with Grandpa and the payment of a large amount of money did Grandpa give me back to Father. My mother never got any reward because Grandpa introduced himself to my father as the one who saved my life. My life with Father was difficult because he was a stranger to me, plus he remarried a very disturbed woman who was an Auschwitz survivor.

My life after liberation was to me as tragic as the Holocaust.

Figure 43. Ida and Adam Paluch's family, Sosnowiec, Poland, 1940. Their mother, Ester Wajntraub-Paluch, holds Ida and Adam on her lap.

Lfd. Nr.	Zu- und Vorname		Geburtsdatum und Ort	Frühere Adresse	Jetzige Adresse
207.	PARYZER	Nasyn Israel	8.6.1918 Bendsburg	Marktstr.18	Grabenzeile 27
208.	"	Ruchla Sara	7.3.1916 Pilica	"	"
209.	PINCZOWSKI	Szlama Israel	21.3.1897 Szczekociny	Marktstr.14	Petrikauer.9
210.	"	Chawa Sara	5.4.1927 Sosnowitz	"	"
211.	"	Hendla Sara	10.2.1928 Sosnowitz	"	"
212.	"	Majer Israel	8.1.1931 Sosnowitz	"	"
213.	"	Israel	2.9.1936 Sosnowitz	"	"
214.	PARYZER	Pesla Sara	20.5.1913 Pilica	Tuchgasse 12	Sandzeile 42/8 c
215.	"	Szlama Isr.	31.7.1937 Sosnowitz	"	"
216.	FRESAJZEN	Gitla Sara	1884 Lelów	Breslauer.23	Taubenweg 5
217.	"	Jacheta Sara	6.11.1922 Sosnowitz	"	
218.	PYTOWSKI	Dawid Israel	9.8.1893 Rozprza	Böhmisches	Zeilenweg ↓ 11
219.	"	Roza Sara	27.11.1903 Opatów	"	
220.	"	Arno Israel	20.1.1927 Breslau	"	
221.	"	Leo Israel	29.4.1939 Sosnowitz	"	"
222.	PALUCH	Genia Sara	8.10.1931 Sosnowitz	Modrowgasse 43	Hügelzeile 11
223.	"	Abram Berek Israel	3.5.1937 Sosnowitz	"	"
224.	"	Ida Sara	3.5.1939 Sosnowitz	"	"
225.	PARYZER	Nusyn Israel	4.5.1906 Sosnowitz	Tuchgasse 10	Petrikauer.8
226.	PACHTER	Rózia Sara	3.3.1897 Pieczkowice	Marktstr.4	Zeilenweg 4
227.	"	Abraham Isr.	4.6.1919 Sosnowitz	"	"
228.	"	Josek Israel	29.10.1923 Sosnowitz	"	"
229.	"	Mojżesz Isr.	22.3.1922 Sosnowitz	"	"
230.	PULKA	Hersz Israel	1.7.1889 Działoszyce	Breslauer.11	Hügelzeile 61
231.	"	Gitla Brajndla Sara	10.7.1894 Lelów	"	"
232.	"	Moszek Israel	8.8.1923		

Figure 44. Ida Paluch and her siblings listed on the Środula Ghetto roster, Poland, 1941–43: No. 222–Genia, No. 223–Abram (Adam); No. 224–Ida.

Nr. 394 **C**

Sosnowitz, den 20. August 1942

Die Estera Sara Paluch

, jüdisch,

wohnhaft in Sosnowitz, Mochowgasse 23

ist am 14. August 1942 um 12 Uhr Minuten

in Sosnowitz, Marktstrasse 8 verstorben.

Die Verstorbene war geboren am 13. April 1906

in Szczekociny

(Standesamt Nr.)

Vater: unbekannt

Mutter: unbekannt

Die Verstorbene war — nicht — verheiratet

Eingetragen auf ~~mündliche~~ — schriftliche — Anzeige der Staatlichen Kriminalpolizei in Sosnowitz

~~D Anzeigende~~

~~Vorgelesen, genehmigt und unterschrieben~~

Der Standesbeamte

In Vertretung: A. Wilhelm

Todesursache: Selbstmord durch Sprung aus dem Fenster vom 2. Stockwerk des Hauses Sosnowitz, Marktstrasse 8

Eheschließung de.... Verstorbenen am .... in ....

Figure 45. Ester Wajntraub-Paluch's death certificate in Sosnowiec, Poland, 1942.

Figure 46. Jozefa and Wilhelm Maj, Ida Paluch's rescue parents, in Częstochowa, Poland, 1942.

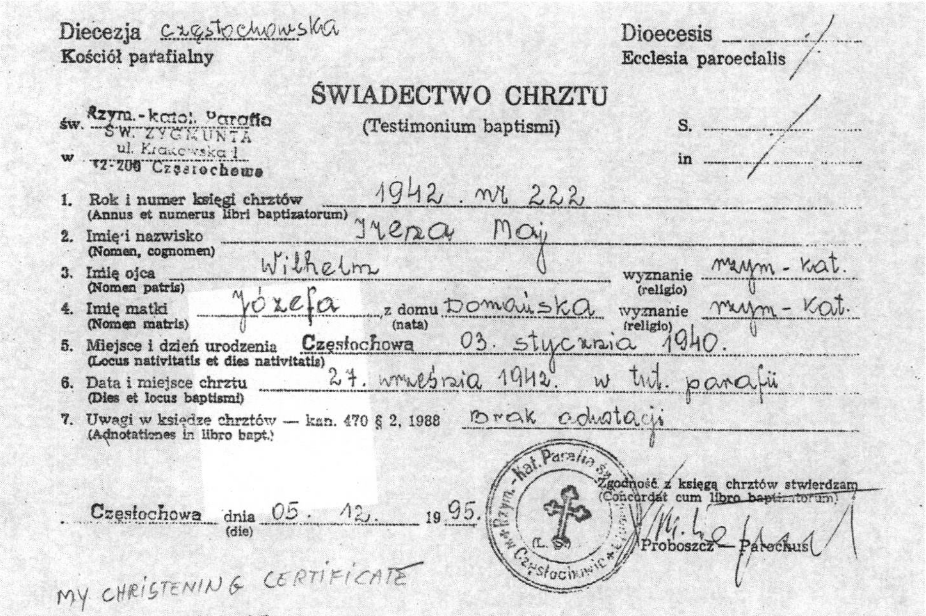

Diecezja częstochowska — Dioecesis /

Kościół parafialny — Ecclesia paroecialis /

ŚWIADECTWO CHRZTU

(Testimonium baptismi)

św. Rzym.-katol. Parafia ŚW. ZYGMUNTA ul. Krakowska 1 — S. /

w 42-200 Częstochowa — in /

1. Rok i numer księgi chrztów (Annus et numerus libri baptizatorum) 1942. nr 222
2. Imię i nazwisko (Nomen, cognomen) Irena Maj
3. Imię ojca (Nomen patris) Wilhelm — wyznanie (religio) rzym.-kat.
4. Imię matki (Nomen matris) Józefa z domu (nata) Domańska — wyznanie (religio) rzym.-kat.
5. Miejsce i dzień urodzenia (Locus nativitatis et dies nativitatis) Częstochowa 03. stycznia 1940.
6. Data i miejsce chrztu (Dies et locus baptismi) 27. września 1942. w tut. parafii
7. Uwagi w księdze chrztów — kan. 470 § 2, 1988 (Adnotationes in libro bapt.) Brak adnotacji

Częstochowa dnia (die) 05. 12. 1995.

Rzym.-Kat. Parafia św. Zygmunta Częstochowa

Zgodność z księgą chrztów stwierdzam (Concordat cum libro baptizatorum)

Proboszcz — Parochus

MY CHRISTENING CERTIFICATE

IDA PALUCH-KERSZ

Figure 47. Ida Paluch's christening certificate, Poland, 1942.

Figure 48. Ida Paluch after her father took her from her rescue mother and placed her in an orphanage in Poland, 1946–47.

PART 5

Hiding in Plain Sight

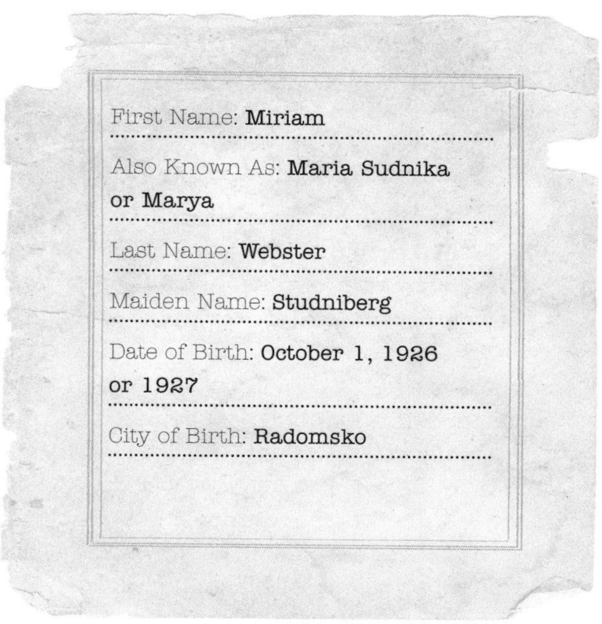
First Name: Miriam
Also Known As: Maria Sudnika or Marya
Last Name: Webster
Maiden Name: Studniberg
Date of Birth: October 1, 1926 or 1927
City of Birth: Radomsko

As told to Haim Levendel

From Radomsko to Chicago

Miriam Studniberg Webster

The Radomsko I Knew

I was born Miriam Studniberg, but at home, they called me Marisha, as it was customary for Jews to have both a Hebrew and a Polish name. I was born on either October 1, 1926, or 1927. I am not sure, because the Łódź Hospital where I was born made a mistake on my birth certificate. The question of my exact age did not come up until later, when I could not ask my parents anymore.

We lived in Radomsko, a large town in central Poland. It had a Jewish population of ten thousand out of twenty-five thousand people. I grew up in the "Park Avenue" section of the town, a predominantly non-Jewish area, but we had a few Jewish neighbors. It was a tree-lined boulevard with wooden benches lining the street and fancy residences with beautiful windows and doors facing the street. Our home, an apartment building, was nothing spectacular, but we owned it and lived in one of the units while renting the rest. There were a few stores scattered in the building and in the neighborhood.

We had electricity, but no water or plumbing. My mother always had help in the house. Our live-in maid brought water in buckets to our house. She started the fire in the morning, brought wood, prepared food for breakfast, cleaned the house, and washed the clothes. When I was not feeling well, she walked me to school. She was a nice person who was eager to convert me to Catholicism when my parents were away, but I was not interested. I loved being Jewish. All my girlfriends were Jewish, and I went to a Jewish school. My parents observed all the Jewish holidays. The holidays were beautiful. We prepared for weeks cleaning the house for Passover. Even as a child I understood the meaning of the holidays. I remember the house was filled with geraniums and white tablecloths. My father was dressed up in his white *kittle* (a cotton smock) for the seder. I understood what Catholicism was and had been inside a church, but it did not give me the same warm and loving feelings as my family's observance of Judaism.

Over the years, we had a number of maids who came from a small rural village close by. They were trying to improve their lot. The girls came from homes that did not have electricity, and they had never even heard a radio. They were looking for exposure to a modern lifestyle and the opportunity to find a husband to go with it.

We enjoyed a comfortable life. When I was young, I spent a considerable amount of time in parks. My mother would wheel me there in the company of other mothers from the neighborhood. When I became older I went to a Jewish elementary school. The father of one of my best girlfriends, who now lives in London, was the school principal. Although the students were all Jewish, it was a public school. We had small classrooms and great teachers. I was considered an excellent student in elementary school. Even as I was passing secret notes to my friends during class, I was always able to answer questions when the teacher caught and tested me. I was able in math, but geography was my favorite subject. I remember studying about North American cities, but we talked a lot about Chicago because it was "the windy city." At the end of the school day, I went ice skating in winter and bike riding and playing volleyball in the summer. My parents could not get me home on time for dinner. I attended the school until seventh grade, and after the end of that school year, I registered for a private high school in Radomsko. I did not attend high school because the war broke out on September 1, 1939, the day I was supposed to start.

My parents had Jewish and non-Jewish friends. I did not experience any antisemitic incidents, except once. On the way to school, a girl told me, "Wait until Hitler comes. You will not be as well as you are." She was one of a few *Volksdeutsche*—that is, an ethnic German, a member of a German colony outside Germany but still connected to Germany. I brushed off her comment like it was nothing. There were rumors about what was happening to the Jews in Europe. I knew about Hitler, and my family had donated coats to the local *gemander*—a local Jewish social services organization for the unfortunate German Jews. It never occurred to me that I might suffer the same fate.

My father's name was Abraham, but everyone called him Abe. He was born in the area, where his family had lived for several generations. His mother had died. His father, a Reform Jew, had retired in Gdynia, a free port called Gdańsk in Polish, and he had remarried. Many people came to play bridge all afternoon on my grandfather's large enclosed porch. He had a beautiful garden. Although it was quite far from Radomsko, I did visit him. He helped his widowed daughter, Chaja Fischalter, run a mineral-water bottling plant. Grandfather David and his daughter did not survive the war. They were sent to Treblinka with the rest of my family and the other Radomsko Jews.

Before the war my father and his brother took over their father's business, feather and down exporters, in Radomsko. They would buy the feathers from the farmers, separate the down, and pack and ship it to different countries, usually outside Poland: Germany, the Baltic countries, the USA, and Palestine. Their customers used these feathers to make all kinds of items, like pillows and bedcovers. In the late thirties, the business thrived. We were unaware that Germany was buying this raw material in preparation for the war; they made bedcovers for the German officers.

My father, a Zionist and active member in the Radomsko Conservative synagogue, was considered a smart man. The people in our community sought his advice on various matters. He attended services every Saturday where men and women prayed together.

We spoke Polish at home, and a little Yiddish. My grandparents spoke Yiddish. My maternal grandfather, a pious Jew, studied the Torah. He died in the Warsaw Ghetto. I don't remember his name.

My mother's name was Stephanie, née Wolfstein—Stefa for short, and her Jewish name was Esther. Born in Warsaw, she had seven brothers and sisters. She did not work outside the home. She had received a scholarship to the Warsaw Conservatory, where she studied opera singing and was the only Jew in the conservatory because of *numerus clausus*. *Numerus clausus*, from the Latin meaning "closed number," was a method, even before the war, that was used to limit the number of Jews in universities, schools, and other institutions. After she married my father, she moved to Radomsko.

I admired my mother, who had a beautiful voice, and I remember her singing around the house. *Carmen* was her favorite opera. Besides singing, she loved to walk. She kept a kosher home.

Before the war, I remember preparing for the Sabbath days in advance, cooking fish, duck, goose, and chicken, and baking challahs, because everything had to be prepared from scratch—we couldn't purchase challah or matzo in a store and our oven wasn't big enough to make all the food we needed. We celebrated all the Jewish holidays. For Passover, my father led a beautiful seder that lasted until midnight. We lived next door to a bakery and had a wonderful relationship with the baker. He allowed my mother and the maid to use his ovens at night because during the day his ovens were filled with bread and pastries for the baker's customers. They would go into the bakery at night after hours, heat the stove very high to "kosher" it, and prepare our holiday food. For Sukkoth, we invited our neighbors into our sukkah. For the High Holidays, I did not go to the synagogue. Instead, I played in our yard. We picked chestnuts from the tree, and the winner was the person who could throw them the farthest. It was our horseshoe game. These were annual events that I took for granted until the Germans invaded Poland.

My only brother, Izja, or Yitzhak, his Jewish name, was two and a half years younger than I. We got along well; he was a darling boy. A *melamed* (teacher of Hebrew and Yiddish) taught him his prayers for his bar mitzvah. I remember the ceremony, which was nothing like what is customary here in the United States. We all went together to the synagogue. He delivered a speech and recited a prayer, we all had dinner at our house, and that was it.

A melamed connected to the synagogue gave me Hebrew lessons. Unlike my success in regular school, his teaching was insufficient for me to learn to read and to speak fluently. I learned a few prayers, and that's all.

Poland Invaded

Our meaningful Jewish life ended when Poland was attacked on Friday, September 1, 1939, while we were at the Kaminsko Resort. Kaminsko, in a wooded area, was a popular destination for Jewish families, who went there to enjoy fresh air and the beautiful forest. It was named for the town it was in, about twenty minutes by train southwest of Radomsko in the Częstochowa region. Częstochowa was an important tourist destination featuring the Black Madonna statue. We always had private rooms in a cottage behind the main building. Under normal circumstances, our recreation would include playing volleyball, resting on blankets, and hiking through the woods. We would have our afternoon meal in the dining hall with the other families. The rest of the time we ate in our cottage. My mother would take my brother and me to the resort when school was out in May. We would spend the summer there. My father would come to the resort after work on Fridays to spend the weekend with us. He returned home Monday morning.

On Friday night, September 1, my father arrived for our final summer weekend. The plan was to return to Radomsko on Sunday to prepare for school. All day warplanes had been flying overhead, and we were worried, but my father reassured us. He was convinced the planes were Polish fighter planes on maneuvers. We still did not believe that anything bad would happen. Looking back, while my father was reassuring my brother and me, he was making plans with the other fathers to hire a horse and buggy to take all the families to Łódź, where they felt it would be safer to be in a city farther from the German border. We left that night, joining a long stream of people fleeing east to Łódź. There we stayed with my father's relatives for about a week. A few days later, the Germans captured Radomsko, on September 3. Łódź was taken a few days later. All I could think about was going home—to Radomsko—and it did not occur to me to consider anything else or expect anything to be different. All of Poland was conquered by October 6.

As things quieted down, we decided to return to our home. Radomsko looked like a ghost town when I got there. The streets were empty. The houses seemed intact, except for windows that were broken during the invasion. People were scared and would not come outside. Nobody knew what to expect. But over time, life started again.

The Jewish school was closed. My brother and I were forbidden to go to school, and we stayed home for about four months, until the beginning of January 1940. The Germans immediately confiscated our business and forced my father to hand over the keys to his feather import-export business to a young, inexperienced administrator. He was nice to us when he needed my father's help in the plant. My father was not employed anymore. We Jews were adversely affected by all these regulations.

The *Judenrat* (Jewish Council) distributed white armbands with a yellow star. I went with my family to a small office to get ours. The man who gave them to us was a Jew. We had to wear the armband when we went outside. Suddenly I was marked. I was not like the other people.

A Jewish family from Germany came and stayed with us for a few days. When the Germans needed twenty-five people to work, they demanded it from the *Judenrat.* Everything went through the *Judenrat.*

Germans physically abused people. Sol Studniberg, my father's brother, was ordered to excavate a road. The Germans claimed that he did not do a good job. They made him run around a courtyard, and he and a few other people were whipped on the head. He was released that evening.

Once, two German soldiers came to our apartment. I stood in the living room with my mom, dad, and brother. I was terrified and just stood there holding onto my mother while they pulled open our drawers and cabinet doors. They pulled out everything and threw it around. They thought we were rich, and they were looking for anything of value. They found and took my father's beautiful stamp collection. My father was extremely upset.

Life in the Radomsko Ghetto

Shortly after the establishment of the ghetto, like many other people, we were evicted in January 1940. My father said to my mother, brother, and me, "You go to your cousins in Warsaw until I find a new place." In Warsaw, conditions had deteriorated; rationing was severe, and typhus had started to spread. We were happy when my father found a place, and we were able to return to Radomsko.

My father found us a single small room in the Radomsko Ghetto. It had a sheet separating the "bedroom" and kitchen. The only good thing about our living quarters was its location. It was at the edge of the ghetto. It was owned by some farm people who rented it to us. Because of its location, our Christian friends could smuggle a few of our belongings from our house and bring them to us. They brought us the blankets, sheets, and pillows from our beds, my mother's pots and pans, and some of our own clothing. This was an extraordinary luxury, because most people had nothing at all.

My family was in the ghetto from January 1940 until October 1, 1942, my birthday. Those two years were nothing like my life before that time. Leaving the ghetto was forbidden, and we had to wear white armbands with the yellow star. The Germans shot anyone who did not abide by their rules. We did not observe Jewish holidays, and I doubt that other families did. Families doubled up in small living quarters. We had our own space, and my parents tried to normalize our lives.

What stands out is that even under these horrific circumstances, my parents said they were ready to forgo all kinds of other needs, but they were not ready to deprive me of an education—and I gladly went to learn every day. Every morning I got up, dressed, hid my books under my arm, and went to the teacher—a woman who had worked as a high school teacher before the invasion. It was against the law to go to school, and I had to hide my books. If they caught me, I would be hanged. She taught me math, Polish grammar, Latin, and German. It was not easy to study Latin on an empty stomach. She was an expensive private tutor—not all of my friends went to school. Class lasted just a few hours each morning. Then I would spend time with my friends in an outdoor area where kids gathered. I would like to say that we still managed to have some fun and enjoy some laughs as teens, but we did not. Fear was mounting. Every day was very scary. We stayed together just holding onto each other. Although there were no fences or guards surrounding the ghetto, I did not try to escape because I feared the patrols. The police shot anybody except people who had special passes, and there were not too many of those.

Because my father was able to buy some food, we were on one meal a day, which was good compared to what other people had. There was a soup kitchen established by the *Judenrat* for people who did not have anything to eat. Fortunately, we did not need to go to the soup kitchen. My father was able to leave the ghetto to help the German administrator of our business, and on his return, he had the opportunity to buy some food on the black market. We lived on potatoes, bread, and whatever else we could find.

The *Judenrat* had set up a minimal first aid station, but no hospital. Fortunately, we remained healthy and did not need medical care. There were no deportations until the end, when they were going to liquidate the ghetto. Jews were brought to Radomsko from other cities and villages on horse-pulled wagons when the Germans designated Radomsko for liquidation.

No news came into the ghetto; we were sealed off from the rest of the world. Occasionally, someone would come in from the outside and tell us that hard times were coming for the Jews. But we all hoped that the American planes would come and bomb.

I did not hear about people escaping from the ghetto, but at the beginning, when we were in Łódź, some people did not return to Radomsko. They went east to the Russians, and it was only after the war that I learned that they had survived in Russia.

A Narrow Escape

On the morning of September 30, the day before my birthday, I woke up. My mother and father were already awake. We were together as a family in our living space. My father had just had a visit from the young German man who had taken over our family's feather plant. He had come to see my father to get as much information about the business as possible, as he knew the liquidation of the ghetto would happen soon. He also gave my father the opportunity to purchase false identification papers for me for five thousand zlotys. The man told my father, "You know, things don't look good for Jews; they are going to empty the city of Jews. I cannot do anything for you, your wife, or your son because he is circumcised, but I can take care of your daughter. She does not look Jewish. I can get some papers and we can help her."

After the man left, my father told me in front of the family, "We want to save you," and explained that I would leave the ghetto and my family. Although I was fearful of leaving my family behind, I convinced myself that I was tough enough to survive. My father sold some items for five thousand zlotys on the black market to obtain the false papers for me.

The next day, the man came back with false papers in the name of Maria Sudnika, two years older than I. He brought with him a big cross and a prayer book. Now in a twist of fate, I would be Catholic. He said, "With this you can run away from the ghetto and try to save yourself." My father had contacted Christian friends who would arrive that night to take me out of the ghetto and to a train bound for Warsaw.

When they came to get me, I was wearing a babushka tied under my chin and lipstick. I looked much older than sixteen. My brother said, "I am so young. Why do I have to die?" I could not answer him. I didn't say anything. I knew I would just start to cry. I knew that if I left the ghetto crying with red eyes, the guards would view me with suspicion, and I might get caught. I just had to turn away and say nothing. For the same reason, I did not kiss anyone good-bye. Not my mother, not my father, not my brother. By that time, we knew through Polish acquaintances that Jews were being targeted.

One of our Christian friends, Maria Kałuszynska, took me away to her house and kept me there until midnight. It was safer to take a midnight train to Warsaw. Even at that time of night, the train was surrounded by SS carrying machine guns. Another Christian friend was brave enough to pass through the cordon; he pretended that I was his daughter. He put me on the packed train. Every seat was filled. The other travelers were squashed together. A young policeman noticed me getting smashed between the other riders and felt sorry for me. He put me on his lap and unwittingly saved me from all the spot checks for Jews during the ride to Warsaw. My thoughts were racing ahead to Warsaw. I prayed that the woman scheduled to meet me at the station would not lose her courage and would show up to take me to my next hiding place. I was shocked when I got to the station and she was waiting for me. She was happy to see me and said, "I'm glad you showed up." She probably thought that I would never make it.

She had previously come to collect feathers from our business. My father had sent her a letter about my arrival in Warsaw. She took me to her house, where I stayed several weeks. Later I learned that she was collecting merchandise for the Germans, but her husband, a high-ranking officer in the Polish Army, was in hiding. She sympathized with me. She often said, "Whenever you need to escape, my house will be open to you." She was a caring woman.

Conditions worsened. Posted street signs stated anyone keeping Jewish runaways would be shot. When I left the ghetto, my father had mapped a plan for me. "First, you stay with the Polish people as long as there is no danger for them. If you see danger, go farther away. If it gets really bad, go to work in Germany. And if you go to Germany, go toward the French border, where they are friendlier." Berlin, Hamburg, and inner towns were known to be more dangerous.

When I told my hostess in Warsaw about my concerns, she told me, "Don't worry! My parents are farmers near Lwów. I will send you there and you will be able to work, but don't tell them you are Jewish. We will tell them that you were one of the Girl Scouts whose mother I knew." I traveled toward the farm by train until Lwów. I was sixteen and looked like a Polish peasant with my big cross and babushka. Although I was scared, I felt that I had the strength to make it through. I was determined to survive because my family had appointed me to be the family member to stay alive. They told me, "If the war ends and we don't make it, tell the world what happened to us and the Jews."

The farmers picked me up from the train station. When I arrived, they were happy with me and never knew I was Jewish. I worked on the farm, milking cows and feeding chickens. I had to learn everything from the ground up. Even in the ghetto, I could sleep until eight A.M. At the farm, I had to get up with the sun and dress for the weather. No matter if it was rainy or snowy or nice, I had to milk the cows, pick up the eggs, and put down food and water for the chickens. The first time I tried to milk a cow, it didn't work. No milk came out. I had no idea how to do it. The farmer came out to see what was going on and had to show me again. Eventually, I got the hang of it.

At the farm, I would go to church like a good Christian. I was afraid that one of the workers would want to go out with me and would discover who I really was, but nothing happened. Within a few weeks, the same signs appeared in the streets warning people not to take in Jewish runaways. I had arranged with my father that I would write to a mutual friend and he would relay letters back and forth. But that arrangement could work only after I arrived in Germany and would have a permanent address.

After leaving the ghetto, and throughout my travels, my only thought was to move on. Of course, I was hoping to be reunited with my family one day, but there was no assurance. In fact, two days after I escaped, there was the big *Aktion*. The ghetto was emptied. The Jews were assembled and sent to Częstochowa, except for a few Jews, among them my father and my uncle Sol. For a short while, my father was able to hide seventeen people, including my mother, brother, and grandfather, in an attic nearby. Everything would have been fine, but an older man who could not take it anymore ran out and was caught by the Germans. After being beaten, he showed the hiding place to the Nazis.

My father and my uncle, who saw my mother and grandfather before they were transported, were able to smuggle some bread to them under the fence. At least they would not go hungry on the train. Then everyone who was gathered in Częstochowa was deported to Treblinka.

A New Destination: In the Lion's Den

Because I wanted to leave, I said to the farmers, "I am homesick and I don't think I can stay any longer. I have to go back to Warsaw." On arrival in Warsaw, I went straight to the German military office that was recruiting Polish workers. Given my need to constantly be on the move, there was no opportunity for me to luxuriate in having "feelings" about what was happening around me. It was just a given that I had to keep moving, and I had to stay safe. I couldn't indulge in self-pity or fear. I had to stay alert and smart so I could plan my next move.

In the office, I observed a mixture of working-class people who badly needed income and some members of the intelligentsia who were fleeing persecution. Although my Polish was perfect and I did not have a typical Jewish accent, I was still afraid of being detected. At this gathering point in Warsaw, I met a few Jewish people whom I easily recognized; I confided in one of the girls, but we didn't keep in touch after the war. I found some comfort in knowing there were other runaway Jews.

The German military did not ask many questions; they needed workers and seemed happy to get me. They showed me on the map several factories where I could go to work, and I chose a huge ammunition factory in Mannheim, near the French border, as my father had suggested.

They put me on a train to Germany. We had to stop in Berlin for identity checks. I was scared. They took everyone off the train—hundreds of people—and brought us to an office. We all had to line up. As they ordered, we took off all of our clothes down to our bra and panties. All the women were given vaginal exams. I had never had a female exam before, and my mother never mentioned anything like this. I didn't know what was happening. Afterward, I thought I would never be able to have children. We all got dressed and got back on the train headed for Mannheim.

When I arrived in Mannheim, I was brought to the Heinrich Lanz A. G. Aktiengesellschaft factory that made guns, bullets, and various parts for German military vehicles. There were many foreign workers—Poles, French, Russians, Yugoslavs—because of the workforce shortages caused by the massive mobilization of German men.

A German restaurant prepared breakfast and dinner that were delivered to the barracks. So I asked if I could work in that restaurant and prepare food for the French. I was following the advice of my father to stay away from the Poles to avoid being detected. They accepted me and gave me a room together with a German girl, who was also working there. All day long, we peeled potatoes, washed the dishes, and did any work needed for the restaurant. The French would probably be unaware of any sign that could give me away as being Jewish.

The restaurant had regular customers. I had to make sure that I didn't make mistakes. The owner of the restaurant behaved like an SS man—mean. The owner was an older man, married with a daughter, who was a little younger than I. Although he wasn't an officer, he wore the uniform and participated in Sunday meetings. Every time I turned around, he seemed to be saluting "Heil Hitler!" To him I was just one of the girls in the kitchen. I took orders from his wife. I was scared of him—and I was scared of all Germans. When the phone rang in the restaurant, I jumped. I worried it was someone calling him to tell him I was Jewish. I didn't cause any trouble. We got along well, but I hated his guts and was in constant fear of being discovered.

I had to wash out big soup kettles that sat on the floor. The kettles were too big to lift, so the water had to be siphoned out with a hose. One time while I was getting the siphon started, it backflowed, and I swallowed scalding hot water and had to be rushed to the hospital. I had to keep my mind completely blank from fear or worry so that I could quickly recover and get out of the hospital before I was discovered. As I lay in the hospital bed, I thought, if they knew I was Jewish, they would just as soon kill me. I returned to my job the next day without incident.

I did not go to church at the beginning. I knew somewhat how to behave in church, but being a foreigner was an advantage. During confession, before Easter, I said to the priest that I did not know how to do it in German; I was holding on to the cross, so he gave me his blessing and let me go.

Periodically, I received communications from my father, which meant he was still alive. The letters were not real letters, just a few words. "Dear Marish, How are you? I'm fine." When I wrote back, I wrote the same brief words. I did not raise any questions, but deep down I had a feeling that something had happened to my mother and to my brother because his letters never said, "*We* are fine." It wasn't like my father to think only of himself. When I learned the truth after the war, it was not a shock to me, but it was a terrible blow to lose the people I so dearly loved.

Mannheim had constant air raids during the time I lived there. During one attack, the restaurant was bombed while we were in the bunker. The next day we were still in the bunker because our living quarters also had been destroyed and the Firma Lanz factory vice president came to see us. His name was Mr. Buchholtz. He was there to assign jobs to all the restaurant workers. He offered to bring me to his home to work as a maid for his wife. She was a French teacher and they had two sons. Unlike the restaurant owners, the Buchholtz family were nice people. They lived in Zweibrücken, not far from Mannheim. They did not know I was Jewish. Had they known, they probably would have kept me anyway, but I was terrified about anyone knowing because I understood it was a death sentence for me and anyone who kept me. Life with them was pleasant. Their boys were a little younger than I, and they were nice to me. I made their beds, dusted, and did the laundry. I helped Mrs. Buchholtz shop for groceries. I was their only household help. They made sure that I went to church every Sunday. Mr. Buchholtz had a beautiful garden where he grew tomatoes, lettuce, carrots, and other vegetables.

During that time, I never heard about the concentration camps or about what was happening to the Jews. No one talked about it. I heard on the radio that the Americans were getting closer and closer. Mr. Buchholtz caught me once listening to the news reports. He told me not to listen to the radio any more, but he didn't report me.

I stayed with the Buchholtz family until the end of 1944, when orders came to gather all the foreigners back to Mannheim ahead of the Allied advances. There they sent me to work in another restaurant where I stayed until the Americans liberated us in March 1945.

The U.S. Seventh Army Takes Mannheim on March 29, 1945: My Father and I Reunite

I was hiding in an underground bunker with German civilians because the U.S. Army was advancing when someone called us to come out. I saw the Americans holding machine guns going from house to house searching for German military. I didn't see them catch anyone. I ran toward them because I was not afraid. I was happy to see them. I knew the Americans were here to defeat Germany and that was good enough for me. A few days later, I went to the American office and told them I was a Jewish refugee. The army gave me a job to work in the mess hall immediately because at the beginning they did not want to employ Germans.

I was eighteen when I was liberated. I did not want to go back to Poland. My father, who had survived with his brother Sol, came over to Germany and went straight to my last address in Zweibrücken. Mr. Buchholtz told my father where to find me. Later, after my father and I were reunited, he told me that Mr. Buchholtz was very nice to him and asked why I had never told him I was Jewish. It is true that he was a good, family-oriented man who was deeply religious. Nonetheless, I would never have told him I was a Jew. It would have endangered both of us. That war was not the time or place for sharing these confidences.

This is when I learned that the Germans had murdered my mother, brother, grandfather, and my mother's brothers and sisters. My father, my uncle, and my aunt had spent the war hidden in a farm under a haystack. At night, the Polish peasants brought them food and any letters. My father was all swollen from malnutrition and immobility. His arrival at my apartment was a wonderful day that I will never forget. There was a knock on the door, and my roommate Chana answered it. I looked up and ran to the door, hugged him, and said, "*Tatusiu!*"("Daddy" in Polish). I was so happy to see him. We cried when we saw each other. He looked terrible—he was white as a sheet. He told me the story of how he survived by hiding under the ground, under a haystack on a farm for two years. The only food he had came from Polish peasants who brought it to him with my letters. Over and over again he said to me, "You survived, you survived." We were filled with joy and relief to be able to be together again.

My father got an apartment, while the other two Jewish girls, whom I had met earlier, and I lived together and worked for the Americans. Little by little, I picked up English. I cooked for the Americans at the canteen. Eventually, the troops moved on, and one of the officers, Lieutenant Hutler, who was Jewish, told me that, in Aglasterhausen near Heidelberg, the United Nations operated a camp for Jewish orphans. He told me I could apply for immigration to the United States there.

The Orphanage

I was too old to live in the children's camp, but the director, Rachel Green Rottersman, liked me and thought I could be helpful with translation because I could speak Polish, German, and English. She gave me a job interviewing the children in their native languages, translating their statements, and typing up their profiles in English. She nominated me as a second-class officer in the United Nations Relief and Rehabilitation Administration (UNRRA). She gave me a uniform and access to the American rations and the PX. It was heartbreaking to hear the children's stories. I remember the sadness in their eyes when they told me their stories. Most of the children were Jewish survivors who had lost their parents. But once in a while, a non-Jewish orphan showed up. These children were placed also.

My time at Aglasterhausen was pivotal to the rest of my life. Rachel became like a mother to me. I witnessed how she changed children's lives by ensuring they were adopted into safe countries like the United States, Canada, Australia, and Palestine instead of being shipped back to Russia or Poland where they might be harmed under Stalin's rule. One group of boys from Estonia were safely shepherded to the United States and featured on the cover of *Life* magazine. It was thanks to Rachel that they were saved. It was that article that captured the attention of the filmmaker Fred Zinnemann, who came to the camp and created the movie *The Search,* based on the people and children in the camp. There were people from all nationalities, British, French, and many others, working for UNRRA.

Rachel and her husband, a Jewish displaced person, returned to the United States. I had a strong desire to come to the States, and my father approved. Rachel had sponsored my immigration to the United States. As part of my false identification process, my original birth certificate had been destroyed to deny my existence. It took years to gain permission to come to the United States. I did not leave Germany until 1949. I arrived in Boston on one of the last refugee trips of the USAT *General Howze.* The ship was full of survivors.

From Boston, I moved to New York where Spary, a social worker and friend of Rachel's, met me. Rachel had friends all over. I stayed one day and went to Chicago. There, I rejoined Rachel, who practically adopted me, and I stayed with her until my father arrived. Rachel found me an apartment, a small place with a room and a kitchen, near the University of Chicago, where Rachel lived and worked. She also

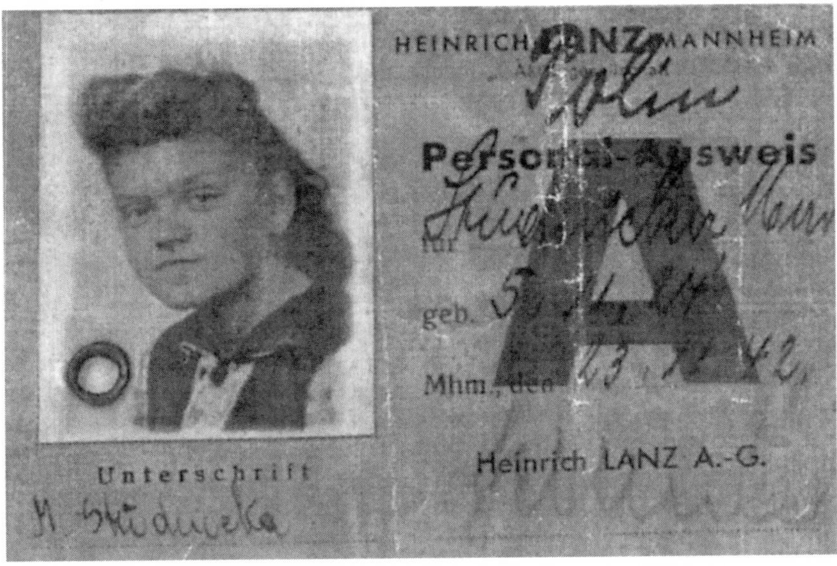

Figure 49. Miriam Studniberg's identification card with her false name, Marya Studniceka, when she arrived in Mannheim, Germany, to work at Heinrich Lanz, 1942.

Figure 50. Miriam Studniberg, *center front,* with friends "Coca Cola," Kasia, and Peggy, when she was living and working for the United Nations Relief and Rehabilitation Administration (UNRRA), Aglasterhausen Displaced Persons Camp near Heidelberg, Germany, 1945.

found a job for me. She and her husband had a child, and they shared their lives with me. When my husband and I had our family a few years later, Rachel and I raised our sons together—sharing holidays like family. She was like a mother to me and a grandmother to my children.

My father arrived in Chicago but could not adjust. He stayed briefly. My father said that he had always lived without a boss and that the language would make it difficult to succeed on his own. The climate of Chicago did not agree with him, and his health was failing. He was a broken man. He could make a better living in Mannheim, partnering with other Jews he knew.

He decided to return to Germany where his brother and wife lived. My uncle's son, born after the war, still lives in Mannheim, where he has three children and three grandchildren. We stay in touch.

Figure 51. Miriam Studniberg, Aglasterhausen, Germany, 1945.

First Name: Amos
Also Known As: Mieczyslav
(Mietek) Lemanski
Last Name: Turner
Date of Birth: February 18, 1926
City of Birth: Tel Aviv
Country of Birth: British Mandate
for Palestine

Pretending to Be a Pole

Amos Turner

I survived the Holocaust pretending to be a Pole.

Before World War II, five thousand Jews and thirty thousand Poles lived in my hometown, Zawiercie, an industrial city in southwestern Poland. Jewish life centered on the synagogue; life cycle events; Hebrew, Yiddish, and Orthodox schools; and Zionist organizations. Most Jews lived in the Jewish section of Zawiercie that contained clothing and shoe stores, bakeries, groceries, and meat markets. Once a week, Polish farmers came to Zawiercie to sell eggs, milk, cheese, vegetables, fresh fish, and poultry. I attended the secular Tarbut School, where we spoke and learned in the Hebrew language. I celebrated my thirteenth birthday and my bar mitzvah in February 1939.

The German Army, which included Austrians, marched into Poland on Friday, September 1, 1939, and three days later they entered Zawiercie. The German Army overtook the people who tried to escape the night before and forced them to return to Zawiercie. Britain and France, honoring their commitment to Poland, entered the war on September 3, 1939.

Germany decided to annex southwestern Poland, including Zawiercie (Warthenau in German), and sent the Gestapo, police, and border guards to control the civilian populations. The Gestapo forced the Jewish community to form the *Judenrat* (Jewish Council), which consisted of leaders of the prewar Jewish community. The Gestapo informed the Jewish Council that they would have full jurisdiction over

Jews. This was a shocking development as we realized that practically overnight we had lost all our rights. The Jewish Council tried to establish contacts with the Gestapo and police with bribes.

In December 1939, the SS deported Jews from Bohemia to Poland. We gave up one room of our three-room apartment to an elderly couple from Bohemia. This room contained our kitchen, which my mother shared with them. Because we had to pass through their room every time we entered or left our apartment, they didn't have much privacy. In later years, when the Germans deported Jews to death camps, the Germans pretended that they were deporting Jews to the east to work.

The Gestapo ordered Jews to turn over radios, money, diamonds, gold, silver, and furs. We gave the Gestapo a radio, silver objects, and my mother's fur coat. We hid money, gold, and my mother's diamond ring. Jews complied with the order partially and hid what they could. The Gestapo confiscated Jewish homes and forced Jews to move to smaller and more congested quarters. We were also forced to wear the Jewish star and to perform forced labor. My four uncles and I had to show up every morning, and the Germans assigned us jobs moving furniture, doing repairs, and cleaning German offices and homes. I worked as an electrician, a trade I had learned in the Zawiercie Ghetto.

In January 1940, we became aware of an atrocity committed by the SS. My Uncle Max, who fought in the Polish Army, was taken prisoner and kept in a stalag in Germany. After a few months the German Army transported the POWs to Biała Podłaska in eastern Poland. They separated the Jewish prisoners and turned them over to the SS. The SS marched them toward Lublin and on the way started to shoot the men who walked slowly. One-third of the marchers were killed before the Jewish Council of Lublin bribed the SS leaders. Uncle Max was released and returned to Zawiercie. We assumed at the time that the SS action was an aberration and that bribes could alleviate their abhorrent behavior.

As late as 1941, almost two years into the German occupation, we were still able to walk to a nearby village to attend a Jewish wedding. I was also able to mail food packages to my mother's oldest sister, Esther Goldsobel, and her family who lived in Warsaw and who suffered from hunger. All that stopped when the Germans formed the ghetto in Zawiercie, which happened at the end of 1941. Our apartment was in the Zawiercie Ghetto so we didn't have to move. Although the Gestapo strictly prohibited it, I studied with a tutor, and we prayed on Rosh Hashanah and other holidays. We even had a sukkah in the ghetto. Having no other choice, we learned somehow how to adjust to the horrible conditions imposed by the Germans. We had lost all our legal rights; we were in danger of being arrested, beaten, and sent to Auschwitz. Without enough food, we were constantly hungry. Medication was lacking, and we were always fearful about what would happen next.

Throughout this period, the SS forced young Jewish men and women to work in faraway forced labor camps, from which they were later transferred to death camps. The SS sent the German police into the ghetto to search and arrest the workers. At this time, my parents were safe because the SS only arrested young Jewish men and women. I managed to hide and to stay in Zawiercie. My Uncle Max had suggested that he could build a false bottom in a large wooden container with coal, which we had in our apartment. I helped him build it. We provided an opening in the bottom of the container to enable me to breathe and to get some food and water.

Every night I removed enough coal so that if I had to hide, I could slide into the false bottom and my parents would replace the coal in the container. During SS "actions" we were not allowed to go to work. I hid successfully, even though the Germans raised the cover to search inside. I was scared, but I held my breath and did not move. Lying in the container felt like being in a casket, but the presence of my parents in the apartment and a strong will to survive made it bearable.

In 1941, as the Germans were making plans to attack the Soviet Union, they needed factories closer to the front lines. Luftwaffe (German air force) officers came to Zawiercie to establish a clothing and shoe factory. The Jewish Council assured them there were experienced tailors with sewing machines in the ghetto. Jewish tailors trained others and about two thousand men and women were employed in the factory. I worked in the shoe factory where I met a friendly and decent young Polish girl, Aleksandra Karpeta. We spoke during breaks about the war. Aleksandra showed unusual compassion to the suffering and dangers confronting me and all Jews. She told me that should I decide to escape, I could hide in her parents' apartment for a few days. She didn't divulge then that she had made the same offer to my friend Zosia Borzykowska.

Children and older people lived in the ghetto, where the workers returned at noon and at night. They stopped at a kitchen, where they received hot meals. The Jewish Council bought food from Poles and smuggled it into the ghetto, which was a dangerous task, but the need was great—so it was done.

In June 1942 the Germans evicted two thousand Jews from neighboring villages to Zawiercie and pretended they were transferring them to eastern Poland. A Pole, who was running the train, told a member of the Jewish Council that the train went to Auschwitz (Oświęcim). To the best of my knowledge, not even one person survived from this group. Lieutenant Garbrecht, the supervisor of the Luftwaffe factory, a very decent German, argued with the SS and managed to save a few hundred younger people from their clutches. My parents and I started to worry that someday we might be forced to separate.

There was always hope in the ghetto that the war would end soon and that life would return to normal. One man listened to the BBC on a clandestine radio and kept us up to date on the war's progress. We knew that the United States entered the war in 1941 and that the German armies started to experience reverses in Russia and North Africa, which happened early in 1942. As far as we were concerned, it was only a matter of time until the German forces would be defeated. Working for the Luftwaffe gave us a false sense of security; we believed that we could remain in Zawiercie until the end of the war.

Early in 1943, Mordechai Anielewicz, the head of the Warsaw Ghetto uprising organization, traveled to Zawiercie from Warsaw carrying false papers to seek financial help to buy weapons. My father, who had been president of a Zionist organization before the war, arranged for a number of people to meet Anielewicz in our apartment to listen to the plans for the Warsaw Ghetto uprising and to give him money, which they had been able to hide from the Germans. The Jewish Council bribed the German police and obtained a permit for Anielewicz to travel to Jewish ghettos in Będzin and Sosnowiec and for his safe return to Warsaw. The Jewish Council also paid smugglers to take him across the border between Germany and Poland. It was a difficult undertaking but well organized and coordinated by the various town Jewish Councils.

Our feelings of being secure were shattered during the summer of 1943, when the SS deported all Jews from the nearby communities, Dąbrowa Górnicza, Będzin, and Sosnowiec, to Auschwitz (Oświęcim). My parents encouraged me to make escape plans. My father contacted a member of Hashomer Hatzair, a Zionist youth organization, and asked her if she could eradicate all inked entries from my identification card, which she did. I filled in a Polish name, Catholic religion, and an address in the Polish area of Zawiercie. My family felt that I had the best chance to survive pretending to be a Pole because I had blond hair and blue eyes; I spoke Polish well without a Yiddish accent. My parents also knew that I had befriended Aleksandra, who had told me that if I escaped, her parents would allow me to spend a few days in their apartment, which was not far from the factory.

We continued to work in the Luftwaffe factory until August 1943, when the SS and the Gestapo decided to replace us with Polish workers and deport us to Auschwitz. Luftwaffe officers went to Berlin to prevent it. They did not succeed, but were allowed to keep a Jewish transition team. The Luftwaffe prepared a list of five hundred workers and kept them in the factory. I checked the list but did not find my name on it.

On August 26, 1943, the Gestapo ordered all Jews to assemble in a large square in front of the Jewish Council building. The SS and police searched the ghetto and shot those who were hiding. Lieutenant Garbrecht was not allowed by the Gestapo to enter the square, but I noticed that my Luftwaffe supervisor Zimmerman entered the square and was assembling a group of workers. I asked my parents what I should do. They insisted that I approach Zimmerman. I parted from my parents with a heavy heart and tears in my eyes. When Zimmerman saw me, he motioned for me to join the small group of workers and he marched us to the factory. We were kept hidden and given some food and water by the Luftwaffe soldiers. During the next two days and nights, we were shocked to hear shots and the sounds of children's cries. The SS herded them with their parents into cattle cars. I was in shock, fearing that the worst would happen to my parents, to my family, and to all the others, but I forced myself to function.

Four thousand five hundred Jews—men, women, and children, including my parents, uncles, aunts, cousins, friends, and acquaintances—were taken forcibly to Auschwitz. We found out after the war that the SS kept detailed records of the people assigned to work. Thus, we knew then that a day after they arrived in Auschwitz, only 1,743 people were still alive. My mother, her sisters and brother, my father's six sisters, their spouses and children were murdered on the day they arrived in Auschwitz. From the 4,500 people, 400 were alive at the end of the war. I realized after the liberation that I had lost 48 members of my immediate family.

For a few days after this tragic event, I was in a daze. I was then assigned to travel to the ghetto by truck to move some supplies. On one of these trips, an SS officer used a whip to force us off the truck. I fell on cobblestones and injured my left shoulder. At night a Polish surgeon came to the factory to take care of the wounded workers. He set my arm, put it in a sling, and told me not to work until my shoulder healed.

I was able to walk in the working halls and made contact with many Poles, who told me that more Polish workers were being brought in to replace the Jewish transition team. I decided to try to escape as soon as I was able to work.

A Polish worker named Jan told me that he knew a hotel owner in Gleiwitz (Gliwice), a city in Germany not far from Zawiercie, who needed a worker. At the factory we made plans to take the same train to Gleiwitz on Monday. We would only make eye contact on the train. Once we arrived in Gleiwitz, we would meet on the platform. I knew that the Karpeta family agreed to provide me with temporary shelter in their apartment. I had my false identity card. As I walked around the factory, I noticed a broken window from which I could jump to the street.

I escaped six weeks after my injury, and I went to the Karpeta family. As predicted by my Polish friends, the SS took four hundred ninety Jews away from the factory to Auschwitz on October 18, 1943. Only ten Jews remained in the factory: seven tailors, one electrician, and two children who escaped from the train. They all survived the war.

It was pure luck that I escaped from the factory three days earlier. I hid one night in the apartment of the Karpeta family. The next morning Aleksandra accompanied me to the Zawiercie railroad station. We noticed two German policemen at the ticket office. Aleksandra suggested that she would buy the ticket for me while I would wait in front of the station. We waited for the announcement that the train was arriving, and I ran with the ticket in my hand toward the train. Once on the train, I was able to make eye contact with Jan.

When we arrived in Gleiwitz, Jan and I went to the hotel. The owner of the hotel offered me a job and shelter. The owner tried in vain to obtain a work permit for me; without it he was unable to keep me and gave me thirty days' notice. And so I was stranded with no place to hide.

Four friends of mine—Inka Windman, Basia Weinblum, Zosia Borzykowska, and Mania Lifschitz—managed to escape from the ghetto. They made their way to Germany using false identity cards from Hashomer Hatzair, and they found employment and shelter using a unique idea. They walked into an office of the German Labor Department and pretended that they were in a transport of Polish workers, that they got off the train to buy something, and that the train left without them. Zosia and Mania were assigned to work in a hotel in Hindenburg (now Zabrze, Poland), Inka was assigned to work in a hospital, and Basia in a munitions factory in Tarnowskie Góry.

I was able to make contact with Zosia within two weeks by mail through my friend Aleksandra, who helped Zosia and Mania in their escape. I met with all four of them in Hindenburg in Zosia and Mania's room in back of the hotel where they worked. They told me how they were able to secure employment and encouraged me to try their idea. I spoke German, which I learned in high school and from working for the Germans.

I went to Beuthen (Bytom) and Hindenburg, but I was rebuffed. In Oppeln (Opole), they were in a dire need of an electrician, my story was accepted, and I was sent to a labor camp in Ottmuth, Germany. The camp's population consisted of Poles, Russians, French, Dutch, Belgians, Czech, and Serb workers. The Poles and Russians were restricted more than the other nationals. They had to wear identification badges, and they were not allowed to travel freely or to go to the movies.

I arrived at the camp by myself, which was highly unusual, as others came in groups. My Polish coworkers asked me many questions, and I doubt that I answered them to everybody's satisfaction. I was then told that I would have to undergo a medical examination.

I feared the examination. If discovered, I would be sent to Auschwitz. I took a chance as I had no other options. I do not know whether the doctor was absent-minded, or in the darkness in the corner of the room, he did not notice that I was circumcised.

Two factors played a key role in my being left alone from that time on. First, the Polish coworkers were puzzled by my safe return from the medical examination. Second, there was a feeling of empathy for Jews because the Poles knew the full extent of the Jewish tragedy that was unfolding in front of their eyes. They stopped asking me questions about my past, and they did not discuss the suffering of the Jews in my presence. One Polish worker came from the city of Auschwitz, and he was especially sympathetic to me because he knew what was taking place there.

Once a month the Poles were given a permit to travel home, which was great for them, but a serious problem for me. I did not dare return to Zawiercie as someone could recognize and denounce me. So I had to find a way to spend a whole weekend without raising suspicion. Zosia suggested that I could come to her and Mania on Saturday and stay until Sunday. They were even able to bring some food from the hotel restaurant.

On Saturday morning I traveled to Kattowitz (Katowice), where I met Aleksandra, who brought me some food stamps. Then I went to Gliwice to a bathhouse where I could take a bath in private, but I had to pretend to be a German. I spent some time in parks pretending to be waiting for someone and in movie theaters, where I felt more secure sitting in the dark. To enter the bathhouse or a movie theater, I had to remove my Polish identification badge, which was a dangerous act. I would return to Ottmuth on Sunday afternoon.

This situation continued for about five months until spring 1944. Zosia, Mania, and Inka had no problems working in the hotel and hospital. Basia, however, worked in a munitions factory as a welder. She had a difficult job and was harassed by a Pole from Zawiercie. She was afraid that he would turn her over to the Gestapo.

At the same time, the Soviet Army was moving across Poland. Basia and Inka decided to cross the border into Poland to reach the Soviet Army. Basia knew of a smuggler in Żarki, a village near Zawiercie, and asked me to join her to meet with him to make final arrangements. Basia and Inka persuaded Zosia and Mania to join them. I tried in vain to convince them that Basia could get a job in another city and that this was a much safer way than crossing a border, but they were anxious to be free and not to wait for the end of the war. My friends refused to listen to my pleas.

I stayed with them as long as I could and left them with great sadness. I wished them good luck, hoping that they would succeed, but I was doubtful.

After my friends left, I lost their companionship but also a place to sleep when I had to leave Ottmuth once a month. I still could not travel to Zawiercie, so I continued what I was doing before, but I would sleep at different railroad stations on Saturday nights once a month, even though the German police watched them. I would pretend to be waiting for a train, always carrying a valid travel permit and a ticket. Trying to appear inconspicuous, I would enter a washroom, and I did not hesitate to stand next to a policeman or an SS man. Although I was terrified, I forced myself to act normally, not to show fear, and not to engage in idle conversation. I had to bury my fear to survive.

I received a postcard from Zosia, Mania, and Basia when they reached the city of Tarnow, within seventy miles of the advancing Soviet Army. I was surprised that they did not mention Inka. The postcard was the last message from them. After that, they disappeared without a trace. Even today, thinking about my wonderful friends, I regret not being able to dissuade them from their decision.

I did not hear what happened to Inka until the end of World War II. Inka lost her way trying to cross the border; she was arrested and turned over to the Gestapo. She suffered horrible beatings by the Gestapo for about six months. She was then sent to Auschwitz and assigned to work in a factory, where she met a number of people from Zawiercie, including my father.

Inka told my father that I was working as an electrician in a shoe factory in Germany and that my chances of surviving were good. I believe that the news encouraged my father, who suffered horribly in the camps, to make a special effort to survive the war. He weighed seventy pounds at the end of the war.

I do not remember any of the movies that I saw, but I do remember two newsreels, which I will never forget: the uprising and destruction of the Warsaw Ghetto by SS tanks and artillery and a review of Muslim volunteers to the SS by the grand mufti of Jerusalem.

It was very difficult for a Jew to transform himself practically overnight into a non-Jew and pretend to be of a different religion. One had to look non-Jewish, assume a new name, new personality, new customs, and new interests. I could not undress or shower in front of other people. And I had to pretend constantly that I had family and friends in Zawiercie who would write letters to me. I had to be on my guard all the time, watching what I said and how I said it.

Epilogue

After the end of World War II in May 1945, survivors who were able to travel visited displaced persons camps, their hometowns, the offices of the newly formed Jewish Councils, American Joint, and United Nations Relief and Rehabilitation Administration (UNRRA), in search of their family members. They examined lists of survivors and spoke to survivors from their hometowns. I went to Zawiercie and met with the ten people who survived in the Luftwaffe factory. They told me that my father, my uncles Harry and Max, and Aunt Jadzia survived, and that they were living near Munich in the American Zone of Germany. They persuaded me to travel to Warsaw and to join the Lohamei Hagetaot (Ghetto Fighters) group, which was directed by Icchak (Yitzhak) Zuckerman and a few other survivors of the Warsaw Ghetto uprising. The group was planning to travel to Israel and to form a kibbutz.

The leaders of the kibbutz knew that written memories of life and persecution in the Warsaw Ghetto were enclosed in a steel box and hidden in a certain building. They were eager to retrieve the box, and they determined the approximate location of this building. We went with shovels and picks every morning to dig, but our effort was unsuccessful because after the uprising all ghetto buildings were demolished by the Nazis into a pile of rubble.

Attempting to bring joy in our lives, in the evenings we danced the hora, sang Hebrew songs, and told stories about Israel. After a short time, Aliyah Bet organized a train to take hundreds of young Jewish survivors, including myself, from Poland to Prague, Czechoslovakia, and from Prague by buses to Munich, Germany.

I was nineteen years old when I reunited with my family in an apartment, which my Uncle Max was able to secure in München-Fasanerie. The apartment was formerly occupied by a high-ranking SS official. Our reunion was bittersweet

Figure 52. Amos Turner and his father, Alexander, Truskawiec, Poland, 1938.

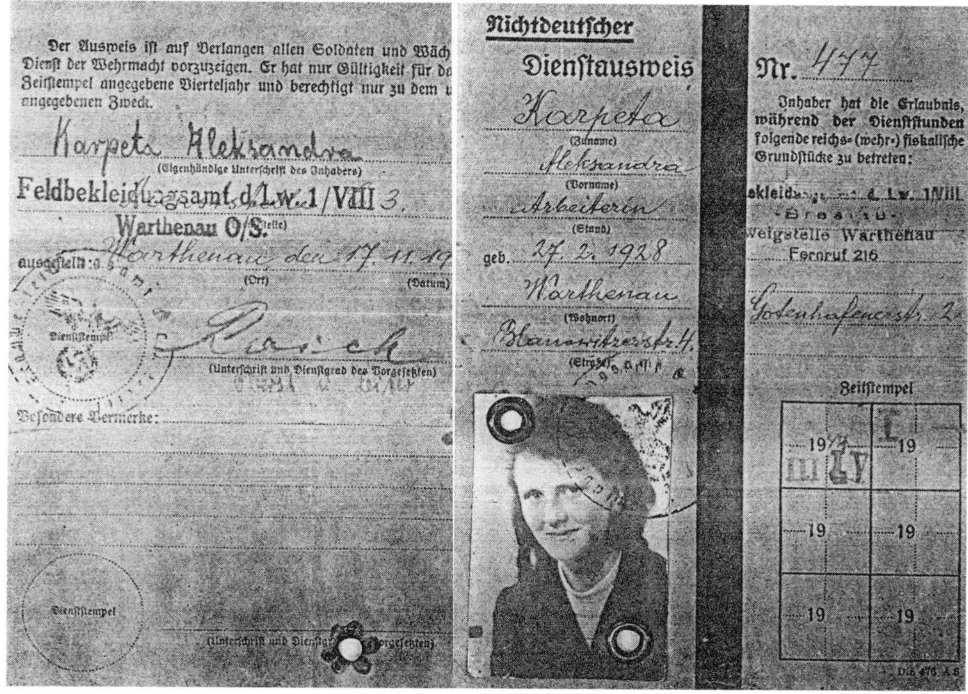

Der Ausweis ist auf Verlangen allen Soldaten und Wäch[illegible] Dienst der Wehrmacht vorzuzeigen. Er hat nur Gültigkeit für da[illegible] Zeitstempel angegebene Vierteljahr und berechtigt nur zu dem [illegible] angegebenen Zweck.

Karpeta Aleksandra
(Eigenhändige Unterschrift des Inhabers)

Feldbekleidungsamt d. Lw. 1/VIII 3.
Warthenau O/S. (Stelle)

ausgestellt: Warthenau den 17. 11. 19[illegible]
(Ort) (Datum)

Dienststempel

(Unterschrift und Dienstgrad des Vorgesetzten)

Besondere Vermerke:

Dienststempel

(Unterschrift und Dienstgrad des Vorgesetzten)

Nichtdeutscher

Dienstausweis Nr. 477

Karpeta
(Zuname)
Aleksandra
(Vorname)
Arbeiterin
(Stand)
geb. 27. 2. 1928
Warthenau
(Wohnort)
Blanowitzerstr. 4
(Straße)

Inhaber hat die Erlaubnis, während der Dienststunden folgende reichs- (wehr-) fiskalische Grundstücke zu betreten:

[illegible]ekleid[illegible] d. Lw. 1/VIII
Breslau
Zweigstelle Warthenau
Fernruf 216

Gotenhafenerstr. 2

Zeitstempel

19	19
19	19
19	19

Figure 53. Amos Turner's Polish friend Aleksandra Karpeta's work permit, 1944.

Figure 54. Amos Turner and Edith Singer meet on the USS *General R. M. Blatchford* coming over to the United States, 1950.

as we suspected we were the only survivors from my father's side of my family. We discussed endlessly what happened during the war.

The Polish people who helped me acted selflessly, and they risked their lives in the process. I had no money to give them, and they did not expect any compensation. After the war, my father and I presented information to Yad Vashem Holocaust History Museum in Jerusalem, which honored Aleksandra Karpeta Borkiewicz as a "Righteous Gentile." She received a gold medal, a memorial plaque was placed on the Wall of Remembrance, and a tree was planted in her honor. Yad Vashem also honored five thousand other Poles who helped Jews. I helped Aleksandra financially until her death.

Only Rudolph Schneider, one of the three Gestapo leaders in our city, received a death sentence and only because a friend of mine, Heniek Landau, recognized him and got him arrested by U.S. Army Intelligence. He was held in the Dachau Concentration Camp near Munich. My father, Uncle Max, and I as well as a number of other survivors from Zawiercie went to Dachau to testify against Schneider.

We succeeded in persuading the U.S. military commandant of the camp to extradite Schneider to Poland. Schneider was tried in Częstochowa; he was found guilty and sentenced to death by hanging. The other two Gestapo agents were tried in German courts. They did not spend a day in jail, even though my father and other Jewish witnesses testified about their crimes.

I followed my father's advice to continue my studies. I enrolled in the UNRRA University in Munich for one year, and I transferred to the German Technological Institute in the same city. I graduated in 1949 with a degree in electrical engineering. I studied with a group of Jewish survivors, and we had no social contact with the German students. The American Jewish Joint Distribution Committee (JDC) helped all survivors with food and clothing, and they also organized two kitchens for the students.

Our family gave serious consideration to immigration to Israel. My father was a Zionist all his life, and as a child I attended a Hebrew Zionist school. But after Uncle Harry left for the United States in 1946, the family decided, after years of separation, not to split up and to follow him. I visited the Lohamei Hagetaot group and explained why I had to stay with my family and that I would not be able to rejoin them. We applied to the U.S. immigration authorities under the Displaced Persons Act. My father, Uncle Max and his wife, Chana, and Aunt Jadzia left for Chicago in 1949. I was delayed by my studies and by a broken leg injury, which I suffered skiing in the Alps.

I was approved to leave for the United States in August 1950. I met my future wife, Edith, and her mother, Miriam Singer, at the train station, and we traveled together to Bremen Port and then went on the USS *General R. M. Blatchford* to New York. Edith stayed in New York with her family while I went to Chicago. Edith and I liked each other very much. I visited New York often and saw Edith during each trip. Our relationship continued to deepen and we were falling in love. I asked Edith to marry me and to move to Chicago. Edith accepted, and we were engaged in 1953 and married on July 11, 1954, in Brooklyn, New York, by my uncle, Rabbi Moshe Turner, the only survivor from my mother's side of my family.

PART 6

In Concentration Camps

The First Night

Judith Levy Straus

The child looks around
With eyes wide open,
But cannot comprehend
What the eyes see
So many in one room . . .
People sleeping in their clothes . . .
And in dirt.
Long lines for watery soup . . .
Grown-ups pushing each other . . .
And yelling.
Beds stacked three high . . .
With straw mattresses that itch . . .
And bugs that bite.
No bathrooms, no kitchens,
No real food, no toys,
And grown-ups crying.
The child closes her eyes
She does not want to see,
She does not want to hear.
She does not want to feel
How afraid she is.

A Child's Confusion

Judith Levy Straus

Mother always said:
It's very important to be neat and clean.
Yet Mother says now:
It really does not matter very much.
Mother always said:
Don't shove; never push those ahead of you.
Mother says now:
Make sure you don't end up last in the soup line.
Mother always said:
Never take what does not belong to you.
Mother says now:
It's all right to take potatoes.
Mother always said:
Good friends never hurt each other.
Mother says now:
Your friend stole your bread because she is hungry.
Mother always said:
Tell the truth, never tell a lie.
Mother says now:
Tell them you are ill,
Then we won't go on transport.
So many changes.
What happened to Mother?
What will happen to us all?

The Transit Camp

Judith Levy Straus

Every Monday it arrives
Gaping and empty
The long snake of cattle cars.
Every Tuesday it leaves
Locked and full
With human cargo going east.
Every Monday in overcrowded barracks
Terrified faces
Full of worry, fear.
Every Tuesday, the faces of those left
Expressionless, empty . . .
Only six more days till Monday.

Westerbork, 1943: Monday Night in the Big Barracks

Judith Levy Straus

A single railroad track bisects Camp Westerbork in Holland. It was the main transit camp for Dutch Jews. From there they were sent to concentration and extermination camps, east. Regularly, every Monday I saw the arrival of a long train composed of cattle cars—their doors wide open—all empty. When people were finished with their work assignment, they would see the train, and the expressions on their faces would change. The mood and noise level in our barrack was different, too: more tense, more urgent, more anxious.

Every Monday night after curfew, when everyone had to be in their own barrack, some men in ordinary clothes would enter. They held sheets of paper in their hands. These men were not Nazis, nor Dutch police: they were part of the Jewish Council of the camp, and we all knew why these men were there and what was on their papers. When the men arrived, the noise level in the barrack changed—then all sound stopped, as though turned off by a switch. It became so quiet I could hear people breathe! Then the men would start to read from the sheets of paper. They read names—only names. They read the list of names of the people from our barrack who were to be at the train early Tuesday morning. The men added that those named would go to a work camp and that they could take only one suitcase or rucksack and a blanket roll. The men added that if someone did not show up, a substitute would be selected at random.

These were not work camps; they were death camps, Auschwitz and Sobibor. Some transports went to Bergen-Belsen and Theresienstadt. To go on these was considered a privilege. The first few transports to Bergen-Belsen and Theresienstadt even went in regular passenger trains rather than cattle cars, and people actually volunteered for these transports.

The dreadful silence continued as long as the men were there, but after they left, pandemonium broke out. I will never forget the indescribable combination of crying, shouting, and wailing.

I was ten years old at the time. We were very lucky: none of our names—my father's, my mother's, or mine—were called during the four months we lived in the big barracks, but I remember being terrified and bewildered on each of these terrible Monday nights.

Those whose names were not called tried to console and help the ones who were to be on a transport by giving them some of their own hoarded food for the journey and helping some of the young mothers with the packing and dressing their children. By morning everyone was drained, exhausted.

And then it was time for the train to leave. Those not on a transport were not allowed near the train, even if they had family on it. Once from a different barrack, I could see what was going on: How people were shoved into the cars. How the cars were overloaded with their human cargo. How the doors were closed and locked. I still remember hearing the loud clang when the doors were shoved closed.

Every Tuesday, in the morning, the train left. Filled beyond capacity—with more than a thousand human beings.

Those remaining went back to their work. And by Wednesday the mood seemed to have changed again. Westerbork, at least outwardly, returned to its "normal" pace. We consoled one another and ourselves. We had a reprieve—at least until next Monday night.

Figure 55. The star Judith Levy wore in Westerbork, Holland, and in Theresienstadt, Czechoslovakia, from April 1942 to the liberation.

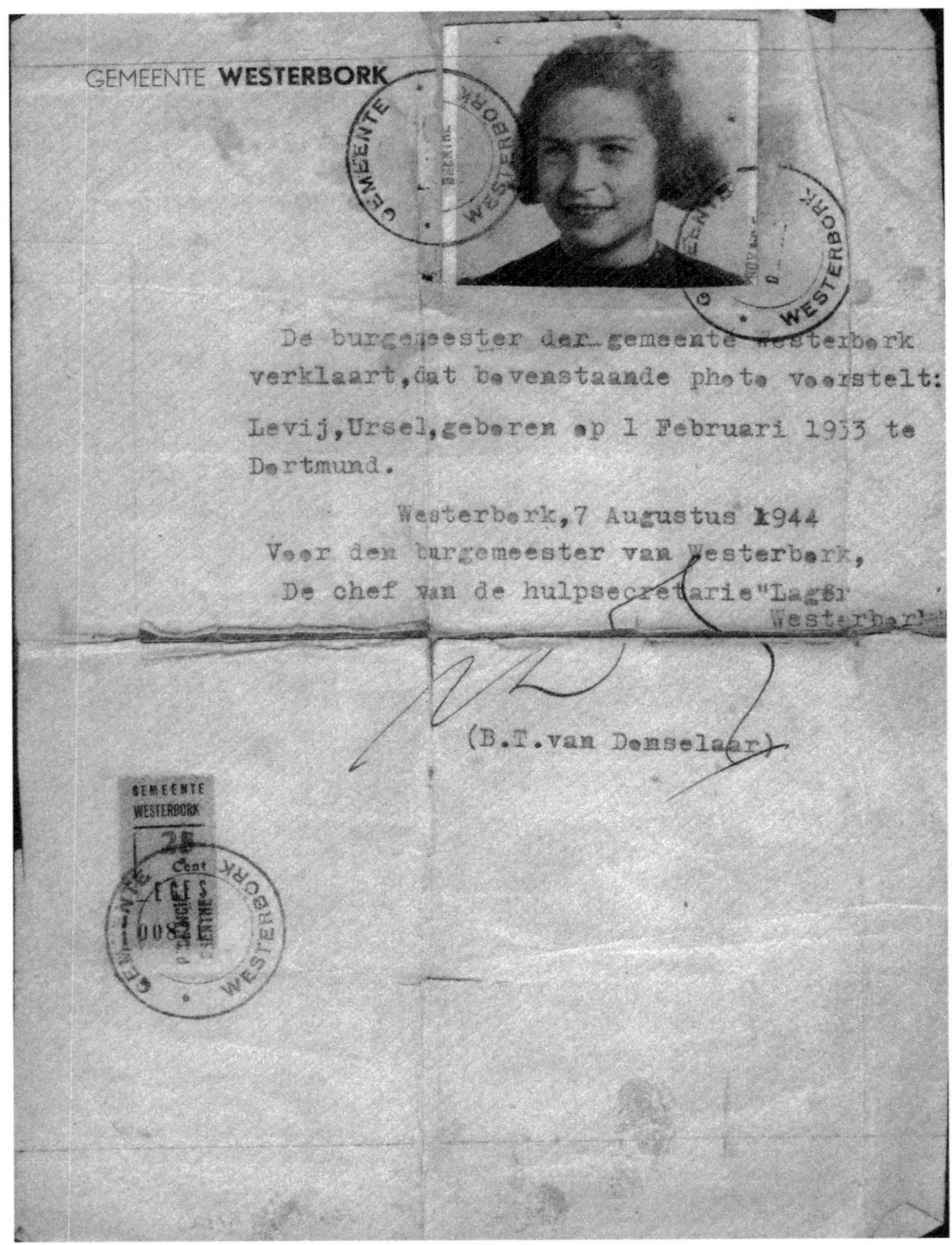

GEMEENTE WESTERBORK

De burgemeester der gemeente Westerbork
verklaart, dat bovenstaande photo voorstelt:
Levij, Ursel, geboren op 1 Februari 1933 te
Dortmund.

Westerbork, 7 Augustus 1944
Voor den burgemeester van Westerbork,
De chef van de hulpsecretarie "Lager
Westerbork"

(B.T.van Demselaar)

GEMEENTE
WESTERBORK
25
Cent

Figure 56. Judith Levy's identification card in Westerbork, Holland.

Figure 57. Theresienstadt food card and camp money.

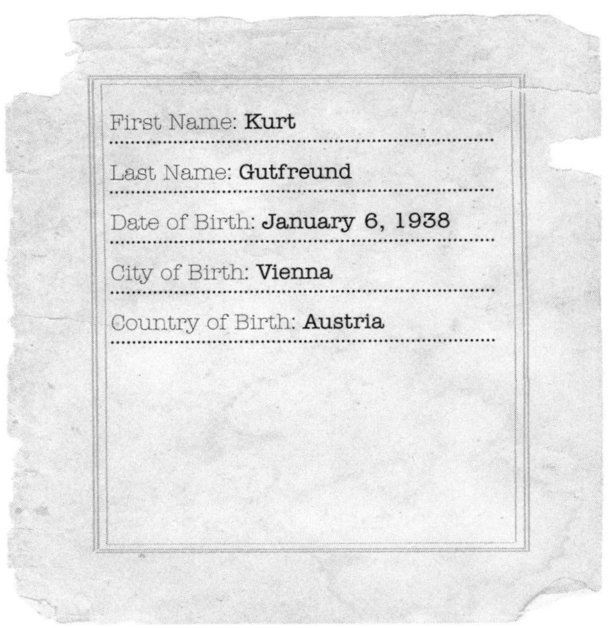
First Name: Kurt
Last Name: Gutfreund
Date of Birth: January 6, 1938
City of Birth: Vienna
Country of Birth: Austria

As told to Elaine Saphier Fox

"One Out of One Hundred"

Kurt Gutfreund

Vienna

Thousands of children were incarcerated with their families between 1942 and 1945 in Theresienstadt, a Nazi concentration camp. According to a quote from *I Never Saw Another Butterfly,* written by Hana Volavkova, only an estimated one hundred children survived Theresienstadt, while Yad Vashem estimates 1,234 children survived. I, Kurt Gutfreund, am one of those surviving children.

I was born in Vienna, Austria, on January 6, 1938, just two months before the Nazis invaded Austria on March 11, 1938. My father, Heinrich Gutfreund, a goldsmith, and my mother, Hildegard Grasel, who had been voted the prettiest shop salesclerk in Vienna, were both Viennese and German-speaking. Father went to trade school and Mother attended high school. My parents both enjoyed music. Mother loved opera and the theater. They loved each other dearly and had a wonderful marriage until the Nazis intervened. They were not religious Jews, but I had a bris (circumcision rite), and we observed the High Holidays.

Father's relatives were Jewish on both sides of the family, whereas only Mother's mother, Hermine Abeles, was Jewish. She married Otto Grasel, a Catholic who was a newspaper journalist. Under the Nuremberg Laws promulgated in 1935, my maternal grandparents' mixed marriage made my mother a *Mischling,* a "mixed breed" and not a pure Aryan. Another law later required that all Jews wear a yellow Jewish star on their outer clothing. At first, Father thought we were safe from arrest and deportation because we were Viennese.

During my mother's pregnancy with me, my father had a stroke, which permanently disabled him and prohibited him from working. He was still hospitalized when I was born. By necessity, Mother worked to support our family. Some people remember Father picking me up from kindergarten and recall that he had a lame arm. I have no recollection of my father, kindergarten, or anything else concerning my first few years in Vienna. Subsequently, I have learned that I had a kindergarten friend, Peter, and we were both noted for crying the loudest in class. Mother, whom I called Mamschi, often told me how Father adored me. I only know what Mamschi or others told me about Father and my early life.

Mamschi related an incident about my first encounter with a Nazi. I was a blond, curly-headed two-year-old playing in a nearby park. A Nazi soldier walking by stopped, approached me, and told me I was cute. According to Mamschi, I replied, "Don't touch me, I am a Jew." Mamschi never told me what his reaction was, and I don't remember. In another incident that did not turn out as well, a Nazi ordered Mamschi's sister Aunt Hermine and her husband to clean the streets with a toothbrush. Shortly thereafter, they fled to Bogotá, Colombia. Recognizing the gravity of the situation for the Jews, Father instructed Mamschi that "the little boy must live."

In June 1942, when I was almost five years old, upon returning to our apartment from an outing, Mamschi noticed police nearby. Waiting until they were gone, she returned to the apartment and found a note on our apartment door. The Nazis had arrested Father. On June 15, 1942, according to official records, he was shipped "east," deported with nine thousand other Viennese Jews to Maly Trostinec, a death camp near Minsk, Russia, on a par with or worse than Auschwitz. In 1941, Maly Trostinec was established as an extermination camp. As I learned later, transports of Viennese Jews began in May 1942 and continued through October 1942. Jews were taken directly from the trains onto trucks and transported to an execution site in the nearby forest, where five squads shot them into pits. Despite his disability and religion, Mamschi kept up her hope that Father would return. He was not among the seventeen who survived. People who could not work were the first to be liquidated.

After his deportation, we immediately went "underground." For a few months we lived in several different apartments with increasingly more people in each apartment. Because I was only four years old, I don't remember the apartments' locations. We lived in the Jewish section, the second district; so I assume that is where we remained. Mamschi hoped that because she had a Catholic father she would not be considered a Jew. Those hopes were soon squelched. She tried unsuccessfully to get Aryan papers and to leave Austria. In December 1942, we were arrested. I do not remember the hiding or the arrest.

Theresienstadt

Although I do not remember being deported, I subsequently learned that in early January 1943, Mamschi and I were put on a transport. We arrived on January 8 at

Theresienstadt on Transport 114 IV-14B, approximately seventy kilometers from Prague, Czechoslovakia. It was a walled fortress the Nazis used as a "model camp." Theresienstadt, however, was a concentration camp used to transport Jews to the death camps like Auschwitz and Treblinka, where my paternal grandfather was murdered. In addition, it provided slave labor for the Nazis. Originally built as a soldiers' garrison, the Nazis crammed into tight quarters tens of thousands of people under extremely harsh conditions. In the latter part of the war, the Nazis deceptively used this camp to quell reports circulating that the Nazis were exterminating Jews by inviting the Red Cross to inspect how well Jews were treated. I do not remember seeing the Red Cross or being aware that it was there.

Perhaps we were transported to Theresienstadt rather than to a death camp because Mamschi was a *Mischling* and other *Mischlinge* were sent there. But at five, I knew I was there because I was Jewish. Mamschi, thirty-seven at the time, learned that to assure survival, she should volunteer for work. Her job was to split mica, which was used for making radar and other electronic items for the Luftwaffe, the German air force. Mamschi believed that her ability to work in the mica factory saved us from being shipped to the death camps. Never having been sent to the children's camp, I lived with Mamschi in a tiny room. She hugged and kissed me when we spent the evenings together. She taught me how to read, write, and gave me math lessons. During the day, I would walk through the woods to see her and watch her work for a while. I cherished and loved Mamschi.

After visiting her, I played in the narrow streets. Although Theresienstadt was not an extermination camp, many people died of illnesses, starvation, old age, and the extreme conditions. There were meager food rations causing near starvation. We prisoners did not have warm clothing or sufficient medical treatment. People collected corpses on the street, put them on wagons, and pushed them through the streets. As young children do, my friends and I mimicked what we had witnessed. We pretended that we were carrying dead bodies off the street, putting them in carts, and carrying them away for disposal. Also we climbed into a dark coal cellar and stole coal to give to old people so they could keep warm. Once I heard some Nazis approach the coal cellar where I was picking up pieces of coal. Terrified, I hid. The SS marched around with growling German shepherds and other large dogs. To this day, I am afraid of big dogs.

One day, my closest friend and his mother received a notice to appear at the train station to be transferred. Not wanting to lose my friend, I cried and begged Mamschi that we must go with them. Mamschi finally succumbed. We went to the train station and boarded the train. The Nazi in charge asked Mamschi for her documentation; because she had none to present, he slapped Mamschi and ordered us off the train. At that time, Mamschi was unaware that the transport's destination led to mass murder of Jews at death camps like Auschwitz. My friend never returned.

Because Theresienstadt was a "model camp," Mamschi could receive gifts of food, and she sent preprinted postcards acknowledging our receipt of packages that Aunt Renée had sent. Unlike Mamschi, Aunt Renée, Mamschi's youngest sister, was Catholic. She had been raised by her Catholic aunt, my maternal grandfather's sister, and attended school in a convent. She remained in Vienna working for attorneys who kept her safe throughout the war. Mamschi and Aunt Renée established a code because the cards' contents were written by Germans and reviewed by their censors prior to being sent. In her postcards Mamschi would indicate what foods we needed by incorporating her request in the address. Aunt Renée's food packages helped supplement our meager provisions and kept us from starving. Watery potato skin soup and a slice of bread was our daily fare, insufficient for long-term survival. Aunt Renée saved all those cards, and I have them now. I also have Mamschi's wedding ring, which is inscribed with my parents' names and their marriage date. Because Father did not put the gold mark for authenticity on the ring, the Nazis never confiscated it. Mamschi later tried to trade it for bread, but no one would take it because the gold mark was missing.

Many Czech Jews were interned in Theresienstadt. As a result, I learned how to speak Czech, which became a valuable asset when we finally fled.

Liberation

At the end of 1944, most of the Theresienstadt inmates had been transported to the east and certain death. We were lucky to remain. Although the average length of stay for inmates was four to six months, we were there two-and-one-half years. Mamschi credited her job splitting mica and being a *Mischling* for our survival. On May 8, 1945, I saw a Russian tank rolling by outside the camp and an SS guard fleeing from the camp across the field to get away from the Russians. Although I observed no actual fighting, the Russians did shoot at the fleeing SS guard. The Russian soldiers kindly took me, this blond, blue-eyed little boy, inside the tank's cramped, dark quarters. We communicated in Czech. They showed me the control panel and generously shared their food with me, and I looked out the front window. We were free at last.

Before Theresienstadt was liberated, the inmates of the concentration camps in the east were liberated, and the death march of survivors began. Many arrived at Theresienstadt seriously ill. Mamschi learned through a posted Jewish Council leaflet advising us of an epidemic. Rather than waiting to be repatriated and fearing we would become ill if we stayed, we fled, hitchhiking and walking to Prague. We stole apples along the way and sold them to earn money. Again, my ability to speak Czech came in handy for translating and negotiating the sale of the apples.

When we arrived in Prague, Mamschi hired a small truck with a soft roof and sides to take us to Vienna along with six or eight other people. We returned to Vienna during the summer of 1945, when I was seven years old.

Return to Vienna

After our return, we stayed in a comfortable pension. Mamschi rarely talked about Theresienstadt after the war. She sought to wipe out all the bad memories of that difficult period in our lives. I coped as well as I could, knowing that Mamschi did everything in her power to give me the best of what was available. I could not and have not forgotten those scary moments in the dark cellar and watching people picking up the dead bodies in the street.

We were joyfully reunited with Aunt Renée, who had sent us all those food packages and with whom I am very close to this day. Mamschi traded clothes for food to supplement the small government pension that she received. I believe she may have given her jewelry to someone to hide for safekeeping before we were deported and was able to retrieve her jewelry when we returned. It helped supplement her small income.

I started second grade in the fall. Due to Mamschi's tutoring, I was well prepared for school. For about two years I lived in a boarding home, while Mamschi worked. I saw her only on weekends. Then she enrolled me in *Lycée Français* because the school served a wholesome lunch, and I would learn a foreign language. Eventually, Mamschi managed to get an apartment, and I moved there with her. Most of the children at school were gentile. I was always aware of antisemitism. When I met new people, I let them know immediately that I was Jewish because I did not want to hear any antisemitic remarks or jokes. When I was twelve, I joined Hashomer Hatzair, a Zionist youth group, and thought about going to Israel.

I had my bar mitzvah in Vienna. Mamschi's Buenos Aires cousin came to Vienna and bought me a bar mitzvah suit. He took Mamschi and me to a restaurant afterward to celebrate.

Mamschi's sister Aunt Hermine, who in the late 1930s fled to Bogotá, had given birth in 1926 to a baby boy, Fredl, out of wedlock and given him up for adoption. During the war he wound up in a youth concentration camp, Möhringen, Germany, and had a very tough life without a loving mother. After the war, Mamschi found her nephew Fredl. He adored Mamschi and has become like a brother to me. I still talk to him every day. He and his family are Christian and live in Vienna.

In the 1950s, life in Vienna was very difficult. At fourteen I wanted to leave school and go to the United States, but Mamschi insisted that I must have a usable trade. She believed a trade was necessary for survival. Complying with her wishes, I finished optician school but never worked at that profession. This job was not my dream; my dream was to go to the United States and become a merchant. I applied for a visa to seek my fortune in the States and took an English course to prepare for life in the States.

United States at Last

In April 1958, when I was twenty, Aunt Hermine signed the required United States affidavit of support stating that I would not become a burden. I finally received the visa. I was thrilled. First, I went to England where my paternal uncle, Paul Godfrey, had lived since escaping Vienna in 1938. From there, I left for the United States. After a week in New York, I went to Chicago, where Aunt Hermine had lived since 1946 or 1947. I stayed with her and her husband for a year. She worked at the Fair Store, a discount department store on State Street. Despite my poor knowledge of English, she helped me get a job there. My first challenge was learning English because it was essential to a sales job. Upon arrival in the United States I watched television, which helped me understand the language. Seen as a refugee, I worked hard to adapt and fit into the American culture. My ability to understand numbers and customer requests for merchandise enabled me to pick up English quickly.

My second challenge was learning American sizes that are measured by inches rather than centimeters like European sizes. I worked three months in the men's department, at first for the minimum wage of one dollar an hour. In the fall, for the back-to-school trade, I worked on straight commission in the boys' department. The Fair Store then sent me for executive training. Finally, apparently mastering retail sales, I became an assistant buyer in the children's department.

Making friends as a newcomer, however, was a third challenge. Work provided me with the opportunity to make friends with colleagues, including the woman who became my first wife. In 1961, I left the Fair Store to work for one of its wholesale suppliers. Nineteen years later, I bought that company, changed it from a wholesaler to an import business, and imported children's outerwear from the Far East. I traveled extensively on business and prospered. Subsequently I sold and bought back the business a few times. I arrived in the United States with five dollars to my name. Now I have a home in Vail, Colorado, and a condominium on Chicago's Gold Coast.

My first wife and I had two children, a son, David, born in 1961, and a daughter, Leslie, in 1965. Leslie has two daughters, Danielle, who is twelve, and Alexandria, who is eight. They live in Highland Park. My son became a bar mitzvah at the Western Wall in Jerusalem. Mamschi had come to visit us every year, stayed for long periods, and was very close to her grandchildren, but always returned to Vienna. Mamschi died in 1988. After twenty-eight years of marriage, my wife wanted a divorce. It was amiable, without lawyers, and we are on good terms. Sometime later, my daughter Leslie introduced me to my present wife, Nancy Schwartz, a retired lawyer. We have a fifteen-year-old daughter named Hedy after my Mamschi, Hildegard. My grandchildren and Hedy love one another and play together often. I frequently return to Vienna, from where I have so few memories, and yet such close family: Fredl, Aunt Renée, and my many friends.

I have gone back to Theresienstadt three times, the first time in the 1970s (then under Communist rule). We had a private tour. I was shocked and angry that the tour guide's emphasis was about the interned partisans rather than the countless Jews imprisoned there. I informed our guide that it was primarily a concentration camp for Jews. The second time I returned was in 1991 or 1992. Then the tour guide gave the true story about the Jews and Theresienstadt. When I told her I was there during the war, she thought I made a mistake and thought I meant my father. Apparently she had not met many child survivors.

The third time I returned was in 1995 for the fiftieth anniversary of the liberation. I visited the place where I thought we had lived and saw the coal cellars, but I was unsure which cellar was the one I crawled into. Upon seeing the cellars, I felt an odd feeling arising in my stomach. I also saw the place where the trains came in from different cities and countries with their cargo of Jews and then departed with them for the east and death. I visited the small museum in the children's home where child inmates' pictures were displayed. The same children's opera, *Brundibár,* performed in Theresienstadt for the Red Cross in 1944, was also staged for us. Although I have no recollection of seeing *Brundibár* as a child, the opera was very emotional for me.

Eventually, I also visited Auschwitz. The most moving and poignant feeling aroused in me was when I saw the small suitcases that belonged to children from Theresienstadt who were murdered there. I was horrified at what happened to those children and recognized how fortunate I am.

My early experiences with the brutal Nazi regime did not crush my belief in mankind. I believe that people should be tolerant of one another. I came to this country a poor German-speaking refugee. I got a job, was promoted, and was valued at the Fair Store for what I could produce. Unlike my childhood experience during World War II, here in America I was judged by my worth and as a valued human being and given the opportunity to forge a successful career and close family.

I have been lucky. I had a mother who would have given her life for me and who assured my survival. My early experiences created the need to be independent, not to count on others, and to become successful to care for my family. Having known starvation, I am concerned about having enough food. I hate to waste food or throw it out. I am still wary of big dogs. My children believe that I have been greatly affected by my childhood experiences because I do not exhibit many emotions, but they know I love them dearly. Also, I know that they are affected by my painful past.

As a practicing Jew, I currently belong to Temple Shalom, a Reform synagogue. I believe in God. I have a strong bond with Israel and am usually a liberal on most issues. I want my children and other generations to remember the Holocaust and for no one else to experience what we went through. I still marvel about how Mamschi and I survived. I would like Father to know that Mamschi followed his instruction—“the little boy must live!” And yes, the little boy did live, with a lovely family and good fortune.

Figure 58. Kurt Gutfreund's mother, Hildegard, and father, Heinrich, Vienna, Austria, 1935.

Figure 59. Kurt Gutfreund and his mother, Vienna, Austria, 1940.

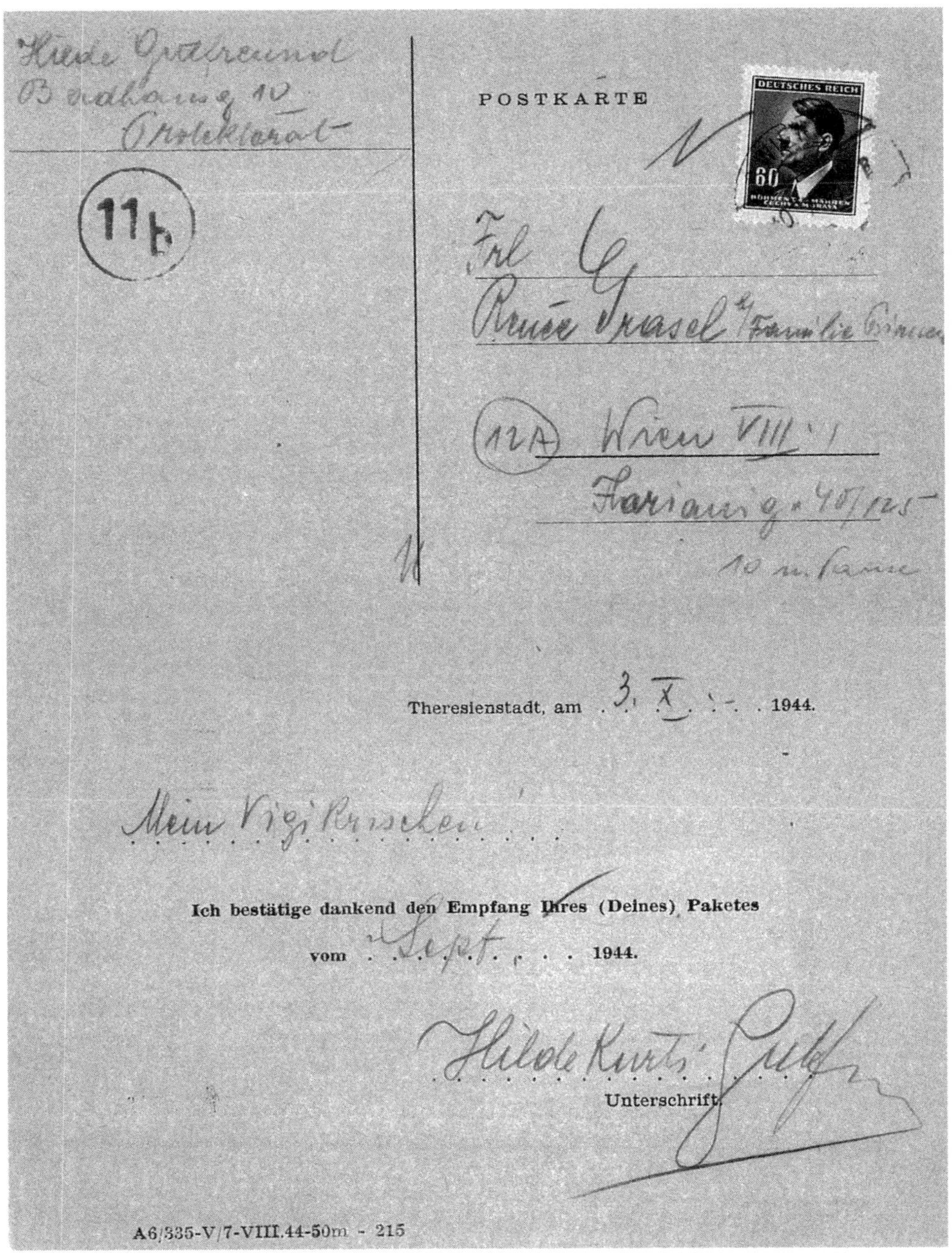

POSTKARTE

DEUTSCHES REICH 60

11b

12A Wien VIII

Theresienstadt, am 3. X. 1944.

Ich bestätige dankend den Empfang Ihres (Deines) Paketes

vom Sept. 1944.

Unterschrift

A6/335-V/7-VIII.44-50m - 215

Figure 60. Postcard Kurt Gutfreund's mother, Hildegard, wrote to her sister Renée, while Hildegard and Kurt were inmates, Theresienstadt, 1944.

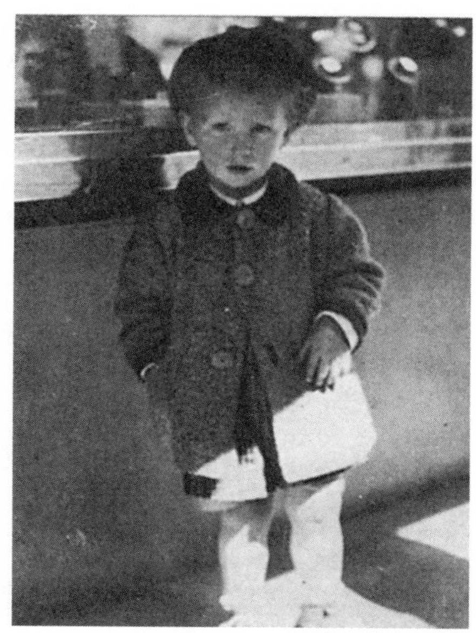

Figure 61. Kurt Gutfreund in Austria, 1941.

PART 7

Aftermath

Fall 1944 Rixensart

Henry Stark

First: fields of wheat and dandelions
The smell of hay
Country roads and abandoned gliders
Chickens squawking in the yard
Later: country roads and fields of snow
Children on their sleds
I have one too; mine is
Handmade, wood, solid
Beautiful, my first toy
I'm smiling
That's what freedom does.*

*After the liberation of Antwerp, the author, Henry Stark, and his family moved to a small rural community near Brussels called Rixensart to avoid the bombing of Antwerp by the Germans. After being in hiding nearly four years, the author recalls his first opportunity to live life in the same manner as non-Jewish children did.

Charcoal

Aaron Elster

> Why do I tell my story?
>
> We are the last of the survivors and we have an obligation to tell the younger generations of the atrocities that humans are able to inflict on others.
>
> When I speak to children, I ask that they take away two ideas from my story. First, you must believe in yourself. You must trust that you are stronger and smarter than you think you are. In the end, it is essential to love, appreciate, and respect yourself above all. Second, I want children to learn that prejudice and intolerance against others can lead to another Holocaust. As the decision makers of tomorrow, children must understand the consequences of indifference and hate. They must not be bystanders: they must always be proactive and have the courage to speak up and care.
>
> —*Aaron Elster*

The Russian Army bombed our town before its liberation in August 1944. Certain smells, sounds, sights, tastes bring me back to a time and place of my early childhood—a childhood that I try to keep buried and leave hidden in my past. More often than not my past reemerges, and I am suddenly twelve years old. It is September 1944, when the Russians liberated us in the town of my birth, Sokołów, Podłaski, Poland. Most of the twenty-nine Holocaust survivors attempted to establish some type of normalcy despite having lost their families and possessions.

A Russian soldier guarded our building against our former neighbors, who were unhappy that we had survived and returned to reclaim what was ours. The curse of antisemitism still existed. Because of all we went through to survive the Germans' attempt to exterminate us, we lived in fear. My sister Irene, fifteen years old, and I were the only two children who survived in this community and existed among these broken human beings. From a thriving population of six thousand Jews, we were the remnants. Having lost our parents and our little sister, Sarah, and all close relatives in the gas chambers of Treblinka, we had become a burden to those Jewish survivors.

Suddenly, a kind and loving Polish woman, Mrs. Kuczewiczowi, who was a friend of the family, appeared. This woman still owned and operated a restaurant. She is the same woman who gave me a loaf of black, round bread when I had escaped from the 1942 massive deportation. On that same night I had used the bread as a pillow when I slept in the forest. Now she helped Irene wash and be deloused. She poured naphtha on Irene's hair, and although it was very smelly, it got rid of the lice that had been nesting there during our hiding time.

Mrs. Kuczewiczowi took Irene under her wing. She put her to work in her restaurant while I became a "street kid." Word spread among the remaining survivors that two orphans had survived, and one child needed a daily meal. They decided that each survivor would provide a meal for me on a daily rotation. Some insisted that I perform chores before I was given my meal. It certainly was not the life I had imagined after escaping the town's liquidation and surviving the horrors of life hidden in the dark and filthy attic during the war. The winter's freezing cold and the summer's sweltering heat under that tin roof had sucked the air out of the attic and made it impossible to breathe and turned me into a fifty-pound skeleton. I lived with hunger and isolation for two years. My only companions were the lice on my body, the rats and mice, and the daily visit by Mrs. Gorski, who handled my toilet bucket.

The remnants of the Jewish community were busy trying to reconstruct their own lives under harsh and hostile circumstances because antisemitism was rampant. Their former neighbors resented the Jews because they survived, and the neighbors feared that they would lose their stolen Jewish property. Therefore, they had little room for others. I adapted to my circumstances and learned quickly to fend for myself. I became street-smart and learned about survival all over again.

Most of my days were spent on the streets with boys who were in similar life situations. I was enrolled in the fifth grade in grammar school. I had difficulty adjusting because I could not read or spell, causing the other children to make fun of me and call me the "lice-infested Jew." My Catholic schooling ended when the town priest asked me to stay after school. He suggested that my life would be much better if I converted and came to live in his church. I believe the priest wanted to help and show me the "way of the Lord," and for me to seek salvation through Jesus Christ. "After all," he said, "they have been killing Jews for years, and twenty years from now the same thing will happen. So why would you want to remain a Jew?" That was the last day of my school career. My education came to an abrupt end.

One survivor, a tailor, lived with his sister in a small house down the street from the rest of the survivors. When we lived in the ghetto, surrounded by brick walls and barbed wire, he worked for the *Judenrat* (Jewish Council) as a ghetto policeman. Rumor had it that during the final roundups of the Jews deported to Treblinka for extermination, he assisted the Gestapo by pulling his own parents and family out of their hiding place. He believed that he would be spared because of his loyalty to the Nazi killers. Most of the survivors shunned him.

To exact payment for my meal, this tailor made me go into the burned buildings to collect charcoal. He used the charcoal to press the garments that he made for his local customers. The charcoal was ignited in a pressing iron that became red hot. Another chore he ordered was to prepare slaughtered chickens for their meals. I hated the process of ripping off the feathers and submerging the poor chicken in boiling water until its white skin was ready to be cooked.

When it was time for me to receive my meal, I was sternly told that my food would be waiting as soon as I completed my task and brought him a basketful of charcoal. I developed a deep resentment toward him and his sister. I walked down a small hill to Ulica Krutka (Krutka Street), as far as Ulica Piekna (Piekna Street), to a burned-out house that once was my home.

During the Russian bombing in August 1944, when the Germans were retreating, our house was bombed and caught fire. Now another homeless boy followed me into that burned house. The remaining burned walls stood tall, and the black, shiny charcoal gleamed in the sunlight like some ancient monument. It was a scary job as often the balance of the walls would collapse as I ripped the charred wood from those walls. As I tore the charcoal from the walls, black soot engulfed me. I was very hungry and wanted to get this chore over with so I could get something to eat. The boy who was keeping me company was wandering around the ruins, keeping busy kicking objects in his path.

The ruins were full of burned possessions, which included twisted beds, stoves, broken discolored fixtures, and fragments of pots. People who had occupied our house after our expulsion and deportation had owned these objects. They were scattered among the bricks that were once part of our home. The wooden floors were gone and only garbage and filth remained. I was almost finished. My basket was overflowing with burned remains, when suddenly a powerful explosion created a darkness from all the dirt, wood, and brick particles that erupted into space. When the darkness and smoke abated, I no longer saw my companion alive. He was dead, with his stomach partially opened, exposing parts of his insides. While kicking all that was in front of him, he managed to kick an unexploded grenade.

I still delivered the basketful of charcoal.

And I survived.

Figure 62. Aaron Elster, Łódź, Poland, after World War II.

Figure 63. Aaron Elster on the soccer field in a displaced persons camp, Fürth, Germany, 1946.

Fading Memories

Aaron Elster

I recall intimate details of bygone years in vivid colors and sounds. Dreams and nightmares coexist, creating blissful or horrifying moments in my present life. Of particular significance is my memory, or lack of it, relating to my father. Scenes of the Sokołów, Podłaski's marketplace in September 1942, are real and yet recede into a painful oblivion.

The ghetto is now *Judenrein* (free of Jews). The Final Solution to the Jewish problem here has been carried out. In September 1942, on Yom Kippur, escaping the first liquidation, I eventually return to the ghetto to find my mother, who was part of a work detail to cleanse the ghetto of any Jewish belongings.

I block all memory relating to my return to the marketplace. Did I see my father in a separate work detail? Fleeting sights appear and disappear of his gaunt and sad face. Yet, when I tell my story of escape, I say that I believe my dad was shipped to Treblinka with my little six-year-old sister, Sarah. My hope has always been that she did not die with total strangers, but with someone who loved her—someone to assure her that all will be well and hold her lovingly as she gasps her last breath in the gas chamber of Treblinka.

I refuse to accept that my father was in the group that was destined for immediate death. Instead, I want to believe he was put on a work detail and is still alive. My tormented vision of Sarah's brutal murder tears at me; it is unbearable. The pain doesn't subside. In my mental image Sarah is pushed into a cattle car with many frightened adults and children, squeezed against one another.

In my mind the smaller children have trouble breathing; they are crying and moaning. People push one another to gain some breathing space. Children fall or are pushed to the ground and perhaps unintentionally stepped on. The cries are deadened by the rumbling of the cattle cars that take these condemned Jews to Treblinka. Upon their arrival I picture them shoved into the dreaded showers where the poison gas chokes life out of them. I visualize little Sarah in pain as she suffocates.

Figure 64. Aaron Elster's mother, Cywia, cousin Hannah, and sister Sarah, Sokołów, Poland, Ghetto, 1941.

The Haul in the Wall

Henry Stark

I knew that something big was up. Mrs. Kappendijk, the lady in whose house we were hiding, was in an agitated celebratory mood. I didn't quite know what to make of it. The fear that was—until then—our constant companion had lifted, to be replaced by a kind of nervous, but not unhappy, expectation. It seemed that everyone knew what was going on except me.

The year was 1944, the place was the outskirts of Antwerp, and as I later found out, it was the first week of September. My parents, father Paul, age forty-five, mother Anna, age forty; my sister Edith, age thirteen and seven years my senior; and I had been in hiding since the end of 1941, or maybe early 1942. Mrs. Kappendijk, an elderly Flemish widow, had been our last hope to escape from the Gestapo and the SS. Until recently, Carl deFuchs, a former colleague of my father's in the diamond industry in Antwerp, and his new wife had been hiding us in a small house in the town of Boom, an industrial backwater of Antwerp on a tidal estuary of the River Schelde. As far as I know, Boom was of little interest to anyone, except possibly the regional employees of the big Agfa-Gevaert factory complex. At that time Agfa-Gevaert, a leader in the production of photographic film and imaging technology, was owned by the notorious I. G. Farben Company and was considered an enemy institution. Its assets in the United States were seized by the American government.

We lived on the top floor of a creaky, otherwise silent house that had a ceiling trapdoor that could be opened to admit fresh air and give us a rooftop view of the surroundings. From the outside the upper floor of the house looked deserted. Allied airplanes regularly bombed the area at night, their target presumably being the Agfa and Minerva plants. The Minerva plant had been taken over by the Germans to repair and service Luftwaffe airplanes. Faulty Allied bombing killed hundreds of local civilians, including over two hundred children in one raid alone. After these bombing raids the various fires around the region would color the sky a glowing red, a color that to this day I associate with night and danger.

Our "toilet," such as it was, was a version of a short steel barrel, the kind they might use for shipping chemicals, paint, and other material. It was obviously not easy to use, and I "held it in" for as long as possible rather than have to climb on it. Campers have a word for such a contraption; they call it the "groover" because it tends to leave grooves on tender behinds. When the barrel was loaded, or the smell became unbearable, my sister, father, and mother emptied the thing in the mudflats adjacent to our house. At low tide the mudflats became exposed, ready to accept our family "gift." As the tide went in, the waste made its way to the sea.

Giving in to the daily threats made by the Germans against those hiding Jews, deFuchs ordered us to leave. His wife was terrified that they would be exposed as Jew hiders and bear the dreadful consequences of such a crime. Who could blame deFuchs for throwing us out? The Germans were good at using terror as a weapon and deFuchs was no hero, nor a moralist; just a guy seeing an opportunity to make some money in return for providing bread and board or, putting it more accurately, leasing out a dump with bread and margarine and some soup for sustenance. I suffered my share of illnesses due to malnutrition.

It is very difficult to judge other people fairly unless one has been in similar circumstances. To my father, deFuchs was a crook who deserved to be vilified. Years later, when we talked about our years of hiding, it came out that I didn't share my father's view of deFuchs. I saw what deFuchs was doing as risky for himself and his wife. He stood to lose everything, possibly his freedom, even his life. He may have exploited the situation, but at least he didn't sell us out. The Jews of Holland should have been so fortunate!

Even as the war was lost, the Germans went on an insane murder spree against Jews. They used all strategic means at their disposal to kill as many Jews as possible. On the same day that we were liberated, the Frank family was deported from Westerbork to Auschwitz. They were sold out by a neighbor who didn't have the courage to identify himself or herself. In a microcosm of how countries behaved during the occupation, this episode sharply illuminates the difference between the way Jews fared in Belgium versus the way they fared in Holland. Of the estimated 137,000 Jews in Holland, only some 25,000 survived the war.

Anyway, we were in an existential bind—a real one, not the kind that they talk about in Philosophy 101. We had largely exhausted our connections with friends and those that might have been able to save us. Communication with the outside world was difficult for us: there were no phones, no mail service, no way to seek help except, possibly, through clandestine visits or word of mouth. Somehow, and I don't know the details, word about our situation got back to a Catholic priest who, in turn, contacted Mrs. Kappendijk. That sweet lady decided to take us in at great risk to herself. This is how we ended up with her in the days leading to our liberation by the Allies. It is to my everlasting sorrow that Mrs. Kappendijk never was nominated to be a "Righteous Gentile." Perhaps one day someone in her family will be there to accept this honor in her place.

"It's OK to come out now," Mrs. Kappendijk told my father, and, sure enough, the Stark family took their first tentative steps into the outside world in broad daylight. In short order we went back to our apartment in Antwerp. There were British troops all over the place and large crowds in the streets. Nearby there was still plenty of shooting, but the shooting was coming from the Allies at the retreating Germans. The war was still raging in many places. For example, one of the most notorious concentration camps—Bergen-Belsen—nearby in northwest Germany, wasn't liberated by the British Eleventh Armored Division until April 1945.

I witnessed an amazing sight: a British tank was firing a machine gun down this straight avenue and a reddish bullet from the gun was slowly making its way down to the target. "How could such slow-moving bullets ever hurt anyone?" I wondered. Someone, maybe a brainy bystander, explained to me that the machine gun was firing tracer bullets that produced a stroboscopic effect, much the way the blades on a high-speed fan look as if they are hardly moving when illuminated by a light almost in synchrony with the speed of rotation. In fact, the bullets were going at close to three thousand feet per second!

Now we were about to begin the rest of our lives. But there was great uncertainty about our future. Before the war my father was a reasonably prosperous diamond dealer and the Stark family didn't lack for the basic necessities of life. The family ate out occasionally, took vacations at the seashore, and there was even a nanny to help my mother take care of me. At the time we went into hiding, my father had converted most of his wealth into diamonds and jewelry, but where to hide it? Whom could you trust? He decided that the wisest course was to wrap the whole stash in a sock and entomb it behind a brick in our cellar at 18/20 Steenbocken Strasse. This procedure required some care because the Gestapo and their Belgian collaborators knew all about the diamond dealers in Antwerp and where they had lived before being deported or having gone into hiding. Finding this loot meant sudden personal enrichment or—if you were a loyal Nazi—you gave it to the Gestapo or the SS who needed money for their various enterprises. Thus, one could expect that the Nazis and friends would go over these vacated Jewish dwellings with a fine-tooth comb. My father, not well educated, but bright and resourceful, divined this. So he took much care in doing it right.

The big moment had come. Would we start the second half of our lives in penury or would finding the treasure enable us to continue to live as we had lived before the war?

We were all in the cellar and my father, using a chisel-like instrument, freed the brick that entombed the stash. All over the wall there were signs that someone had been looking for loose bricks. But *the* brick had been left alone. And the sock and its contents were still there!

The destruction of the Third Reich and finding our valuables intact did not mean that the Stark family lived happily ever after. There was much antisemitism in Europe after the war, and Belgium was not immune to it. I got a good strong taste of it when my father enrolled me in Antwerp's foremost French-culture-based school, the *Lycée d'Anvers.* I encountered bullying both from students and from teachers because I was Jewish. Ironically, during the period of hiding, I was aware that a terrible danger lurked in the "outside" world, but I never encountered an antisemite in person. For me direct antisemitism became a fact of life after the liberation. Later, when my father decided to immigrate to America, I encountered a rather brutal environment at the Orthodox yeshiva in Washington Heights in New York City that my father enrolled me in. Knowing next to nothing about Jewish rituals and not being able to pray in Hebrew branded me an unacceptable "goy" (non-Jew) in the eyes of my classmates. This was a difficult time for me. My parents, meanwhile, had truly become displaced persons. Failing to learn English and overcome both by the strangeness of America and their own postwar exhaustion, they created a miniuniverse of their own choosing. Their only friends spoke Yiddish, they nearly never went out as a couple, and when they did, it was often to sit in a little treeless concrete pedestrian plaza bordered by Broadway and 157th Street in Washington Heights.

I was eleven years old when we came to America, and soon after I realized that a role reversal was taking place with my parents. I was the one who could speak English; I was the one who began to understand how things were done in America. I was assimilating and my parents were not. It was they who came to me for advice.

We had been lucky: we had survived Hitler, we had not been deported, and our period of hiding was relatively short compared with that of our Jewish brethren in the east. But the Holocaust had left us wounded, and it took a long time for the wounds to heal; and some never did.

Disillusionment

Judith Levy Straus

It all happened during World War II, in Holland. The year was 1941. I was eight years old, and I became the owner of a beautiful doll. She had real blond hair, eyes that opened and closed, and a pretty smile on her face. Her dress was light blue, and she wore tiny socks and shoes. This doll was very special to me. Actually she was special for reasons that had nothing to do with her looks; she was special because of the why and where and how I got her. At that time it was not possible to purchase dolls, especially for Jewish children. So this doll was not bought by my parents, and she was not new; she was a hand-me-down. Family friends had a daughter who had outgrown the doll, and I became the lucky new owner.

I was the only child of parents who had lived in Germany and who had attempted to escape Hitler by fleeing to Holland. But now Hitler and the Nazis were in Holland, and by 1942 the persecution and deportation of Jews was in full force. At age nine I could not share or even comprehend my family's anxiety about deportation or survival. What I felt was loneliness. The adults in our home were always so busy with discussions that stopped when I came into the room. Their voices were filled with emotion, which they tried to hide from me. They wanted to shield and spare me, but instead I felt excluded—threatened by something unknown—and lonely. This is why the doll became so important.

I had no brothers or sisters to share time or feelings with. I had learned that friends, at my age, are really only playmates. We children usually tried to hide our fears from one another. Playing with friends was also limited by Nazi restrictions as to where Jewish people were allowed to be and at what hour of the day. And so my doll became my sister, my brother, my confidant. She became a very important and special doll.

My doll and I were separated in June of 1943, when my parents and I were deported to the Westerbork camp. Westerbork was a transit camp in Holland where the Nazis incarcerated Dutch Jews before sending them "east," which turned out to be the concentration and extermination camps of Auschwitz, Sobibor, Bergen-Belsen, and Theresienstadt.

I was ten years old when we came to Westerbork. A concentration camp has its own horrors for each person. The horrors of a ten-year-old are probably quite different than those felt by adults. For me, the fear of being alone, of being separated from my parents, was overwhelming. I am convinced my parents sensed this because miraculously, one day my doll appeared in our barrack in Westerbork.

I do not remember the exact circumstances of her arrival. We were allowed to receive packages from relatives or friends still in Amsterdam, and the doll must have arrived in one of these packages. No one can imagine the joy I felt upon receiving this doll. I can only say that, no matter how long I will live, I will remember that feeling.

I remember more. I learned what disillusionment and betrayal feel like.

In 1944, my parents and I were scheduled for a transport "east." My parents felt this would not be the right place to take the doll, so I asked a girlfriend to keep the doll and take good care of her until I returned. Her father had a very important job at Westerbork, and she was not likely to be transported anywhere. And she promised me that the doll would be taken care of.

Our transport went to Theresienstadt, in Czechoslovakia. After three weeks my father, along with thousands of other men, was transported farther "east." My mother and I stayed in Theresienstadt until the camp was liberated by the Russians in 1945. Shortly after that my mother and I returned to Holland. Just my mother and I returned, but not my father.

One of my first missions after we came back to Amsterdam was to find my friend and reclaim my doll. I went to their apartment, rang their bell, and my friend and her mother came to the door. I could not quite understand the look on their faces. I expected a happy welcome. Instead their mouths sort of dropped, and I thought I saw surprise, even shock. Why were they not expecting me?

And my doll? My friend said that her parents had told her to leave the doll in Westerbork after their liberation. "Why?" I asked. Silence. "But you promised!" I said. Silence. "But I told you I would come back for her when I returned." Only silence . . .

"When I returned"—there it was. There is such a fine line between "when" and "if," but such a great difference in meaning. "When I return"—when I left my doll with this friend, I did not know exactly what her father's important job in the camp was. Later I learned that he was one of those who made up the lists of his fellow Jews for deportation to the concentration camps in the east. He helped decide who would go where, and when. This man knew! He knew where the trains were going. Yet he, and others like him, kept putting names on these lists: our names—my father's and grandfather's names, the names of aunts and uncles, my school friends' names. This man knew enough to substitute "if" she returns for "when" she returns. And thus my doll was left on a garbage heap in Westerbork.

I was twelve years old at that time. Still a child, more or less. Learning about the world, trying to understand and comprehend. Knowing the terrors of two years in concentration camps. Knowing the intent of Hitler and the Nazis.

And here is where disillusionment enters my story. My disillusionment was not in learning that there were people like Hitler. Like most Holocaust children, I had learned that lesson well. All the protective parents in the world could not shield their children from that. Nor was the disillusionment caused by the loss of my doll. It was produced by the sudden and ugly realization that there actually were some among our own, fellow Jews, who were willing to cooperate with the Nazis to the fullest. They knew all along, and they betrayed us.

First Name: Ava
Also Known As: Eva Hegedis
Last Name: Kadishson Schieber
Maiden Name: Hegedis
Date of Birth: April 12, 1926
City of Birth: Novi Sad
Country of Birth: Yugoslavia (now Serbia)

Bond with Rain

Ava Hegedis Kadishson Schieber

A rainy day is usually an incentive for me to leave my comfortable dwelling to welcome raindrops on my face. My lifelong joyful theme of water has many variations. From my early childhood in Novi Sad, Yugoslavia, Mother, with her engaging smile, would regularly rinse my hair in rainwater, which was collected in wooden buckets for that purpose. She would warm up and then pour what she called "soft water" to rinse my hair to make it beautifully soft and shiny. Rain became my friend.

Besides bringing relief from the summer heat, downpours created glorious puddles in front of our house, where, contrary to the usual family rules, we were allowed to frolic barefoot in the water. Growing into my teens, I found that rain could be at times a chilling precursor of frost and mud. Weather, however, was the least worry of the wartime conditions shrouding my life. Even some fierce stormy rains became my blessing. They justified my indoor chores for the farmers who provided for my shelter. Indoor work was easier than my outdoor work, allowing me to take care of personal necessities like making my clothes and canvas shoes. Best of all was the opportunity to read my encyclopedias.

In the late spring of 1941, at fifteen years old, I had to run for my life from Belgrade. It was an impulse that drove me to take those books from my home into hiding; they became my most precious possession. Those volumes became a raft, keeping me afloat—preventing me from sinking into an isolated disconnect on the small rural farm. I had the books safe in a closed trunk to keep the rodents out. Reading reminded me of my former life. Education had been the backbone of my prewar routine. The diverse information in those books engaged my mind and created an anchor to sanity as I and my surrounding existence were losing a foothold. At times I welcomed the freezing rain that chilled my body. After I had finished the essential outdoor chores, I could stay in my shack. On the farm I pretended to be a deaf mute. In spite of the short winter days and frequent lack of kerosene for my lamp to provide light, I could in dimming visibility view the marvelous and abundant illustrations in my books. I would collect rainwater, warm it on my tin stove, and wash myself. This provided me with an illusion of being clean. Rain remained my ally.

The distance from Belgrade south to the farm was only a couple of hours' walk, but for the duration of almost four years, my life in hiding was one hundred and eighty degrees opposite of my former reality. Being a Jew, I had lost the right to live. Father, a veteran from the First World War, understood the dire future for us Jews under Nazi occupation. If we did not register as Jews, which was mandatory, he believed that we had a better chance to survive. Instead, he advised us to hide individually underground. It must have been difficult for Father to say this to me. It was my choice, but he advised me to leave the family and hide with complete strangers. My family separated in 1941, and Father fled from Belgrade back to Novi Sad sixty miles north.

The Danube region of Yugoslavia was part of Hungary until the end of the First World War. In 1941, World War II rewound the history clock and returned that region to its previous borders. My family's cultural roots were there in that former Austro-Hungarian Empire. The era following my grandparents' and my parents' youth was a time of momentous political changes. National aspirations were carried out with bloody encounters but never solved disputes. Instead, as with the inextricable history of such disputes, they forced the survivors into migration or alliances they neither understood nor craved. Those unfortunate generations of long-reigning empires experimented with creating mixed unions of minority groups, who hated one another, but who were coerced or forced to unite. In those maladjusted environments, radical political movements rose to fight once more for optimal power. Nazi ideologues rekindled old fears, breeding hatred, superstitions, and pseudoscience within a formidable militaristic force.

I was born in Novi Sad and in a newly created monarchy called Yugoslavia, a nation that fell apart into its cultural and ethnic fragments and suspicious neighboring differences. When the Nazis started the war, once again Serbia became a merciless battleground. When the belching German Army guns turned silent, I was one of the extremely few Jewish survivors in Serbia, cautiously testing the air to learn if I could freely inhale again.

In the fall of 1944, I felt happy to have been reunited with Mother. The death of my sister, to whom I was very attached, was a pain I kept hidden from Mother, who found solace in perpetuating the self-deception that her child would return from the partisans. I too naively indulged myself in the irrational hope that Father and Grandmother might have escaped the last roundup of Jews in Hungary. I was confident that Father's intellect evaluated the hazards, and he escaped once again. Unwilling to face reality or logic, I used hope as my antidote. I hoped, I was young.

After the war, rain mixed with snow accompanied me on my journey to Novi Sad, the city where I was born. I had hoped to find Father and Grandmother, or information about where they were. My persistent stubbornness at the partisan headquarters in Belgrade had helped me obtain travel papers, and a Russian Red Cross convoy commander agreed to take me to Novi Sad. The road showed evidence of recent fighting caused by the German units left behind. On the road were soldiers' corpses from both sides, including horses. In death all uniforms blended into a unified color of lives lost mercifully covered by falling snow. My long-lasting impression from that journey was a conversation with the Russian medical commander of the unit during a short break off the road. With the obvious intention to talk to me, he came out of the truck's cabin. He handed back my papers, saying that I was going to need them in Novi Sad, adding that he wrote a recommendation, which would help me return to Belgrade. I thanked him for his help. I was not accustomed to thoughtfulness anymore. The soldiers kept a respectful distance from where we stood. Russian discipline was rigid compared to the partisans' unrestricted behavior.

The doctor told me that my papers revealed that I was a Jewish survivor searching for my family. He advised me not to talk to the soldiers; definitely not to say I was a Jew. Furthermore, he said he was a Jew as well, but the soldiers did not know that. As it was very cold sitting in an open truck, he took off his fur coat for me to wear. I was moved by his kindness and grateful for the coat, but aghast at his words. That high-ranking medical officer confided in me, an incidental stranger, that he was a Jew. This was a fact he concealed from his comrades all his years in combat. That was puzzling for me and left a deeply disturbing impact. On that rainy day my arrival in Novi Sad had already drenched me with controversial emotions.

I was walking in the direction of the house we lived in before we moved to Belgrade a year before the German invasion of Yugoslavia. I was on the Jevrejska Utica (Jevrejska Street), looking at my grammar school, adjacent to the synagogue. This was a soft ground of memories. I was on my home turf. Broken pavement around the synagogue compound showed ominous signs of neglect and decay. Plaster was crumbling from the facades of buildings; here and there were shattered structures. Broken windows stared at me with a vacant gaze as all life was extinct behind the frames. Those empty sockets represented reality. Throughout the war years I experienced highly disturbing feelings I didn't know how to deal with; therefore, I let them sink into a semidormant state within my mind when they occurred. I knew I would have to retrieve them from hibernation later on and hopefully clarify my hurt and bewilderment. Meanwhile, more confusing events were piling up. I had no opportunity to talk about my thoughts or ask for advice. I could not burden Mother, the only person I trusted with my numerous perplexities. She was carrying her own burden of irreversible shattering losses.

As I was taking in the ominous evidence of what the Novi Sad Jews had suffered, suddenly a pleasant surprise of that day was walking toward me. Edith Reich, my friend from the carefree elementary school days, was approaching. She had not recognized me. When we were face to face and I had blocked her way with a smile and started to talk, her eyes widened in utter disbelief. Looking at me as if I really should have been a ghost, she blurted out that every one of my former classmates believed I was dead. I had recognized my friend, while she still was some distance away. Edith looked as I remembered her: neat, poised, and I thought elegant the way she held her umbrella high above her head, gripping the nice wooden handle with her gloved hand. I had not thought about umbrellas or gloves for years.

She wore a barrette tilted to the side as we used to wear, being part of our school uniform. I felt good seeing Edith. It reassured me that the entire prewar reality had not disappeared forever. Edith said she couldn't recognize me the way I looked. She could not take back her words, which had slipped out. She seemed a little embarrassed. I knew I was dressed in my hand-stitched garment from faded old fabrics, improvised, not flattering at all. I was wearing my homemade canvas shoes. I was proud of being able to make my shoes. They were comfortable and dried fast after I washed the mud off. Of course, I did not look the way Edith knew me from the prewar years. I used to be a rather well-groomed student, with a flair for an individual touch in spite of our strict uniform. I enjoyed looking different, even combing my hair in a manner that was not trendy. Unlike the Shirley Temple corkscrew curls the girls were wearing, I wore my hair in long braids. I was presenting my personal unorthodox views in and out of the school, and both ways usually got me into trouble. Some of my teachers complained. The principal regularly called Father to his office. Father would reassure me the principal mainly talked to him about music, as it was known that Father was a good amateur musician. My parents and some teachers indulged me by accepting me as an equal in some discussions. Yet, I must have been a headache for other teachers, as even mothers of my friends, including Edith's, were equally ill at ease if I frequently visited. All this had made me feel good. I could in my rebellious, immature way unbalance some of the adults' authority. But very soon I had learned, if I wanted to stay alive, I had better be mute.

In spite of my gloomy premonition about the unknown destiny of Father and Grandmother, simply being on the familiar street in Novi Sad, seeing and talking to Edith, made me content. I had not had the pleasure of talking to a friend for years.

Momentarily everything else seemed less relevant and was recoiling into the distance. Edith personified the preadolescence we had shared. We used to be as close as girls that age would get. We spent summer vacations together on the Danube beach. Mostly swimming and gossiping, we carefully observed indiscretions of those older girls. We watched their behavior and envied them in their already developed maturing bodies. We still were at that edge of our hormonal upsurge but knew what was going on behind the planks of the changing cabins. Edith and I used to shamelessly eavesdrop and giggle, titillated about what we had heard.

There was a row of especially large, elaborate, comfortable dressing and lounging cabins, those rented by the financially privileged in our town. In particular we were targeting the elegant cabins to observe and listen to what was going on between those adults. That kind of information represented the prime subject Edith and I would talk about. We felt powerful and almost grown up with our fragmented knowledge. Guards, protecting the privacy of those expensive enclaves for intimate endeavors, used to doze off in the midsummer heat, which of course became opportune for Edith and me to listen to the secretive activities. We knew about the indiscretions and clandestine affairs taking place in Novi Sad's high-society cabins. We were proud and felt sophisticated within our worldliness. Fleeting memory images dashed through my mind, seeing Edith so close, but far away.

The past felt so unreal on that rainy afternoon. Edith's frightened face was staring at me from underneath her umbrella. Of course I did not realize how run-down and shabby my appearance must have been for her when we met. She didn't know that during the war years my concern was to successfully blend into the deaf-mute farm girl part I was playing. To invite a second look from anyone was hazardous. I must have succeeded so well to be indistinct, I had become unrecognizable. Even my once close friend mistook me for one of the many displaced people in rags no one wanted to pay attention to or get involved with. Thus, people looked the other way simply not to notice their existence.

Edith stiffly said she had finished school. She looked somewhat ill at ease, but talking about her studies must have been a comfortable subject for her, and she became more relaxed and ceased fidgeting. It seemed odd that she did not show any interest or ask any questions about my war experiences. To interrupt our stagnant dialogue I tried to bring into the conversation some of our mutual prewar memories and mutual interests but met Edith's uncommitted reaction. I congratulated Edith for having finished high school and asked her about her plans to continue her studies. I remembered some of our prewar dreams and aspirations. We both had a flair for the arts and used to talk about imagining ourselves within our respective fields.

Edith wanted to study classical ballet, and I remembered her as a very good dancer. I asked her if she had continued with her art and the theater. She seemed confused, as if my question was something utterly novel and had never been considered. Edith noticed my surprise. She added that dance was one of her childish whims. She had not yet decided what to study. Our conversation was dragging on, being one-sided. Her attitude became remote, her answers hesitant. Thus, in spite of my years in isolation, and having been deprived of the dynamic of regular interaction—it hit me. Edith just did not want to talk to me. We were standing at the opposite side of a hole in the broken pavement not to stop pedestrian traffic. People were walking between us, stepping over that hole. I did not want to let go of Edith. I tried briefly to tell her about my hiding on a farm, during the occupation. It felt good to see her, and I wanted to prolong our encounter. I tried to reach her by explaining how I hoped to start school and study art at the academy in Belgrade. Art used to be the field I always was involved with; therefore, I was going to study art and become a set and costume designer. Besides my feeling of well-being while creating, I knew I wanted to express what had happened within and around me during the war, and I was going to convey what I thought and felt through my paintings. I owed this to the lives lost—and to my life that by chance was spared.

Edith seemed so utterly uninterested in anything I was saying. It made me wonder if I was speaking in a language she had never heard before. Or maybe she was not listening at all to what I said. It was not that difficult to understand that I had to hide on a farm, and played a deaf-mute farmhand to escape the Nazi dragnet. All Jews who registered in Belgrade were murdered in Zemun Region at the Saimishte,

БРОЈ 42 Год. 1939/40

КРАЉЕВИНА ЈУГОСЛАВИЈА
ДРЖ. ЖЕНСКА РЕАЛНА ГИМНАЗИЈА НОВИ САД

ЂАЧКИ ЛИСТ

ученице .... разреда, рођене

.... 1926 у ....

.... бановине

У Новом Саду, ... 1939

Разредни старешина: Директор:

Figure 65. Ava Hegedis Kadishson's student identification card, Belgrade, Yugoslavia, 1938.

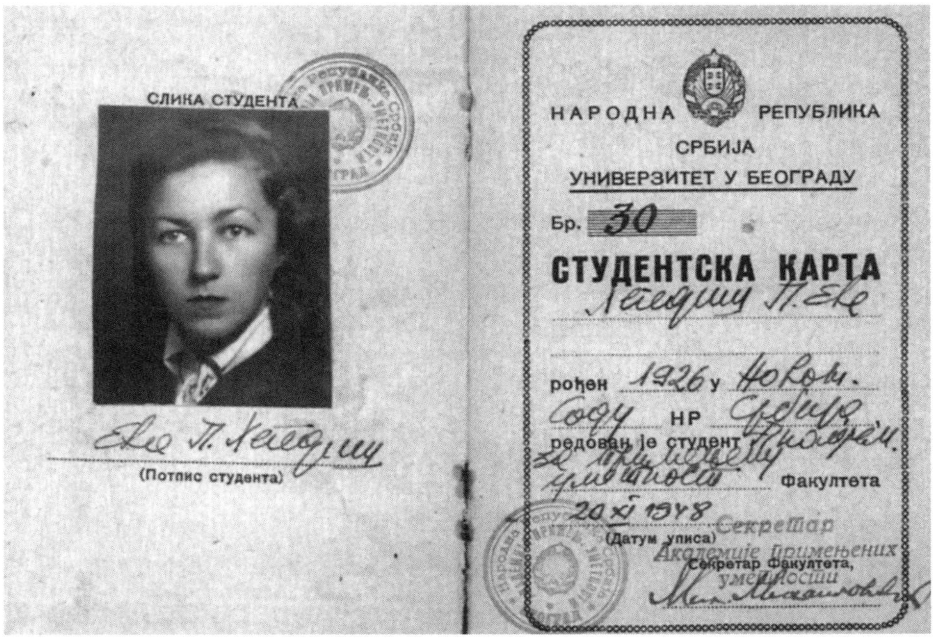
СЛИКА СТУДЕНТА

(Потпис студента)

НАРОДНА РЕПУБЛИКА
СРБИЈА
УНИВЕРЗИТЕТ У БЕОГРАДУ

Бр. 30

СТУДЕНТСКА КАРТА

рођен 1926 у ....

.... НР ....

редован је студент ....

.... Факултета

20 XI 1948
(Датум уписа)

Секретар Факултета,

Figure 66. Ava Hegedis Kadishson's identification card while working in the film industry, Belgrade, Yugoslavia, 1948.

the place for agricultural fairs before the war. Why was she so indifferent to what I was telling her? Maybe she didn't want to hear me—the witness.

Standing not far from each other, I felt we were miles apart. Was it possible, I wondered, that I had changed so much she couldn't understand me anymore? Have I gone through a reversed metamorphosis? I believed I had been the butterfly, but I might have undergone a change that had transformed me into a worm. I did not feel that way, but I possibly lost contact with reality.

For years, I even hid my thoughts to avoid pain. I sketched some small drawings in hiding, which represented my silent monologues, but with no sounding board and no echo. This encounter with Edith, talking to someone I knew well, felt uplifting until I realized Edith's continuous nervous side glances. She really wanted to leave. I stopped talking.

In the brief silence that followed, Edith finally blurted out, "How did you arrive in Novi Sad? Battles are still being fought in the area; only the military moves through." I told her about the Russian Red Cross convoy I traveled with from Belgrade. As I said it, Edith fell silent, staring at me from underneath her lowered umbrella, which sank so close to her head it became like the brim of an enormous hat surrounding her face with darkness. I hardly saw her features, but noticed that her lower jaw was trembling; she was afraid. Why would she be afraid of me? I was a friend out of her childhood. I reappeared from years of hiding my identity to stay alive. I looked downtrodden, but was not asking anything from her, not even for advice as I had already laid out my plans. I was simply happy to talk to her.

When we met I had the feeling that Edith acted fear-ridden from the start, but I discarded that thought as it did not make any sense to me. What could have been the reasons for her fear? I had no idea what had scared her. After an uneasy silence, in a hardly audible voice she said, "No women would travel with Russians as everyone was afraid of them. They were raping all the women in their path." She ended whispering. "How did you dare travel with the Russians?" I was not sure if what she said sounded concerned or accusing. I tried to convince her that none of the soldiers had even looked at me during the journey. And how the officer was kind and gave me his fur coat as it was cold traveling on the open truck.

While I was speaking, Edith was physically retreating from me until she had reached the wall of the house behind her. By the end of my explanation, she was visibly shivering, and I felt sorry for her. It was not that cold. Questions raced through my mind. What was her trepidation? I had been her friend, yet she obviously wanted to run away, get rid of me as fast as she could, and I did not understand why.

I appreciated her candor, but felt hurt by the obvious disgust in her voice when she said, "I cannot possibly invite you to my home, you look so unkempt. You have changed into someone so different than who you had been. I am looking at you standing in a puddle of water ever since we started to talk and you are even not paying attention to it. What kind of a world are you coming from?"

Visibly trembling with both her gloved hands holding the umbrella, Edith walked away.

A Passion to Tell

Chaya Horowitz Roth

This is an autobiographical essay about recurring memories of events that took place during the Holocaust and World War II and my passion to speak about them: first to my children, then to friends, students, adults, and other children who wanted to hear the stories of the war's witness.[1]

September 8, 1939

My name is Chaya, a name given to me by my mother and father, Hannah Fale and Aron Jakob Horowitz, so that my name, Chaya (meaning life), should help heal my great-grandmother, Hanah Hinde, who was ailing when I was born. This was a custom among Jewish people to ward off the *yetzer harah* (evil eye).

It is September 8, 1939, the eve of the High Holidays. The Gestapo haul off my father from our Berlin apartment. They take him to an *Umschlagsplatz* (gathering place) and hold him there. Later, he and the other Jewish men of Polish origin, including the Polish Christian men who were also rounded up, are taken to Sachsenhausen Concentration Camp, about thirty-five kilometers from Berlin.

Throughout the years, I have often wondered why my father was beaten to death ten days after his arrival and incarceration in Sachsenhausen, September 18, 1939. What happened to the other men during the early days in Sachsenhausen following Hitler's invasion of Poland? I knew about the ignominy, the disregard for human life in the work and death camps. Moreover, I thought that my father was not the type of man who provoked rage in anyone, not even in the most ruthless men. He was a gentle soul; a polite, caring, studious man. What could he have done to deserve a deadly beating?

Only recently did I discover in Richard Evans's book *The Third Reich in Power* the reason for the roundups of both non-Jewish Poles and Jews of Polish origin. These were allegedly conducted in retaliation for "staged Nazi stunts" in which small groups of German operatives, disguised in Polish uniforms, seized a number of radio stations in Germany close to the Polish border (like the Gleiwitz broadcasting station in Upper Silesia) and transmitted inflammatory anti-German messages to the outside world.[2] Directed by Heinrich Himmler, Gestapo chief, Hitler fabricated the situation to make the attacks appear to be the works of anti-Nazi saboteurs. Evans and others cited these attacks as Hitler's justification for his invasion of Poland on September 1, 1939. The roundup of Jewish men on September 8 was part of Hitler's antisemitic rampage against Jews who were Polish nationals.

Our family discovered during our most recent visit to Sachsenhausen in June 2011 that our father was caught in the turmoil of this event. His name, Aron Jakob Horowitz, appeared on the list of detainees picked up on September 8. We do know—according to an eyewitness, our cousin, who was incarcerated at the same time as our father—that our father was beaten on his way to stand at *Appel* (roll call) incanting the *Shema Yisrael,* and he was savagely slain.

On September 18, Hannah, our mother, was thirty-one years old; Gitta, my sister, was eight and a half; and I was almost five. So began World War II for us.

September 21, 1939

Our father was buried in a small wooden box at the Adass Yisrael Orthodox cemetery in Berlin, under the watchful eyes of two Gestapo men, in the presence of our mother, my sister, Gitta, and our great-grandfather, the Hasidic *Rav* (Rabbi) Itsche. I stayed with my babysitter. I remember playing with two wooden black and white salt and pepper shakers, shaped in the form of a king and queen. To keep myself content, I invented a story, short and sweet, making believe that I was the queen and the king was my father. My father was home with me and we were playing house in our palace. Meanwhile, at the cemetery, the grown-ups and my sister were burying my father. When my mother and Gitta returned home, I asked about our father, and they said what most people tell their young children when a parent dies, "Your papa is up in the sky, behind the clouds."

I said nothing, but I knew better: My father was certainly not in the sky. Hadn't we been playing together all along, when he was king and I his queen?

November 1939

I do not remember saying good-bye to my mother in November 1939, when our mother sent us to Belgium with a smuggler to stay with our father's family. According to my sister, Gitta, she and I left Berlin with a smuggler, who dropped us off in Amsterdam at a family friend's house. We waited a number of days for the next smuggler to arrive. Wanting to forget about our woes, my only ongoing complaint was that the woolen kneesocks that my mother had made me wear before leaving home were rough and scratchy, and I kept trying to pull them off.

Eventually, the new smuggler arrived. We left by train to the Belgian border, where our smuggler helped us off the train. Once our feet were on the ground, the smuggler explained that we had to run as fast as we could until we crossed the border. My sister remembers, "It was pitch dark outside. I think it was raining; but most of all I remember the cold. You were holding on to me and I was holding on to you, but we did not say a word. We ran in total silence, though I think that you stumbled a few times and I had to pick you up; but no one said a word, and you did not cry. Eventually, we crossed the border. A car picked us up, and brought us to Antwerp, to our father's family. They received us warmly and cared for us, but it took a while until we were able to calm down. This is an escape I will never forget."

This escape that my sister remembered, I totally blocked out of my mind. Thinking about it today, I realize that it was thanks to her support that I was able to blot it out of my memory.

Our mother joined us within three months after her harrowing escape that included being imprisoned by the Gestapo in Aachen, Germany. After a lengthy interrogation, she burst into tears and screamed uncontrollably. "How long are you going to interrogate me?" In response to this outburst the Gestapo decided to let her go and sent her back to Berlin, or so they thought. An officer accompanied her to the train station and put her on a train heading to Berlin. Determined not to give in to the Gestapo's disastrous decision, our mother did not take that train to Berlin. Instead, she left the train and went back to Aachen, where she searched for another smuggler, whose address she knew. This time she arrived in Antwerp at our father's family home in the trunk of a car. It was March or April 1940.

May 10, 1940

On that day, the Germans invaded Belgium, Holland, and France. Soon, a part of the Jewish population in Antwerp attempted to escape to Dunkirk, the port city from which the British were retreating to England. This escape was called "The Flight" (*De Vlucht*). Hundreds of Jews with their children, parents, cars, vehicles of all sorts, bicycles, buggies, and carts, walked on the roads. Some ran on the boardwalks with planes strafing overhead. We were running on the boardwalk, and I remember hearing the planes roaring overhead. People attempted to hide wherever possible.

Arriving in Dunkirk, we saw the British ships pulling away from the beaches, leaving us on the dock. Our mother was able to get some English biscuits and a can of boiled beef from a well-meaning British soldier. For us, this exodus was a failure, not only because the friend who drove us to Dunkirk left us stranded there, but because the British on whom our mother counted to help us escape to England had let us down. Though failure it was, there were some exceptions. Our mother made sure we remembered the bombers that flew overhead on the boardwalks never hit us, and we came out alive from this misadventure. Our mother asserted that she would not be defeated. Stranded as we were, she managed to find her way to the nearby town of Boulogne, approached a German military man of high rank at the newly occupied city hall, and explained her predicament to him. She was a widow, newly arrived from Berlin, her husband was accidentally killed, she got as far as Antwerp, and now she needed to return there. I often wondered how the German understood what my mother had told him, but apparently, she convinced him that she needed help. And so, he wrote out a permit allowing her to buy the benzine (gasoline) she needed that would bring her back safely to Antwerp with her children.

The Antwerp-Brussels Years: 1940–42

Too frightened to live with our Jewish family in Antwerp, Mother moved us away from them. Gitta and I attended a public school as Christian children in Schaerbeek, a suburb of Brussels. We were never to divulge our given names. Still, if we thought that forged papers provided a semblance of security, we were mistaken. A few days after we entered our newly rented apartment, we discovered that our neighbors occupying the house next door were German soldiers of the Wehrmacht. While at first terrified, our mother saw the good in this discovery: "Who would suspect a Jewish family living so close to German soldiers?" All reassurances aside, there wasn't a person among us who was not watchful and worried about the sounds from the other house.

And I, now almost seven, could not learn to read or write. My mind was otherwise preoccupied, and I was unable to focus on numbers and letters. I recited poems and sang songs that I had learned in school, but reading and writing were beyond my capabilities.

Brussels–Nice, March 1942

We escaped together with a Jewish family whom our mother had befriended. The roundups and transports of Antwerp Jews had begun. Fear gripped the Jewish community. With newly acquired documents, we boarded a train to Nice, unoccupied France. Apprehensively, we rode in the train until we came to the border and were ordered to get off for document control. The guard, looking like a French officer, took us into his office, one by one, for interrogation. He called me in last, just as my mother had predicted he would. I remember muttering some answers to his questions, but, in truth, I do not remember what I had said. I spoke as softly as I could lest he discover my mistakes; my heart was pounding in my chest, and I was sure he could hear every beat. By the end of the interrogation, getting up from his large upholstered desk chair, he came over to me and took my hand, "Now we are going to your mother." If he suspected that I was lying, he never let on. But walking me over to my mother, he put his hand in front of his eyes, indicating that what he was able to see, he was not supposed to see, and asked: "So, you are all Catholics, Madame Daveau?" My mother, in her best French accent, replied, "Of course, Monsieur, we are all Catholics!"

"Then you may go," he said. Almost as an afterthought he added, "You have a fine little girl, Madame." In part, I was moved by this man's pity, and, in part, I felt shame. Had I not lied well enough? I knew the rest of the family was relieved at having regained our freedom, but I was frightened out of my wits. What would happen next?

The Effects of Fright and Flight

Because we were prepared for some things and totally unprepared for others, we felt a need to recall the difficult escapes that had transpired. In the 1950s, in our mother's house, we spent many hours clarifying what had happened to us. We spoke about the persecutions, our many flights during the war, and about our fears of being caught, in spite of our forged documents. Being the youngest in my family was like having no head or memory, no understanding or sensitivity to suffering. And because I was never to reveal my true name to anyone, or tell anyone whence I came, I always felt like a stranger (like so many other hidden children). Wherever people got together, whether at family gatherings, in the schools I had attended, or at any gathering where I had been allowed to be, these feelings remained with me for many years, and they tend to reappear when I am stressed or am expected to perform a difficult task.

My Obsession to Tell

When my children were born in the early 1960s, I was overjoyed because in their presence I knew I could be myself. I felt that my children would know me—not the "me" who had been unknown in the past, a stranger, but the person I had been all along deep inside myself. As soon as they were able to understand and communicate, I was driven to tell them who I was and whence I came.

When they were young, I told them about my childhood experiences during the war. We did not speak about the Holocaust or Shoah yet. Jews in Europe spoke about the *Krieg* (war). I explained what had been difficult and painful, such as the interrogations at the borders, the separations, crossing the Alps, and the roundups in Nice, 1942. I also told them how lucky we had been that some good people had come to our aid and saved us, such as the good gendarme who took me away from the roundup in Nice on August 26, 1942, and meeting Andreina in the Italian Alps of Piemonte, who offered us shelter. I did not exaggerate the feats I was involved in, but I felt that each story I told had to be coherent, with a beginning, the danger point, and an ending where the danger had been dealt with, at least for the duration of that story. I did not want to frighten my children. I just wanted to tell them how life had been for us, but I did not know how my stories had affected them.

The children liked to hear my multilingual stories, and they were impressed to have such a "courageous" young mother. I wanted us to be close, as though we had literally come from the same place; but I soon realized that the children, being American-born, and I, a refugee and child survivor, would never share the same past. Because I was aware of this anomaly, rather than accepting my fate that we had come from different worlds, I intensified my mission of talking about my past. I shared with them, almost daily, one event or other that had taken place during the war from the time they were four, five, and seven years of age. And these reminiscences continued, though not as frequently, throughout their growing-up years. When they were on their way to school, or when I picked them up in our car pool, or when I was cooking dinner in the kitchen, should I suddenly remember one thing or another that was meaningful to me, I would ask them if they wanted to hear another story, and the answer was always, "Yes!" Then, I would add, "This I want you to remember." And then, a memory followed.

But I did not stop there. I had to explain to them that technically we were not survivors. Only camp survivors could claim that identity. "Who were you, then?" they asked. I explained that we were refugees who had survived the war the best way we could, and we were never incarcerated by the enemies, whether German, Italian Fascists, Vichy French, except for the Nice roundup. My children tired of hearing my clarifications as to who is a refugee or a survivor. They tired of hearing that they, though born in the States, should remember that they will always be children of refugees. Then, one day, my eldest child lost his cool and told me off.

"Get used to it, Mom. We'll never be like you; you are the refugee, but we are American Jews, born here. And we will always be different than you because we belong here and you don't!"

Passing on Family Values

If transmission of the Holocaust was my leitmotif, passing on the values I had garnered during these early years came a close second. I admonished them to remember the war and the Holocaust. And I told them it is essential to do the "right" thing. Any injustice done to a child brought back to mind the brutality and injustice of the war. For don't we all tear up, or run to break up a fight, when a child is threatened or being beaten on the street? And didn't I push myself against a human chain of policemen on the South Side of Chicago that intended to keep black Americans segregated on the 79th Street Rainbow Beach, in the 1970s? No, I was not arrested for disturbing the peace, but neither did the policemen let me break up their chain and walk with those who were shamed into being escorted away from our beach. I couldn't believe this was happening. It reminded me of the Nice roundup.

Nice Roundup: August 26, 1942

Didn't I tell my children that should someone hurt or frighten them, they should not fear to cry out for help; some good person might hear them and come to their rescue? I used my own experience as an example when I was caught in the big Nice roundup and transported with my new stepfather, Luzer, to the Auvarre barracks. I explained how I panicked and screamed after I was forcibly separated from him. I kept shouting, "I am not Jewish, I must go home, you are making a big mistake, my mother will be very angry if I don't come home right away!" And the tears and screams from a panic-stricken seven-year-old child threatened to trigger disorder, if not outright panic, among six hundred sixty Jewish people who had been rounded up that day. Alert to my panic, a tall gendarme came over to me, and bending down, he pointed his finger at me, saying, "If you stop crying right now, little girl, I will take you home after my work is done. Now, be silent and no more screams!"

I understood that this was a threat, but I hoped it was also a promise. Then, I became mute and my eyes bulged out of their sockets because I had to guard the door next to which I stood, lest the gendarme forgot about me in the midst of his paperwork. And so it was that by the end of the day, the gendarme came out and took my hand, as I still stood standing outside his door, and walked me over to his car. He brought me to our French cousin's home address, and he dropped me off there. He offered to bring me up to my mother's, but I politely refused and walked away. My righteous savior had let me go free, a small Jewish girl from the barracks.

I knew the house and walked up to the landing and saw the seal on her door. French Jews were supposed to be immune to the roundups, if they were French citizens, or so I thought. What was I supposed to do now?

Suddenly, my sister appeared on the landing. Frantic and desperate, our mother had sent Gitta on a dangerous mission: "Find her wherever you can think of, and may God help us!" So, my ten-and-a-half-year-old sister kept her head and decided that if I had run away from the roundup I would most likely go to a safe place, such as our French cousin's house, because she was not yet on the list of endangered Jews. But she too had confronted the cousin's sealed door a short time before my arrival. When Gitta returned to our cousin's sealed door, she found me. On that day, my life was saved twice: once by the French gendarme and then by my brave sister.

September 1943–April 1944

With the Italian occupation in southern France, we lived more peacefully and managed to station ourselves for the summer in St.-Martin-Vésubie with other Jewish refugees. My mother refused to register daily at city hall as was required by the Italian occupation. But because we had our false papers from Nice, I believe she felt we were safer without registering. On September 8, 1943, Italy capitulated to the Allies. Panic and fright fueled this next escape because the Germans were at our backs. We crossed the Alps with some nine hundred to one thousand Jewish refugees and hid in the mountains. A good woman, Andreina, took us into her stone cave. It was a shepherd's stone structure the Italians called a *cava*. We stayed there for about five months.

Although the Germans were losing the war, their tireless search for Jews in the mountains became more crazed day by day. Mother decided we must leave. Life became dangerous not only for us, but also for Andreina and her family, who could have been shot for hiding us. We escaped again, thanks to a brave priest, Don Brondello, who brought us new identity papers.

Our mother had decided that the safest way to travel would be to hitchhike to Rome because all train tracks had been bombarded. As we reached the road, Mother told us to stay out of sight; picking up three people was not as easy as picking up one attractive woman. She put on her black felt hat, and we waited. In time, a German jeep pulled up at the head of a long column of German trucks and came to a halt. My mother introduced Gitta and me. We were both standing on the side of the road, and the German driver examined our papers. A superior officer yelled, "What are you doing?" He examined the papers again. The driver received permission to move on with us in tow. Gitta had to sit on the truck marked "Ammunitions" with other German soldiers sitting in the back, and I stepped into the jeep with my mother. In this manner, we arrived at the outskirts of Rome with a column of the German military. Even as I tell it now, the incongruity of this story is shocking and unbelievable, improbable, but true. Our escape came to an end when our mother found the Dorothean convent recommended by our young priest and the nuns took us in. We were now two little girls, Danish and Protestant, that the Danish ambassador sent to this ultraorthodox Catholic convent.

June 4, 1944, the Allies Liberate Rome

Mother came to the convent to liberate us. But we were not to tell the mother superior that we were leaving the convent for good or that we were Jewish. Would the nuns be offended to know that they had hidden two Jewish girls rather than two Protestant ones, I thought? Our mother insisted we were to say farewell, pretending that we would return to school in the fall. These war lies I could not forget, nor forgive. To lie to save a life is permitted, but to lie to the person who has saved your life seemed wrong to me. Even if Mother had wanted to spare the nuns' feelings for having saved her Jewish children, it appeared to be a double insult. The insult to us was that we as Jews were unworthy to be saved by Christians. And the insult to the nuns was that they were not worthy of our thanks for having saved two Jewish children. Did our mother really think that the nuns had not suspected all along that we were Jewish? I was upset.

As we were walking on the narrow sidewalk leading away from the convent, I decided to tell my mother and Gitta that since we are free now I wanted to take back my real name. "From this day on I want to be called Chaya again, the name I was given at birth." No more Helli, Helene, Elena, Daveau, or Kantor, and no more lies. They were surprised, but did not think this decision was particularly noteworthy.

In Rome, we found an apartment to live in and a school we would attend. We caught our breath, a year's long breath, and attended a French/Italian school. Gitta was fourteen now, and I was ten. Here in a new environment we adjusted quite well. We made some friends, and seemingly, without too much effort, we both made the school's honor roll.

But our days of running were not over. A few well-intentioned soldiers from the Jewish Brigade temporarily stationed in Rome befriended us. They convinced our mother that it would be in our best interest, since World War II had not yet ended, that we should go to Palestine under the auspices of Youth Aliyah. From them we received legal documents as orphans to sail on the ship *Princess Kathleen,* on March 22, 1945. We left our mother and our father's brother, Uncle Herman, and were driven to the Italian port of Bari. Again, I do not remember saying goodbye to my mother, but I was not alone. My sister was with me. From there we sailed to the port of Haifa and arrived on March 27 together with 899 voyagers. A journalist reported in the *Davar* newspaper that all immigrants had official documents, to ensure that our entry into Palestine was legal.

Palestine—Atlit, 1945

Atlit was a temporary holding camp. The reception at Atlit was unsettling. It was a camp with watchtowers, barbed-wire fences, tents, and wooden sleeping berths. Fear erased what little memory I had. Gitta shuttled us around, from one registration table to another where we received toothbrushes, combs, possibly soap, and from there to the delousing center. My mind was a blank or at best in a fog.

The Jewish Agency leaders spoke with Gitta and asked about our family background. Just as the Jewish Brigade had coached her, she told the Jewish agency that we only wanted to go to Ben Shemen. That is what she said.

In Ben Shemen, we benefited from a good agricultural and general education and remained in Palestine for about sixteen months. Still, during the first few months in Ben Shemen, I was ill. Sad, unable to eat, and at the mercy of wrenching stomach pains, I dreamed of my mother. I wrote poems to my mother, in Hebrew, even before I was speaking the language. And slowly the content of my poems began to change from mother-love to the love of country. I made friends and was becoming a patriot. The discovery of that warm and supportive environment in my new school engaged my independence and learning and had given me strength and self-esteem. And that was the beginning of my identification with Israel.

I Am Older Now

When I first began telling my children about the war, I did not see that I was foisting a burden on their young shoulders. But by the time they were adolescents, I could not help but wonder if I had hurt them. Did I neglect their needs for security, love, learning, exploring, and enjoyment? Was the Holocaust the only and central focus in my life? I admit that much of what I spoke about was tied with our legacy, the legacy of the Holocaust and Israel.

"And the Times They Are a-Changin' . . ."

Some years passed before our adult children became parents. I saw and heard their efforts at ferreting out what is good to pass on to their children, when this should be done, and what would be better ways to learn our history than what they had experienced in our family home. Our children are teaching Jewish history in various contexts. While not rejecting ours, their values and beliefs are expanding. Their concerns for today's world and society's ills are paramount. They are formulating their own ideology about parenting and helping their children become who they are. And that is how it should be.

I have come to realize that who one is cannot be given or handed over from one person to another. Each human being has to tackle the task of disentangling the meaning of his or her life. That process is an unending task. Yet, if we stop examining who we are, we risk not being able to reflect on what we have become.

Epilogue

My life, in part, is about transmitting memories, and not to forget. I don't recall ever wanting to consciously forget, and I was passionate about passing on what I had experienced. But there is much that my mind was unable to absorb. I do not remember saying good-bye to my mother every time I left her, when we left Berlin in 1939, or when we left for Palestine. I do know why I could not learn to read, write, or count when I entered first grade in Brussels, 1942. *Tres mal* (very sick) is what clung to my mind. I do not recall what I said to the police at the border between Free France and Occupied France when my family members were interrogated, and they called me in last in 1942. I know I was ashamed that I had not succeeded in fooling the French officer. He was a kind and compassionate man and let us go free. I do not remember leaving Luzer, my stepfather, in Nice in the roundup barracks, but I do remember that the French gendarme set me free, in August 1942. I wondered how my children received these forgotten memories; but now I know because they have shared them with me.

Notes

1. This essay is based, in part, on the book *The Fate of Holocaust Memories: Transmission and Family Dialogues* (New York: Palgrave Macmillan, 2008) by Chaya H. Roth, with the voices of Hannah Diller and Gitta Fajerstein-Walchirk.

2. Richard J. Evans, *The Third Reich in Power, 1933–1939* (New York: Penguin, 2005), 699–700, 702.

Figure 67. The Horowitz family in hiding in Nice, France, 1942. The woman in white seated at the table is Chaya and Gitta's mother, Hannah Horowitz, Chaya is next to her mother, and Gitta is in the back, peering over her Uncle Herman's shoulder.

Figure 68. Chaya Horowitz with members of the Jewish Brigade, Rome, Italy, 1945.

Figure 69. Chaya and Gitta Horowitz, Palestine, 1946.

Figure 70. Gitta Horowitz's identification card from Ben Shemen Children's Village, 1945.

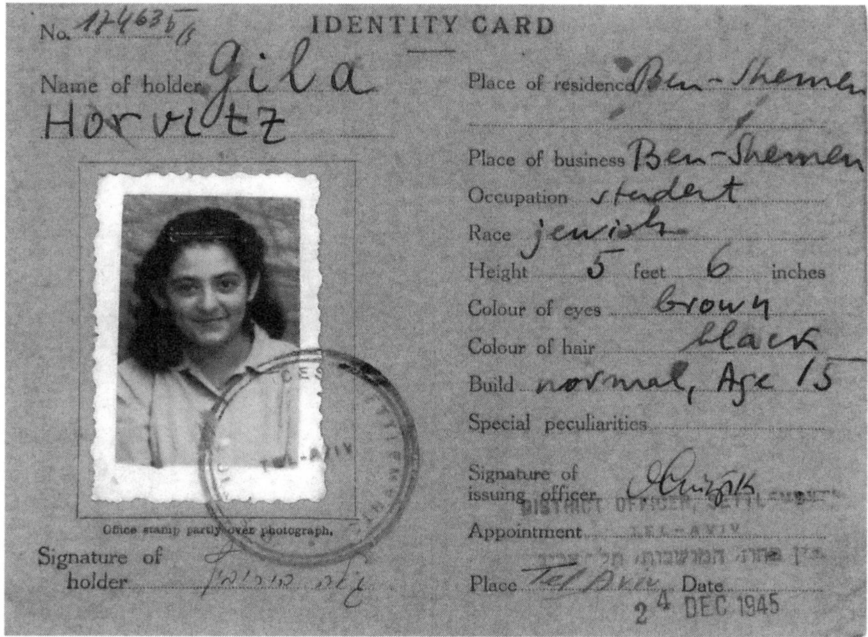

No. 174635/8

IDENTITY CARD

Name of holder Gila Horvitz

Place of residence Ben-Shemen

Place of business Ben-Shemen

Occupation student

Race jewish

Height 5 feet 6 inches

Colour of eyes brown

Colour of hair black

Build normal, Age 15

Special peculiarities

Signature of issuing officer

DISTRICT OFFICER, SETTLEMENT

Appointment TEL-AVIV

Office stamp partly over photograph.

Signature of holder גילה הורביץ

Place Tel Aviv Date 24 DEC 1945

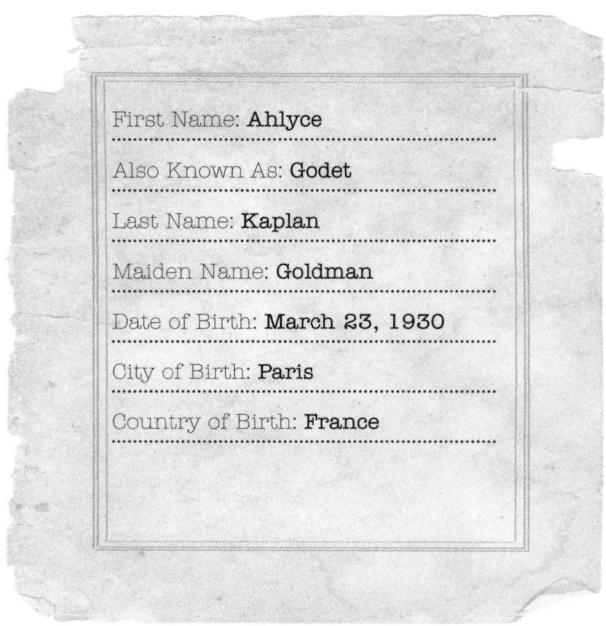
First Name: **Ahlyce**

Also Known As: **Godet**

Last Name: **Kaplan**

Maiden Name: **Goldman**

Date of Birth: **March 23, 1930**

City of Birth: **Paris**

Country of Birth: **France**

A Dog

Ahlyce Goldman Kaplan

We lived in a town house in Hyde Park, on the South Side of Chicago. The house faces Hyde Park Boulevard, and beyond the street is a large park. The house had a separate basement entrance, also facing the street, and its small stairwell provided relative safety to stray dogs, cats, and sometimes birds that sought refuge from the cars and the wind coming off the lake. My husband, Marvin, and I once nursed a sickly bird that flew away after we cared for it. Others that we cared for died.

Once I found a stray dog in the stairwell. He looked like the dog in the movie *Benji,* so we simply called him Benji. He huddled by the door; he was dirty and sad, so I let him into the basement. I could tell there was something special about that dog, so sweet and gentle and affectionate, we loved him then and there. We kept him in the basement that first night, but the next day, when I opened the door, he ran up the basement stairs and settled in the kitchen. I found him wonderful. We had other dogs in the family, but he was fine with them and they with him.

I walked my dogs in the park across the street. It was a hot summer night in the 1980s, and as I was walking Benji, he settled down on the grass, and I sat down next to him. I gave him a hug and said, "You see, you are lucky, someone is taking care of you." And with that I remembered 1942 and the beginning of my terror. I started to sob, screaming sobs, the dog in my arms. I cried for a long long time.

Two days later, I took him to the vet and was told Benji had severe internal injuries. He had to be put down . . . and I am alive.

Figure 71. Ava Hegedis Kadishson Schieber's illustration for Ahlyce Goldman Kaplan's "A Dog."

Untitled Poem

Ava Hegedis Kadishson Schieber

Hello fellow traveler in the future reality,
tread softly over crushed spring sprouts
and multilayered mounts of lost childhood.
In hope we trust our memories upon the water
and the currents we shall not encounter
including the unexpected events that may flow
to swells of turbulent torrents of
recurring outbursts in human frailties.
Our past testifies how in the blink of an eye in time
wanton killing crushes life leaving sharp-edged shards
scattered over coarse ground of miles and decades.
Hence, we the remainder cast our warning
appeal to life's fragility as we depart into history.

PART 8

Lost and Found

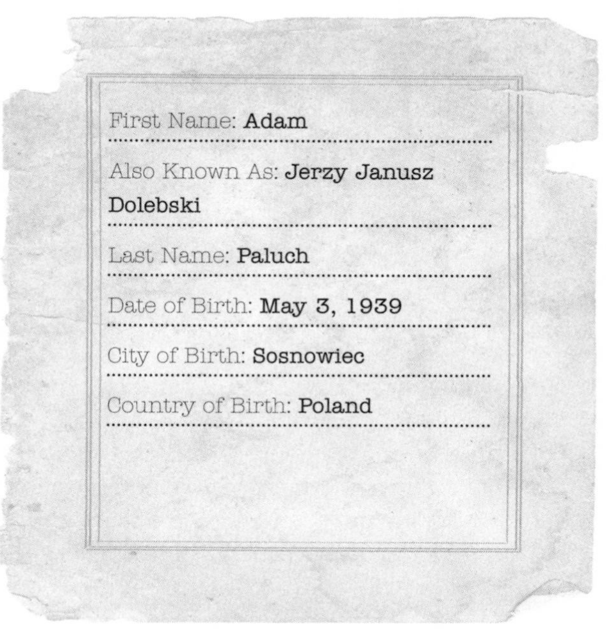
First Name: **Adam**

Also Known As: **Jerzy Janusz Dolebski**

Last Name: **Paluch**

Date of Birth: **May 3, 1939**

City of Birth: **Sosnowiec**

Country of Birth: **Poland**

As told to Henry Stark

The Story of Adam Paluch

Adam Paluch

My name is Adam Paluch, but it was not always so. There are those who say I was born in 1942; others say I was born in 1939. I am a strong, athletic male: a former part-time professional boxer and wrestler. But the paperwork says that I was a girl. I was taunted for being Jewish before I knew that I was Jewish. I was told that I am the child of a childless woman. I was told that my search for my identity was hopeless—that I was "digging in the ashes."

I went to Israel to find my roots, but I found them in America. I am not playing a game of charades. I want only to point out that my life as a Holocaust survivor was unusual, to say the least. It was comical, tragic, serendipitous, average, and extraordinary. There are things that I did that I'm proud of and other things that I regret. But to tell my story, it is easiest to divide my life into three periods: Beginnings—1939 to 1944; Postwar—1944 to May 1995; New life—May 1995 to the present.

Beginnings (1939–44)

This part of my life is very hazy. Years ago while visiting the Majdanek Extermination Camp with my son, I had a flashback: *this* was the place where I was taken as a child. Are there records that prove that I was at Majdanek? And if I was there, why didn't the Germans kill me? Was it because I was going to be a part of their "medical" experiments? A shard of blurred memory: the liberation by the Red/Polish Army, followed by time in an orphanage. But if I was in an orphanage, shouldn't there be a record? Then adoption by Jan and Leokadia Dolebski, a childless Catholic couple living in Lublin. They claim to know nothing about an orphanage.

Fortunately, as I get older, events come into focus and are easier to remember. The rest of the story will be easier to tell.

Postwar (1944–May 1995): The Search Begins

My name is now Jerzy Dolebski and I ask my adoptive parents where I came from. When I am nine years old, I suspect that I wasn't their child because I didn't look like the rest of the children, and, in addition, I was circumcised. They are full of inventive answers. My adoptive mother tells me that I was born out of wedlock (shsh!). My adoptive father tells me that I was found in an abandoned building, and I have a *Yiddish keppele* (Yiddish head) because I am smart. There is talk that I was plucked out of an orphanage (there is no record of this). My adoptive grandmother says that I am a *znajda*—a foundling, which is bad, real bad. It implies in the Polish culture that you were unwanted, even as an innocent child. My adoptive mother is angered and refuses to speak to her mother after this comment.

I am told that I was born in 1942, and a "birth certificate" is drafted on October 15, 1944. Strangely my "birth certificate" says that I am a girl. Starting in 1945, the Dolebskis proceed to have six children in the normal way. I realize that I am different from them—they are blond and fair-skinned; I am dark-haired and swarthy. I am circumcised and their boys are not.

A passing Jewish woman, a neighbor and friend of my father, once tells me, "Do you know that you are a Jewish child?" She knew because my parents told her. Is there such a thing as a Jewish child? A Christian child? If you are a child raised by a Jewish family according to Jewish customs, that makes you a Jewish child. If you are raised by Christians according to Christian customs, you are a Christian child. If I am a Jewish child, where are my Jewish parents?

In October 1945, the Dolebskis move to Lębork, where I am enrolled in grade school. There the kids call me *obrzezaniec*—the circumcised one. I understand that I am different from the other boys. Even my younger brothers are not circumcised. But what does being an *obrzezaniec* imply about my past?

My relationship with my adoptive parents is complicated. On the one hand, they take good care of me, but on the other hand, my feelings of "differentness" grow. I am not allowed to play in bed with my parents and my siblings. My parents keep me busy with chores, unlike their other children. I begin to feel estranged from them, like I'm not really part of this family anymore. My interest in my roots and my own family grows.

I become obsessed with determining my origins. From the age of ten and for another five years, I begin to run away from the Dolebskis' house in Lębork to find my real parents. In addition to Lębork, I search in Warsaw and Łódź. My absence from school does not go unnoticed by my classmates: they call me "the runaway Jew." I have no Jewish last name to give to anyone, so it seems like the search is hopeless. I even look for people who look like me. Nothing doing—no clues, no leads, nothing to bring me closer to the answer of "Who am I?" People begin to think that my search is like that of a crazy person.

After finishing grade school I attend the Technical School of Chemistry in the city of Zgierz. In school I am a good student, doing especially well in math and physics, and earn the respect of my classmates and teachers. But a financial crisis at home requires that I return to Lębork. My father is arrested for some kind of fraud. I go to work to support the family. Then I am drafted in the army to help build bridges. In the army I contract meningitis, which partially destroys my hearing and sends me to the hospital for surgery. That ends my army stay.

When I am twenty-five years old, I enroll in the Polish Naval Academy in Gdynia, about ten miles north of Gdańsk on the Baltic Sea. I graduate three years later and work in the marine rescue unit of the Polish Navy, followed by a stint in the Polish Ocean Lines. Altogether I spend ten years at sea. During this period in 1965, I also marry and have the first of my three children. Eventually we settle in Wejherowo, slightly inland from Gdynia. I am now a family man with family responsibilities. My family knows that I consider myself Jewish and that I am searching for my origins. From the beginning, my wife accepts my Jewish origins and pushes me to continue to search for my Jewish family.

Meanwhile, life goes on. Among other things, I go from being a girl to being a boy. This is accomplished by crossing out "female" in answer to "sex of baby?" on my birth certificate and replacing it with "male." So now it is official: I really am a male. To the Polish bureaucracy I was a girl for the first twenty-five years of my life. Although my birth certificate's incorrect gender designation did not affect me at work, I needed it corrected for school, and it mattered to me to set the record straight as to my correct identity. Originally my parents wanted a girl but chose me. Perhaps the birth certificate was prepared before they adopted me. Further, my father drank a lot and my mother was illiterate, so maybe all these reasons caused the confusion.

The question of who I am still gnaws at me. I need to convince the Jewish community that I am Jewish and that my quest for identity is for real. I meet with the chief rabbi of Warsaw, the head of the Nożyk Synagogue, and he checks to see if indeed I've been circumcised. He is not disappointed. I am now officially Jewish and the rabbi helps me advertise my quest in the Jewish newsletter the *Folks-Sztyme* (*People's Voice*):

> "Jerzy Dolebski is Jewish man who doesn't know who he is.
> Here is a picture of him as a young boy.
> If you recognize this boy please contact . . ."

The line is now baited. A little patience and some luck and I will soon find out who I am. It is now 1990. I have been waiting for nearly fifty years.

The Shapiro Incident

The article in the *Folks-Sztyme* ripples to America. There, someone brings it to the attention of a Mrs. Shapiro in New York City, originally from Lvov (now Lviv, Ukraine), who was separated from her son after the Germans occupied Poland. Mrs. Shapiro hints at the possibility that I might be her son. I become excited and hopeful that she might be my mother. We begin to exchange letters. At one point a friend of Mrs. Shapiro comes to Poland with instructions to look me up. We meet in Warsaw, where the friend takes my picture. At that time I am wearing a beard. The friend returns to the United States. It seems that Mrs. Shapiro, in anticipation that she and her son might be separated during the Holocaust, taught her son to memorize a secret phrase. This way, even if years later they are unrecognizable to each other, the son's knowledge of the phrase will prove without doubt that he is her son. Mrs. Shapiro now asks me for the phrase, and I do not know it.

I am not her son, Mrs. Shapiro concludes. What a letdown! I become depressed about never finding out who I am. Sadly, as I find out much later, Mrs. Shapiro never gets the chance to reconnect with her son in this world.

During 1992, I join a group called the Association of Children of the Holocaust in Poland. One of my friends in the association is concerned about my depression. We talk and I become convinced that I will find the answer to who I am in Israel. There are a large number of Polish Holocaust survivors there, and surely one of them will have the information I need. Moreover, for the first time, my adoptive father comes up with some hard information: I am the child of a Jewish woman named Frieda Nojmark, from Hrubieszów, who gave me to the Dolebskis; by taking me in, they saved my life.

The Dolebski Lie

I then depart for Israel for a period of one month. My search for my roots is helped by Orthodox Jews who arrange to have my story be published in *Yediot Aharonot* (*Latest News*), Israel's second-largest newspaper. In response to the article, there are many inquiries, but none bear fruit. While in Israel I meet a Dr. Kimmelman who is helpful. He has a keen interest in Holocaust survivors and bringing families together. He maintains extensive files and contacts. He helps me to contact Frieda Nojmark's sister (who would have been my aunt) in South America. *Nonsense,* says the sister, Frieda was childless and died in the ghetto, so she couldn't have been my mother. So the Nojmark story is another Dolebski lie. Why did they make it up? To make the claim that they saved my life? To appear as heroes? Under questioning by representatives from Yad Vashem, they finally admit that they took me from an orphanage in Majdanek after the war.

So my hazy recollections about the orphanage were true after all—they were not a product of my imagination. At least I pick up some important pieces of my past.

Despite the Dolebski lies, I feel that I owe them a lot. All human relationships are complicated, and very few people are perfectly good or perfectly bad. The fact is that I was their child, and they took care of me. As an adult I am educated, successful, and independent; would this have happened if they didn't take me out of the orphanage? In Israel the Dolebskis did not meet the standards for "Righteous Gentiles" because they were not my rescuers. However, in gratitude, I planted a tree in their eternal honor and received an official Yad Vashem certificate for doing so. When I present the certificate to Jan Dolebski, he merely tears it up in my presence. Why did he do this? Was he upset by my "disloyalty"? That is, was he diturbed that I was so concerned with finding my roots when—in their view—the Dolebskis were all the "roots" I needed? Was it because my increasing involvements with being Jewish revealed the failure of their attempts to raise me as a non-Jew? Or was it simply plain old embedded antisemitism that rejected the authority of Jews and the Jewish state? I will never know. Possibly the Dolebskis don't know either.

In terms of finding my roots, the trip to Israel is a failure. Yet two important conclusions come out of it: First, Kimmelman makes me aware that other Holocaust survivors in Poland have been displaced and that I might be able to help them upon my return to Poland; and second, I am ready to cut my ties with Poland and start a new life in Israel. But of course, I have a Catholic wife, Danuta, and three children whom my wife raised as non-Jews. Would Danuta like living in Israel? Could she assimilate there? To that end, I arrange to have her join a visit-Israel tour of Polish Jews. Let her see the country and get a taste of the Jewish nation. I have been married thirty years and do not wish to break up my family. Resettling in Israel is not a decision I can make lightly. Moreover, my fur business in Poland is thriving and by Polish standards I live a life of luxury.

I do not wish to dwell on this subject, but I should admit that my private life with my wife is not all that it could be. An eventual divorce is not out of the question.

As Kimmelman's "ambassador" to Poland, I make some inquiries about displaced Polish Jews using a list of names he furnishes. I track down a well-educated woman, who is held in a Polish asylum. Does she really belong there? Was she put there so that others could access her possessions? I talk with her and tell her how to contact Kimmelman. If anyone can help her, it will be him; I feel good about being able to help.

In the meantime, my involvement with the Holocaust Survivors Association becomes even deeper. I am elected the president of the Gdańsk chapter. At this time we are living in Wejherowo, a suburb of Gdańsk.

An Important Interview

A journalist from the New Haven *Jewish Ledger*, Deborah Kazis, is assigned in 1993 to go to Poland to interview child survivors of the Holocaust. She interviews me and takes my picture. Three months later she sends me a copy of her article published in her newspaper. After reading it, I put it in a drawer and forget about it.

Meanwhile, unknown to me, Kazis's article is read by Lucia Weintraub, a good friend of my sister Ida Paluch Kersz. Weintraub is aware that Ida has been searching for her missing siblings. "Read this," Lucia tells Ida, "it might be of interest to you."

In 1995, just before Christmas, I attend a plenary meeting of the Holocaust Child Survivors in Warsaw. Upon my return home from Warsaw—it is very late in the evening—I find that everyone is up and excited. What's going on, I wonder? Then my son tells me that some woman from the United States called and says that she is my long-lost *twin sister*! In retrospect, the call wasn't a complete surprise because I knew that someone from the States was trying to contact me. Ida had earlier written a letter to the Polish Holocaust Survivors Association.

Conversations with My Sister

I return the call to Ida, and right away I'm convinced that I am not her brother. Ida admits to being born in 1939 while my birth certificate gives my date of birth as 1942. How can we be fraternal twins born three years apart? This is a medical impossibility. I offer my help in finding Ida's twin brother. But she persists, "Are you sure that you were born in 1942?" she asks. Actually, when I think about it, I have no proof that my birth certificate is accurate, given my stay in the orphanage and the misinformation about my gender. Moreover, to be born in 1942 *and* to be circumcised doesn't make much sense. The Dolebskis surely didn't have me circumcised. In 1942, most Polish Jews were being sent to the extermination camps at Belzec, Sobibor, and Treblinka under the SS *Aktion Reinhard* implementation of the Final Solution. So who would have been there to circumcise me?

So I tell Ida that I'm willing to concede that I might have been born earlier, perhaps in 1939. I am disgruntled by the fact that I am suddenly three years older. But this age correction allows for the possibility that we are indeed twins. We talk on the phone a lot and find that our thoughts on many things coincide—almost too much so for a mere coincidence. From the first moment we met we sang the same Polish lullaby. Later when I visited the Highland Park, Illinois, sidewalk sale with Ida, we walked in different directions, but we each bought identical shoes. We each have the same favorite colors, foods, and allergies. Often we call each other at the exact same time. Neither of us smokes or drinks despite being with families that did.

But more than anything it is the pictures that tell the story: the amazing resemblance between my son Gregory and Ida's and my Jewish father. My son Peter, at the age of three, bears a strong resemblance to Ida at the same age. The more that we exchange pictures, the more the family resemblances stand out: the same foreheads, jawlines, green eyes, and blond hair when we were young that got darker as we grew up. Like our Jewish father, we are both excellent ballroom dancers. There can be no doubt: we are brother and sister.

And one day I get a letter from Ida that she is coming to Poland. She signs it *Your sister, Ida.*

Reunion

Back in the United States, Ida works for an accounting company. She is eager to come to Poland to see me, but she has to wait until the tax season is over. She arrives at the Warsaw airport on April 28, 1995, by coincidence the same day that my eldest son Gregory has his birthday. She plans to spend two weeks. "After being separated for fifty-three years, you can only stay two weeks?" I say. She changes her plans and stays a whole month. During this period we find the family ties that bind.

Ida invites me to join her and the rest of the surviving family back in the States. I agree to come with her. I leave Poland on May 31, 1995. I now have an extended family reaching from Poland to Skokie, Illinois, USA. There are regrets, of course. I have three grown children in Poland who miss me and whom I would like to see more often. I have lost the proximity of my Polish family and the country of my birth. I have gained a new family and new country in America.

When Ida applied to the government for my immigration to the United States, she submitted old family pictures of the two of us and our Jewish family and my

Figure 72. Adam Paluch with his Polish mother, Leokadia Dolebski, Lublin, Poland, early 1940s.

sons. My older son resembles my father, and my middle son at age two looks like Ida at the same age sitting on our mother's lap. Two weeks later, the Immigration and Naturalization Service sent Ida a letter stating that she could sponsor her brother to come to America. I received a special humanitarian grant to stay as long as I wanted, but I had to renew it every year. It took twelve years to get a green card.

For those people that question whether Ida and I are really twins, we have no doubt about our relationship. Therefore, we decided DNA testing is unnecessary. We believe we have sufficient evidence to verify we are brother and sister.

I have begun a new chapter of my life. If I ever write about it I will call it:
New Life (May 1995–Present)

Figure 73. Adam Paluch with his Polish father, Jan Dolebski, Lublin, Poland, early 1940s.

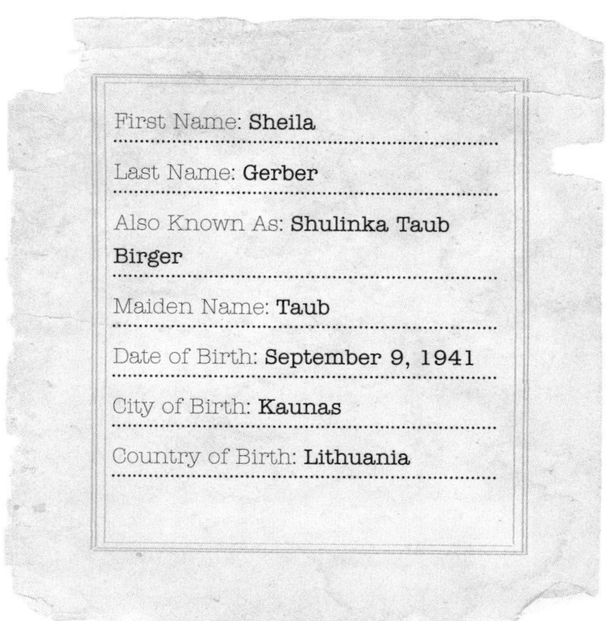

First Name: Sheila
Last Name: Gerber
Also Known As: Shulinka Taub Birger
Maiden Name: Taub
Date of Birth: September 9, 1941
City of Birth: Kaunas
Country of Birth: Lithuania

Secrets

Sheila Taub Birger Gerber

It was the end of June 1967, when I was twenty-six years old. I had just finished another year of teaching. I was home on Chicago's Northwest Side when the doorbell rang. Who could it be, I thought. It was my father. I was surprised to see him because he never came alone. My mother was always with him.

We talked a bit, and then he told me that he was not my father and my mother was not my mother. They were my aunt and uncle, Rosa and Daniel Birger. He said, "Your aunt is your mother's younger sister."

He continued talking, telling me that my parents were killed in the Shoah by the Nazis. We were all in the Kovno Ghetto, his family and mine. I was born shortly after the Jews were forced to move into the ghetto. My parents, Jonah Taub and Fruma Tarshish, kept my September 9, 1941, birth a secret because children weren't allowed to be born in the ghetto. I survived the many *Aktionen* by being hidden. One time when it was not possible to hide me, my uncle saved me from being killed.

He told me that during a selection in the Ghetto Square, he saw me in my buggy in the extermination line. I do not know where my parents were at this time. My uncle grabbed the buggy and pulled it out of the line when a Nazi attacked him. My uncle vigorously fought back. Another Nazi approached the fight and yelled, "Do you know who you are fighting with? He's the middleweight Lithuanian boxing champion." That ended the fight. Uncle Daniel grabbed the buggy and ran away with me. Even when he retold this story to me, he stopped there and wouldn't go any further. He never explained how he was able to flee the Nazis. Perhaps that is all he wanted to tell.

My uncle continued to tell me that my real father learned that the Nazis were going to burn the ghetto and march the survivors out to their death. This news spread like fire in the ghetto. Because conditions were desperate, my parents decided to get me out. My father made arrangements with a Lithuanian farmer, who was a friend, to smuggle me out of the ghetto. I survived in hiding with the farmer until the war's end. Aunt Rosa, Uncle Daniel, and his parents had escaped through an underground tunnel during the burning of the ghetto. After the war my aunt and uncle searched for and retrieved me. My father had been murdered trying to escape to the partisans. It is unknown how my mother died.

My uncle ended the secret story by saying that I had to know the truth and that they should have told me before, but my aunt was against it. I don't know why she was against telling me the truth. Perhaps it was too painful for her to remember those days.

Listening to him, instead of feeling surprised, I felt a sense of relief, and I understood that he was telling me the truth. I thought about my past, about my unanswered questions, and about being told not to ask questions. I was told that I was a child and therefore could not understand. I thought about the secrecy that surrounded me, and about my mother's—no, my aunt's—mysterious tears even at times of joy or even when she looked at me. On these occasions I asked my aunt, "Why are you crying?"

She would say, "You wouldn't understand."

I sensed from my aunt's behavior there was more to my past than I was being told, but I just accepted it when she said, "Don't ask questions." My aunt strongly conveyed to me how much she had suffered and gone through during the war. I did not want to cause her any more suffering by reawakening painful memories. I stopped asking questions.

My uncle got up to leave. I thanked him. He came as my father but left as my uncle. I'm now an orphan—a first-time pregnant orphan about to become a mother to my unborn child. I was numb. I was drained. I sat still for a long while. I understood they were not my parents after all. My parents had been dead since I was an infant. Although I welcomed this information to clear up questions about my past, it was traumatic for me. I was at the end of my ninth month of pregnancy when you are normally more emotional and vulnerable.

I later learned that I had a cousin, Shira, who was also born in the ghetto one month after me. My father found a hiding place for her also with a Lithuanian farmer. After the war, my aunt and uncle searched for and found Shira and me. It took several days of negotiations, exchanging family silverware and other belongings that they had hidden at the war's beginning to get the Lithuanians to return Shira and me. We eventually made our way to Italy, where we lived in several displaced persons camps. At some point a man, unknown to me, came and took Shira away. I was given no explanation as to why—a traumatic event never forgotten.

My aunt's keeping this secret from me did not negatively affect my feelings for her or my uncle. They both saved my life. I do not believe there are any more secrets. I know what there is to be known. I accept that there are gaps in my knowledge because there is no one there to fill those gaps. I continued to call my aunt and uncle Mom and Dad and remained devoted to them as any daughter would be.

I nonetheless continue to crave memory, any memory, of my parents. I want to remember their touch, their love. My young age at the time and the trauma of my experience have erased all memory of them. I desperately want my parents to know that I am alive and that they have Jewish grandchildren and great-grandchildren. I want them to know that they are, and will be, well remembered. My daughter is named after my mother and my son is named after my father. *L'dor v'dor* (from generation to generation).

Figure 74. Sheila Taub's father Jonah's cousin Rivka; her father, Jonah; and her mother, Fruma Taub, Kovno, Lithuania, before the Holocaust.

Figure 75. Sheila Taub's Uncle Daniel Birger, Lithuania, between 1938 and 1940.

Figure 76. Sheila Taub's Aunt Rosa Birger in a displaced persons camp, Rome, Italy, 1949.

Figure 77. Sheila Taub, age nine, when she arrived in Chicago, 1950.

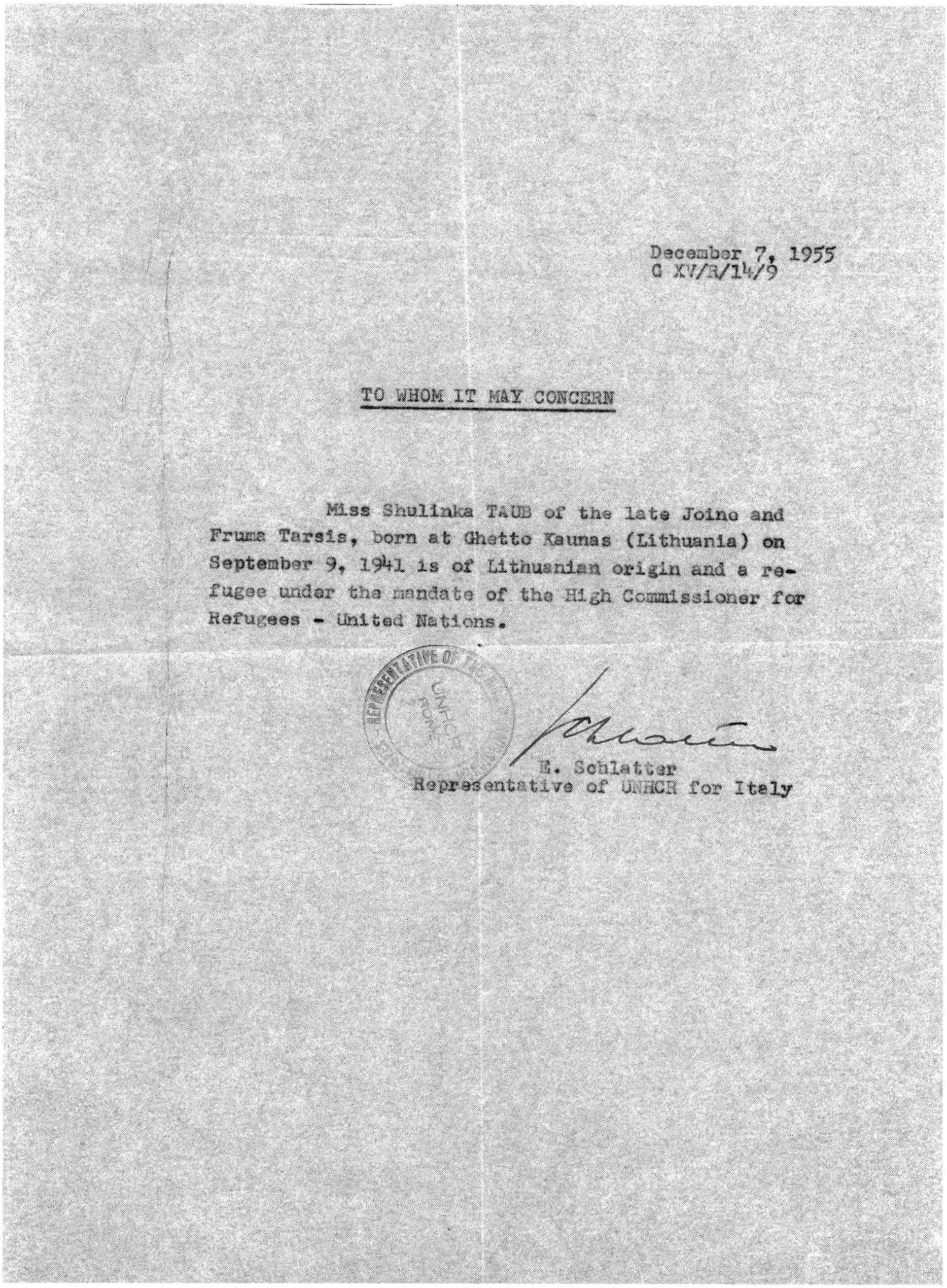

December 7, 1955
G XV/R/14/9

TO WHOM IT MAY CONCERN

Miss Shulinka TAUB of the late Joine and Fruma Tarsis, born at Ghetto Kaunas (Lithuania) on September 9, 1941 is of Lithuanian origin and a refugee under the mandate of the High Commissioner for Refugees - United Nations.

E. Schlatter
Representative of UNHCR for Italy

Figure 78. Letter from the United Nations High Commissioner for Refugees attesting to Sheila Taub's status as a refugee, 1955.

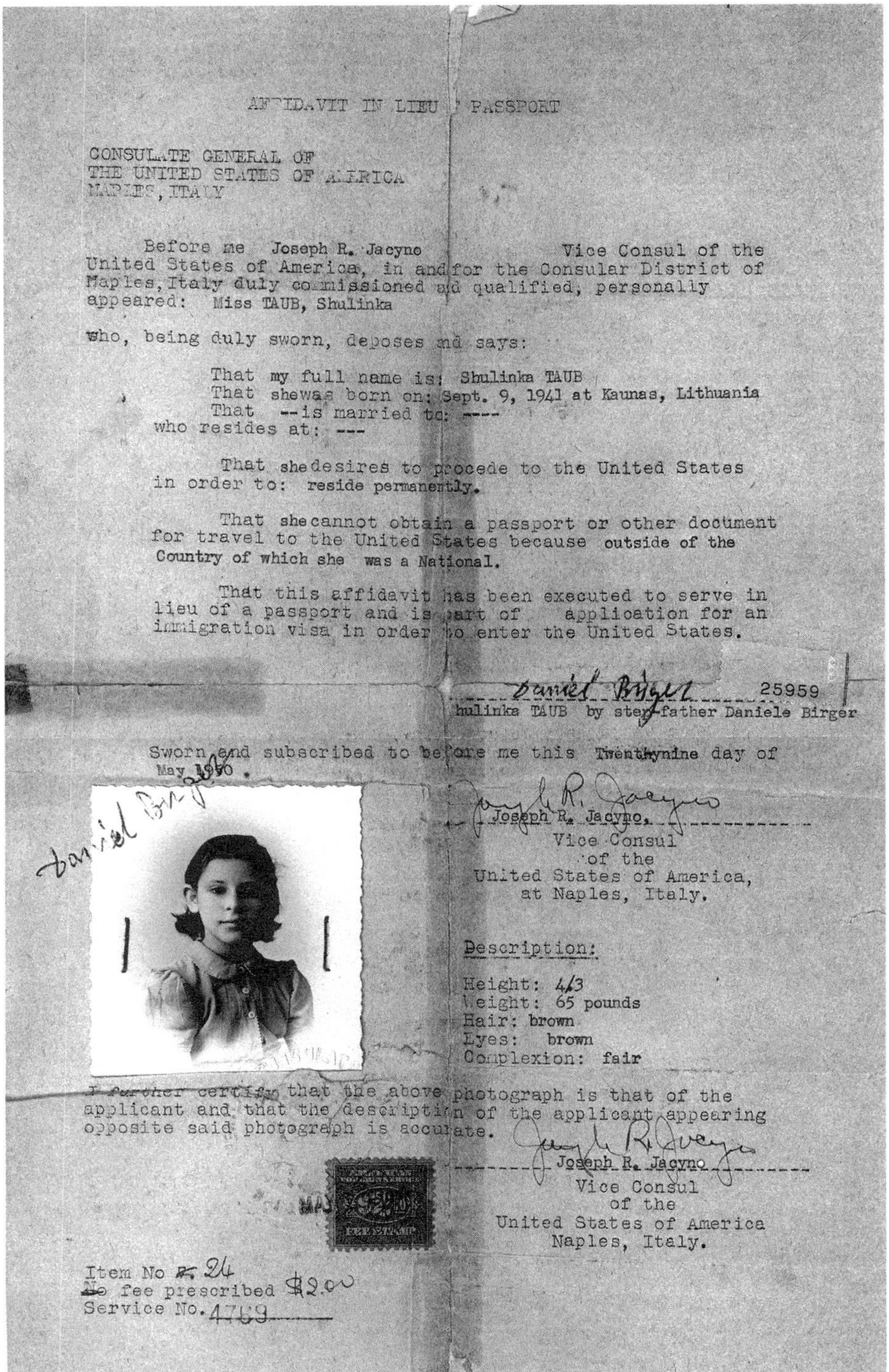

AFFIDAVIT IN LIEU OF PASSPORT

CONSULATE GENERAL OF
THE UNITED STATES OF AMERICA
NAPLES, ITALY

Before me Joseph R. Jacyno Vice Consul of the United States of America, in and for the Consular District of Naples, Italy duly commissioned and qualified, personally appeared: Miss TAUB, Shulinka

who, being duly sworn, deposes and says:

That my full name is: Shulinka TAUB
That shewas born on: Sept. 9, 1941 at Kaunas, Lithuania
That --is married to: ----
who resides at: ---

That shedesires to procede to the United States in order to: reside permanently.

That shecannot obtain a passport or other document for travel to the United States because outside of the Country of which she was a National.

That this affidavit has been executed to serve in lieu of a passport and is part of application for an immigration visa in order to enter the United States.

Daniel Birger 25959
Shulinka TAUB by step-father Daniele Birger

Sworn and subscribed to before me this Twenthynine day of May 1950.

Daniel Birger

Joseph R. Jacyno
Joseph R. Jacyno,
Vice Consul
of the
United States of America,
at Naples, Italy.

Description:

Height: 4/3
Weight: 65 pounds
Hair: brown
Eyes: brown
Complexion: fair

I further certify that the above photograph is that of the applicant and that the description of the applicant appearing opposite said photograph is accurate.

Joseph R. Jacyno
Joseph R. Jacyno
Vice Consul
of the
United States of America
Naples, Italy.

Item No. 24
fee prescribed $2.00
Service No. 4769

Figure 79 and figure 80. Front and back of the affidavit used by Sheila Taub in lieu of a passport.

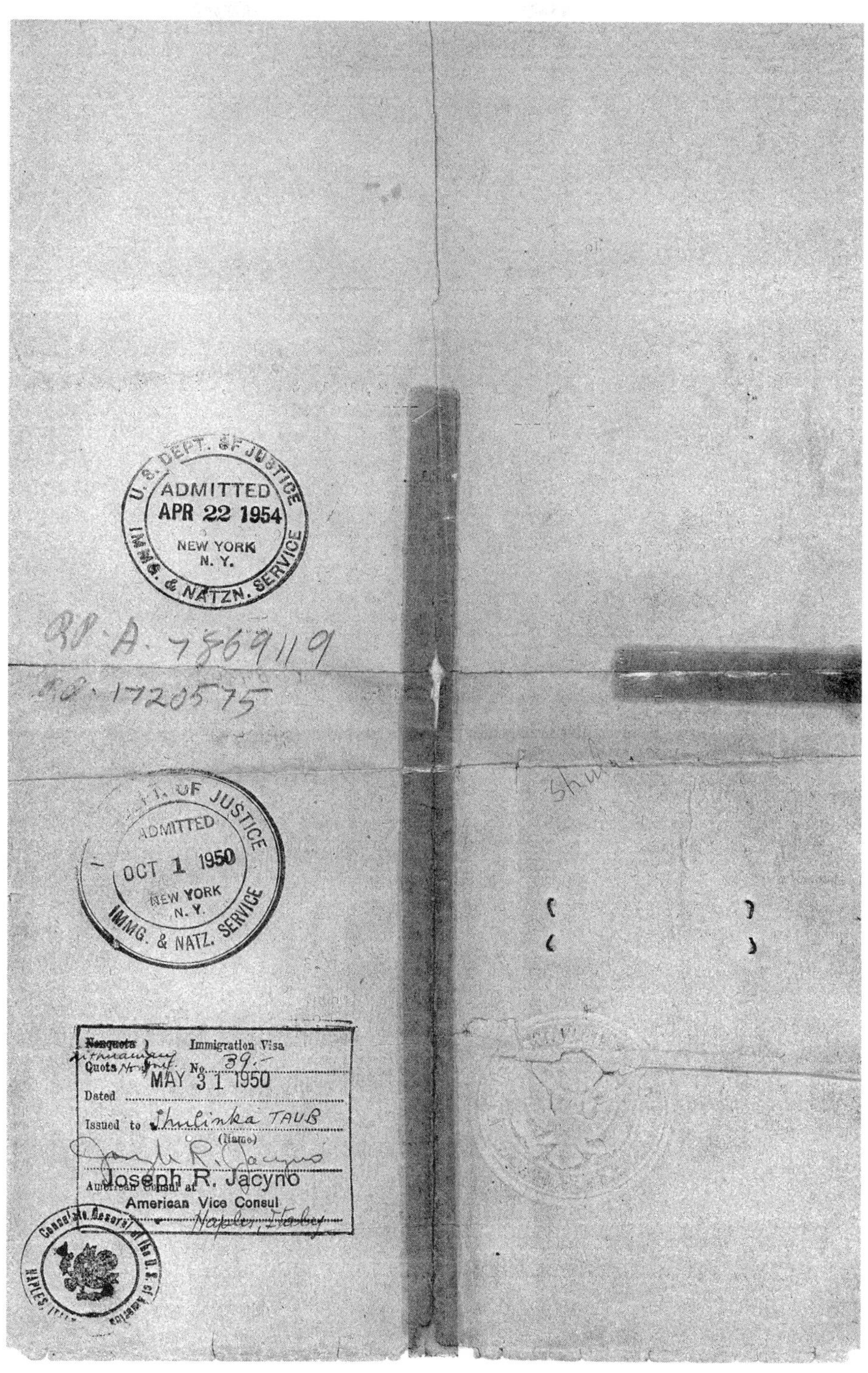

U.S. DEPT. OF JUSTICE
ADMITTED
APR 22 1954
NEW YORK
N. Y.
IMMG. & NATZN. SERVICE

RP-A-7869119
AR-1720575

[illegible] DEPT. OF JUSTICE
ADMITTED
OCT 1 1950
NEW YORK
N. Y.
IMMG. & NATZ. SERVICE

Shula

~~Nonquota~~ Immigration Visa
Quota No. 39.-
Dated MAY 31 1950
Issued to Shulinka TAUB
(Name)
Joseph R. Jacyno
American Consul at
Joseph R. Jacyno
American Vice Consul
Naples, Italy

Consulate General of the U.S. of America
NAPLES, ITALY

An Imagined Conversation, or Perhaps

Leonie Taffel Bergman and Marguerite Lederman Mishkin

Some years ago we two, Marguerite and Leonie, attended a hidden children's gathering. As we began to know each other, we realized that we shared a kinship originating in a terrible happening. Leonie's parents and Marguerite's mother had been taken from the Belgian deportation camp Malines on the last transport to leave from there for Auschwitz on July 31, 1944. All our parents perished at Auschwitz. Together we two decided to create, or possibly re-create, a scenario: Suppose our mothers had met on the transport train that dreadful day of deportation and during the three days of enduring that deportation ride were able to have a conversation. What might they have said to each other at that time? Here is what we imagine they might have told each other.

NUMBER 407: Thank you for giving me some room to stand. It's so crowded in this railcar.

NUMBER 184: We have to do what we can for each other. My name is Adele Taffel, and this is my husband, Pincus.

NUMBER 183: Yes, it is important to remember that we still have names. We are human beings, not just numbers.

NUMBER 407: I agree. My name is Rayzla Lederman.

A. TAFFEL: It's so good to be able to speak—to talk to someone like me. If I could get my hand up far enough to shake yours, I would do so. It's much too crowded for such manners. We came to Belgium for safety we thought, just six years ago, and look what has happened to us. After we left Poland and began to build a life in Germany, we had to flee. And now look at us!

P. TAFFEL: Madame Lederman, where do you come from, or were you born in Belgium?

R. LEDERMAN: No, my brothers, sisters, and I came to Belgium with our parents from Poland after the First World War. If only I could introduce you to my husband, Mordechai. The Nazis took him two years ago, and I have not heard a word about what happened to him.

A. TAFFEL: I am so sorry. What thoughts you must have, day and night. Let us hope he is still alive.

R. LEDERMAN: I can't let myself believe that. If I have any hope left at all, it is for my children. I have a new identity now. I am only Transport Number 407, and my name doesn't have any significance anymore, I suppose.

P. TAFFEL: My God, where are we going? What is happening to us? What will happen to our children? We know only where all the people before us—Transport Numbers 1 through 25; ten, or fifteen, twenty, maybe twenty-five thousand—we know where they went. The same for us!

A. TAFFEL: All these people with us. Five hundred, I'm told. What is there we can do?

R. LEDERMAN: There is nothing we can do now. Everything I've had to do I've already done. I hid my children to give them a chance to live. It was the hardest thing I've done in my life—harder than saying good-bye to my husband. Harder than reporting to the Malines camp. When I last saw my children, Annette was three and my little Marguerite was only two years old. That was some time ago. I know where they are in hiding. Perhaps I shouldn't even have said that much. I won't say any more. God keep them safe. That is all I care about.

A. TAFFEL: That is what my husband and I also did. We have two daughters. They are in hiding, with good people, but they are not together. That makes me so sad, as you can imagine.

Our Loni is almost nine now, and our little Clara is just past four. We haven't seen them for a long time, but some people have told us they are safe. *Zoln zey lebn un zayn gezunt.* (Let them live and be well.)

R. LEDERMAN: The people my daughters are staying with are also good people and very brave people, as you know. We can just hope that they will continue to be brave and kind as times get even harder for them. I'm sorry your daughters are not with each other. My girls are together and can help each other in these bad times, as sisters do, don't they?

A. TAFFEL: Our *kinderlech* (little children) are near enough that, when conditions are safe, arrangements are made for them to see each other. I hope our Loni remembers us, our life together as a family, and tells little Clara about us, their Mama and Papa.

P. TAFFEL: Yes, so that when we do return, God willing, we will not seem as strangers to her.

R. LEDERMAN: My daughters are still so little and young that I don't know if they remember me at all. Maybe Annette does, but my little Marguerite, I am afraid, is too young. The few times I took the risk and visited them, they just ignored me completely. In fact, they made it a point to kiss their foster mother and cling to her. I don't know if they didn't recognize me; maybe they were just angry at me for leaving them.

P. TAFFEL: We have to hope that in the end they will remember us. After all, this war cannot last forever. I've heard that the Allies have invaded Normandy. But it can still take a long time for them to get here—to save us.

A. TAFFEL: Maybe that's going to happen. But we are here, shoved together in this throng, surrounded by the wailing and fear of others, as well as our own. I just can't accept this! But we must try to make the best of this horrible situation. Don't you agree, Madame Lederman?

R. LEDERMAN: I don't care what happens to me anymore. First they take away my Mordechai, who I know is dead, and I won't ever see him anymore. And now I must resign myself to being taken away from my two beautiful baby daughters that I won't ever see again.

A. TAFFEL: Please don't despair and give up on any hope. That is what the Nazis want us to do. We can't let them have this last victory of taking our spirit away.

R. LEDERMAN: But they have already degraded us by making us wear a yellow Star of David and giving us middle names of Israel and Sarah. Then they further dehumanized us by having taken away our names and given us numbers. Now they have put us in these cattle cars where we are stuffed together like bundles of rags. Not only can we not move, but also we have to push and shove one another just to get a little breathing space. We have no food, no water to sustain us, and not even the comfort of privacy for our own needs.

A. TAFFEL: Yet each of us is alone, even in a crowd. Our thoughts, our dark thoughts, come through. But we have to fight despair because of our girls.

P. TAFFEL: Don't forget our faith. In the past God has saved us when other nations tried to destroy us. We had faith; we had hope. Can everything be taken away? During the years we lived with our parents, involved with Judaism, its practices, its wonders, its beliefs—we maintained our faith. Each time we Jews have survived. The hatred, the camps, this is the work of a madman!

R. LEDERMAN: How can you count on God? How can you believe in the Lord? Will God send us help? If God does exist, which I doubt, God has abandoned us. I can't believe that a just and righteous God would allow this horror to happen to us.

A. TAFFEL: Maybe there will be some intervention. Let God intervene and let our children have a good life.

R. LEDERMAN: I still can't believe in a God that allows mothers to be separated from their babies. Your faith seems to be stronger than mine and for that I envy you. All I know for sure is that my Mordechai has been murdered, and I don't have my precious babies with me.

A. TAFFEL: I can understand your despair, but not your bitterness. Think how fortunate we are that our little ones are not on this crowded, filthy, smelly transport, where we can't even take care of them properly. As parents, we must keep their welfare uppermost in our minds. We have heard about work assignments in Auschwitz, and work means survival. We are healthy; we are young; and we are strong. We have survived until now, able to keep from being caught. If we are seen as capable and mentally alert to endure work, we may be selected to work. And that may save us. We have to think that way. It is the big hope we have to be able to survive and to see our children again. If we can prepare ourselves to "look the part" of workers, we will have a chance! We must do that.

R. LEDERMAN: Let me understand what you are trying to tell me. Are you saying that my despair and fear, my very attitude, might influence whether I live or die? I never thought of that; I thought we are all doomed the moment we got on this transport. I still feel hopeless, but now at least I am beginning to wish that I didn't. Thank you for giving me another way to look at this situation. You have certainly given me a different outlook, which I will have to at least consider. Thank you again.

A. TAFFEL: Our children are safe, with people who care for them, sleeping in their own beds. Think about your husband. He would want you to hold on for the sake of your children.

R. LEDERMAN: I have seriously been thinking about what you have said. You have given me two good reasons to try to have some hope; first and foremost, my precious babies, and second, that if we do get on a work detail, we at least have a chance to survive. Hearing all of that, I begin to have a spark of hope. Also,

I'm thankful that I was able to see where my babies are hidden. I was able to leave a few pictures of me and them with the family. Sad to say, I could not find a picture of my Mordechai, so I don't know if the little ones will ever know what their father looked like. I also told the family that in case I did not come back, I want them to keep the little girls.

P. TAFFEL: Don't you want your daughters to grow up Jewish?

R. LEDERMAN: I can tell that you are observant, but my family was not. I care more that my girls are loved and happy than I do about their religion. What has Judaism ever given me, except pain and suffering? I would not be on this transport if I were not a Jew. I just don't want them to suffer. If not being Jewish will keep them safe, let them be brought up as Catholic.

A. TAFFEL: I hope when this is all over and we are all saved we can bring up our own daughters. For Pincus and me, Judaism and its customs has always provided security.

R. LEDERMAN: I can hear that practicing Judaism has given you strength and a belief that the future can be better. But at this time all I can think of is my babies. I don't want Annette and Marguerite to feel guilty or blame themselves if I don't come back. Everything I have done up to this point is to make sure that they will be happy and safe. There is no way that I want what happens to me to affect them negatively. They have nothing to do with whatever unspeakable suffering is awaiting us. The blame for that goes to the Nazis, not those beautiful, innocent children.

A. TAFFEL: I would like you to borrow some of my strength, Madame Lederman.

R. LEDERMAN: I will allow myself to borrow and lean on your strength and faith. If not for my sake, for my daughters' sake.

A. TAFFEL: It is good to know that my words have had an effect on you. I want what is best for you. You are not giving up hope. You are now thinking about the future, Madame Lederman. That is what we all must do, if not for ourselves, then for our little ones.

R. LEDERMAN: I want to think about my darling children. They are so sweet, so wonderful, so little. They are my joy! What else do I have? They have to live! Let us hope we will all be saved. Then our girls, your two and my two, can meet, maybe in Schaerbeek—in some park. My Mordechai and I were married in Schaerbeek.

A. TAFFEL: That is where we lived and worked. Pincus was a tailor, and I was a bookkeeper for a short time.

R. LEDERMAN: That is exactly what my Mordechai and I did. Is it only a coincidence that we should learn about each other, or was it meant to be? I want our daughters to meet, to know each other, and to be together. We will celebrate our reunion, the reunion of our families. Let us hope that the four girls will be able to get to know one another, to become friends.

P. TAFFEL: Yes, if we survive, we must meet again. And with our Loni, Clara, and your daughters. The girls will have such fun together in the park. That will be our reward—the joy of seeing our four girls safe, with us, and playing together.

A. TAFFEL: Let us make that promise to each other, to ourselves. It has been good to talk with you, Mrs. Lederman. No one who has not experienced what we are

Figure 81. Mordechai (Mordka) Lederman, 1906–1942.

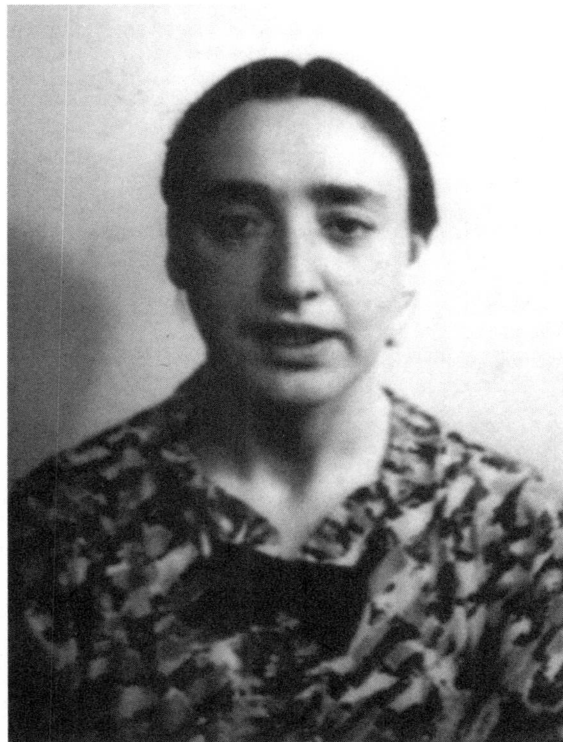

Figure 82. Rayzla Zylbersczac Lederman, 1909–1944.

Figure 83. Pincus Taffel, 1891–1944.

Figure 84. Adele Goldblatt Taffel, 1904–1944.

going through will really understand how dreadful and uncertain our situations are. And how indifferent the rest of the world is to what they must know. Perhaps sometime in the future we will be able to tell this story. Perhaps to each other, on a park bench in Brussels with our children playing in front of us as we talk.

R. LEDERMAN: Please call me by my first name. It feels good to begin this friendship, even in these terrible circumstances. I will keep this image in my mind for now—the picture of our daughters as friends, playing in the park in peace and safety and us sitting there, telling the story of how we survived. It will help me to get through whatever is coming: Or perhaps . . .

A. TAFFEL: Perhaps what, Rayzla?

R. LEDERMAN: Perhaps it will not be us, but our children who will tell this story. May they survive to do so. Maybe the world will listen to them.

Perhaps.

[*The transport stops.* ARBEIT MACHT FREI (WORK MAKES ONE FREE) *reads the sign at the Auschwitz gate.*]

Malines Deportations

No. 604 Mordka Lederman: Transport XVI—31 October l942

No. 407 Rayzla Zylbersczac Lederman—Transport XXVI—31 July 1944

No. 183 Pincus Taffel—Transport XXVI—31 July 1944

No. 184 Adele Goldblatt Taffel—Transport XXVI—31 July 1944

This conversation was written by us, two of the four daughters, all of whom survived the war. We two, Marguerite Lederman Mishkin and Leonie Taffel Bergman, live in the same city and see each other often—at meetings, at some social gatherings, and at friendly get-togethers. We both became teachers in public schools, where we were in constant contact with young people. We survived because of our parents' incredible foresight and fortitude in finding safe places for us, though there were none for them. We tell their stories and ours as an act of our gratitude for that quiet, hidden sacrifice.

We gain comfort in imagining this possible conversation. Because no one can deny that it could have happened, we choose to believe that it might have taken place, and just as described.

Perhaps . . .

Afterword

Elaine Saphier Fox

Why This Project?

Why did I leave my career as a full-time labor and employment law attorney to help a group of Jewish child survivors of the Holocaust tell their stories? It was time. It was time to explore passions that had lain dormant during my child-rearing and career years. It was time to ensure that their stories became part of history.

Like many women, my adult life has been segmented. After college graduation, I began a family and worked as a teacher. When our children were past infancy, but still quite young, I embarked on an enjoyable legal career. But since childhood, I have been intrigued by history, the Holocaust, politics, and human interactions. As a youngster, I remember my parents and grandparents talking about Hitler and his mad scheme to annihilate the Jews, and their concern about my grandmother's Lithuanian family.

As a teenager in the 1950s, my girlfriend Gloria Reiner and I discussed World War II, the atrocities committed, and the injustices perpetrated here at home against the blacks. We vowed that our generation would be different and not allow such evil. We had the youthful exuberance and naïveté to think we had the power to improve human behavior.

In 1963, I experienced another connection with the Holocaust. We had moved into the second-floor apartment of a two flat whose owners, Ella and Leon Krzetowski, were Holocaust survivors. We saw the tattooed numbers on Leon's arm. When they were fourteen years old, they were both forced into the Łódź Ghetto. They came from different environments. Leon was from a large, Hasidic religious family who lived in a rural area. In contrast, Ella lived with her family in Łódź, where her father owned a successful men's clothing store on the main street. They did not know each other until after the war. From Łódź the Germans transported them to Auschwitz. From them I learned firsthand about the gruesome details of life in captivity—starvation, regimentation, inadequate protection from the elements, forced labor from dawn until dusk, and beatings and murders. We heard Leon often screaming in his sleep while he dreamed the Germans were chasing him. A remarkable friendship and bonding began between our families that still exists. My childhood, teenage, and adult experiences set the stage for my involvement in this project.

At the end of 2006, my friend Chaya Horowitz Roth told me about her Hidden Children/Child Survivors Chicago group. They had been seeking someone to help them prepare and compile their war stories into an anthology. Committed to remembering those who were murdered and educating others by telling, writing, or speaking about their war experiences to a variety of audiences, including children, they are among the last Holocaust survivors and witnesses. Their stories must be told.

Through the years I had read several accounts of World War II and the Holocaust, which included works by Elie Wiesel, Lucy Dawidowicz's *The War Against the Jews,* the Theresienstadt children's anthology *I Never Saw Another Butterfly,* and Viktor Frankl's *Man's Search for Meaning.* In preparation for the task ahead, I began to immerse myself in numerous books that included histories of the period, first-hand accounts of survivors, hidden children, and rescuers.

Browsing through our home library, which included books inherited from our family, I made an important discovery—a four-by-six-inch red, thirty-page pamphlet, *Hitlerism and the German Jews,* which replicated a Chicago speech given in April 1933 by Horace J. Bridges, leader of the Chicago Ethical Society. Given the rampant isolationism prevailing in the country, Bridges argued that the United States must abandon its policy, speak out, and aid the German Jews because of Hitler's injustices against them. He said, "It has always been the right of citizens of a free nation to protest against persecutions of citizens of another, whenever such people were being injured 'in mind, body, or estate,' on religious or racial grounds, or indeed in any manner involving manifest injustice."

As early as 1933, before I was born, people in the United States knew about the disastrous circumstances befalling German Jews and even anticipated the horrors yet to come. Some, like my family, were more concerned than others. Not until I found this article did I have a tangible clue as to why my parents and grandparents in the late 1930s and 1940s worried so much about our Lithuanian relatives and European Jews. I was ready to begin.

My Role

Fifteen out of forty-six people in the Hidden Children/Child Survivors group volunteered to form the editorial group. When we began, participants' ages ranged from the late sixties to early eighties. They were originally from Western and Eastern Europe. Although the war interrupted their educations, some members nonetheless went on to earn advanced degrees and even taught in universities, while others started professions or became entrepreneurs. They all speak and write several languages. Three have had their memoirs published.

Most, however, had never written anything of this nature for publication before. Members submitted stories, scenes, and poems about their wartime lives. To help and instruct them, I discussed writing techniques and proper grammar usage. A few members and I worked with those who wanted help. We interviewed, drafted, and confirmed with them that the final product was correct. Prior to the meetings, I circulated authors' written submissions for the group to review for clarity, grammar, syntax, historical accuracy, and content. We discussed the writings at the meeting where the authors always had the final say, unless it involved grammar or accuracy.

Members could not substitute their voices or project what they observed onto another author's voice or experience. At times someone disputed another person's version of a particular event based on what she or he had encountered. Because there were regional differences, writers could not generalize that what they had experienced had been the same for all. For example, the French and Belgian children cheered with joy as the Allies liberated their towns and villages. In contrast, although happy to be free, when the Russians liberated Theresienstadt, the people there did not exhibit the same merriment and adulation.

Writing and rewriting their stories required digging into painful pasts. They uncovered ghosts that had been buried for decades. These ghosts locked tight in a vault were now freed and floated in front of them. At many meetings a member revisited a long-forgotten dreadful experience and broke down. Their original writing did not reflect these insights or memories. On one occasion when Amos Turner was reading his story, he abruptly stopped. When he came to the section about his four friends and what had happened to them, his body tensed up. In another session, Adele Laznowski Zaveduk realized that the trauma of being separated from her mother caused her initially to hold back from showing affection to her children in case they too would be separated. If she wasn't affectionate and another forced separation occurred, perhaps they wouldn't miss her as much. Their anguish and emotional catharsis brought tears to everyone's eyes. Feeling their pain, our editorial group also became a support group.

Childhood Comparisons

They were curious about what life was like for me, an American child, during the war. Listening to and reading their stories, I could not help contrasting their childhoods to mine. Some torn away from family lived alone without any support under the most dire circumstances. Others lived with strangers, or some family, but were terrified of being yanked away. All were in constant danger and knew it. It was like a tornado had devastated their former lives.

I thought how resourceful, disciplined, and brave they were. While they froze, had no playmates, little food, or toys, I lived with my parents and younger sister, Sharon, in a warm apartment and enjoyed extended family nearby. Unlike my friends, I had warm clothes, food, and the safety of a free society with loving parents to care for me. My grandparents gave me dolls and new outfits for Rosh Hashanah. We were free to go to the park, Lake Michigan, museums, and the zoo.

Yet, even before school age in the late 1930s and 1940s, from family conversations, I knew there was something awful happening in this faraway place across a big ocean. I knew about antisemitism directly. Neighborhood toughs with flaming torches chased my younger sister, Sharon, and me calling us "Christ killers" and "dirty Jews." On a Sunday at a suburban Round Lake picnic area with my family, I saw a sign, NO DOGS OR JEWS ALLOWED. I remember my parents' anger and frustration when hearing Father Coughlin preach antisemitic diatribes on Sunday mornings. My parents spoke about the German American Bund meetings here and in Wisconsin. If there were people here who hated Jews, could we in America be safe? Reassuring me, my parents explained that there were laws here that protected us, no Hitler, and here there were more good people than bad. I prayed every night that we would win the war.

I remember butter, sugar, soap, and shoe rationing. There were paper, rubber, and grease collection drives. The only curfews were for brownouts. My father, an air raid captain, patrolled the streets during brownouts. The radio blasted war news. At the movies newsreels showed our planes and ships exploding out of the sky and in the seawater. Headlines screamed about the latest skirmishes. We children sang wartime rants against Hitler, Mussolini, and Hirohito. "Whistle while you work. Hitler is a jerk. Mussolini is a meanie. Whistle while you work."

Then my prayers were answered. Sirens blared, horns blew, and everyone yelled, celebrating the war's end. I saw newsreels showing Mussolini hanging upside down and the skeletal concentration camp victims after liberation. How could people treat other human beings like that, I wondered.

Not long after, my grandmother received a letter in Yiddish from her brother, Birke Rosengarden from Lithuania. I sat on the floor at her feet watching her translate and read his letter. He was the sole survivor of her large family. Transfixed, I watched her shivering body and tears streaming down her face. The Einsatzgruppen murdered her entire family except my Great Uncle Birke. He survived only because prior to the Nazi invasion, the Russians occupied Lithuania. They shipped him to the Siberian salt mines because he was a "capitalist Jew." When he returned from Siberia, he learned that the Germans had murdered his wife and young son. They shot his sister Rivka's husband in front of his store. Birke's mother and eldest brother, Nathan, had been marched to the forest, forced to strip naked and dig their own graves. Collaborators shot them and threw their bodies into the ditches they had dug. Lithuanians shot and murdered my Great Aunt Rivka, who was a doctor, while she was holding her two baby boys and running across a field to escape. All this happened while I was safe in the United States.

Although I was far from the depravity that had smothered Europe, I empathize with my friends who survived so many depredations. They were forced to grow up before their time, always one step away from annihilation. Unlike me, they were compelled to live in strange places with unfamiliar people, or even alone. I was free and far away from the terrors and traumas that they had faced. Despite all these distinctions, there are similarities—importance of family, giving back to our community, searching for knowledge, and working toward a better world.

Separated by thousands of miles, Adele and I witnessed the same events, but under different circumstances. In one of her stories she tells how she and the village people were all cheering when the Yanks, waving on top of their tanks rolling down the street, liberated her French town. I remember sitting in the movie theater on a Saturday afternoon watching a newsreel and seeing the scene she described—smiling Yanks sat on top of their tanks throwing treats to the cheering crowd. Adele was one of the children who caught a treat. In another story she writes about how upset she was when later that same day she saw a group of French women with shaved heads marked with black tar swastikas paraded and pushed down the street in front of jeering crowds. Like Adele, I saw this scene, but in a newsreel, not in person. I too was disturbed and wondered what had they done that was so bad. My mother explained that they had befriended the Germans—the enemy.

Could I have been able to survive like Aaron Elster in a dilapidated attic exposed to the elements and not knowing what happened to his parents or beloved baby sister Sarah? Could I have been as resourceful as Chaya, who screamed her way out of a Nice roundup? Knowing the trauma and fear I felt every time I was separated from my hospitalized mother, I cannot imagine how awful it was for Irma Morgenstern to leave her loving parents, climb over the Warsaw Ghetto wall, jump, and run for her life. Or Gitta Horowitz, lost in the slippery, cold mountains without boots. Or Marguerite Lederman asking, "Who is my mommy now?" Or Judy Levy and Kurt Gutfreund locked in Theresienstadt—their stories go on and on about the perilous lives they had led.

Reflections

We learn from their writings that children know more than adults realize. They carry what they have learned throughout their lives. Their concerns were dismissed. They were told that they were too young to understand what was going on. What did they know about suffering? But they did know. Their stories and poems have given them the voice to expel their anxieties and fears of long ago and to set forth important historical accounts. I am grateful for having facilitated their desire to tell the world what happened.

Their parents and rescuers played a significant part in their survival. These stories are a testament to many of their parents' courageousness and farsightedness. They did everything in their power to protect and save their children, even the most painful act—giving them away. They recognized the impending danger and didn't fall into the trap of believing "it would all blow over." Righteous Gentiles along the way helped them. While the history of this era is replete with villains, we have heroes too—their rescuers. At great risk to their family's lives and their own lives, they helped save and protect these children. In Judaism we believe that every person has a good side and a bad side, *yetzer tov* and *yetzer harah.* Our battle is to ensure that the good side controls the evil impulses. Unlike many, the rescuers' good side prevailed.

Through this experience, I have discovered the resilience of the human spirit in young children. Despite their horrendous childhoods and traumatic experiences, they grew up to lead productive lives and have a generosity of spirit.

It has been an honor to work with my friends and know that their stories are about them—specific children, and what they had endured at the hands of a society ruled by madmen. Their stories are part of history. The purpose of studying history is to learn from the past. Future generations must know how easily civilizations can unravel and affect the innocent. We must continually be on the lookout for demonic despots who imperil freedom and liberty. We can't be blindsided by charismatic leaders.

I am pleased that I have been able to help my friends, who miraculously survived, whose stories now take their place in the history of that bloody period. In some way the survivors' stories memorialize the one-million-plus Jewish children, including my two baby boy cousins and Uncle Birke's young son, who did not survive.

Historical and Personal Timeline of the Holocaust

The following chronology is adapted from the United States Holocaust Memorial Museum's *Teaching About the Holocaust: A Resource Book for Educators* (Washington, D.C.: Diane Publishing, 2004) and from Elliot Lefkovitz, Ph.D., with additions (*shown in italics*) from the lives of those whose stories appear in this anthology.

1933

January 30

German President Paul von Hindenburg appoints Adolf Hitler chancellor of Germany. Within a month, freedom of assembly is restricted, freedom of speech is suspended, and freedom of the press is curtailed.

April 1

Hitler proclaims a boycott of Jewish businesses.

Leah Molton-Motulsky Kadden's family's store windows are smeared with swastikas.

April 7

Germans expel Jews from civil service positions.

Judith Levy Straus's father is dismissed from his position as an electrical engineer at a government agency. The family moves to Holland.

1935

September 15

The Nuremberg Laws are passed. Under these laws, Germany defines Jews on the basis of "race" instead of religion and according to the affiliation of grandparents. Jews are no longer considered citizens of Germany and are deprived of civil and political rights. Jews and non-Jews cannot marry each other or have sexual intercourse outside of marriage. Germany prohibits social intercourse between Jews and non-Jews.

1936

July

The Sachsenhausen Concentration Camp is established near Berlin.

October 25

Hitler and the Italian Fascist leader Benito Mussolini sign the Rome-Berlin Axis agreement.

More than one hundred thousand refugees begin to flee Nazi Germany to other countries.

1937

The Germans confiscate Leah Molton-Motulsky Kadden's family business and property and transfer it to a German Christian.

1938

March 12

Germany annexes Austria in an action called the Anschluss. All German antisemitic decrees immediately apply to Austrian Jews as well.

Kurt Gutfreund is born in Vienna, Austria, two months before the Anschluss.

July 6–15

The Évian Conference, attended by thirty-two countries and convened by U.S. President Franklin D. Roosevelt, fails to find a way to help Jewish refugees. Only the Dominican Republic will accept them. The Nazis conclude that the world is indifferent to the plight of the Jews.

August

The Germans arrest Leah Molton-Motulsky Kadden's father and deport him to Sachsenhausen.

Leonie Taffel Bergman arrives in Belgium from Germany.

August 1

Germany establishes the Office of Jewish Emigration to facilitate forced expulsion of Jews.

August 17

Jews residing in Germany and Austria are compelled to add "Israel" and "Sarah" to their existing names on identity papers to identify them as Jewish.

October 5

The Swiss government requests that all Jewish passports be marked with a large red *J*. Switzerland can then decide whether to admit the holders of the passports. German passports issued to Jews become invalid unless stamped with a *J*.

October 28

Germany expels Jews with Polish citizenship living in Germany to the Polish border. Poland refuses to admit them.

November

Leah Molton-Motulsky Kadden's father arrives in Havana, Cuba. He is able to leave Germany due to Adolf Eichmann's Office of Jewish Emigration, which enforces the expulsion of Jews.

November 9–10

Kristallnacht: the first Nazi government-organized mass pogrom is launched against Jews throughout Germany and Austria. Ninety-one Jews are killed; thousands are beaten; hundreds of synagogues are burned and destroyed. The Germans arrest thirty thousand Jewish men and send most to concentration camps.

Fourteen-year-old Werner Rindsberg, later called Walter Reed, and his father, Siegfried Rindsberg, are rounded up by SA brownshirts and driven to the county jail in Kitzingen, Germany. Werner is released three days later, but Siegfried is transferred to the Dachau Concentration Camp and held for about five weeks.

November 12

A decree is issued forcing all Jews to transfer retail businesses to "Aryans."

November 15

All Jewish children are expelled from German schools.

Germany forbids Jews to attend theaters, concerts, and exhibitions; to drive; to own jewelry; and to have financial investments.

1939

January 30

In a speech at the Reichstag, Hitler proclaims that the next war will see the "annihilation of the Jewish race in Europe."

February

The Wagner-Rogers Bill, which would admit twenty thousand Jewish refugee children to the United States, dies in Congress.

Amos Turner celebrates his bar mitzvah in Zawiercie, Poland.

May 13–June 17

The United States refuses safe haven to more than nine hundred Jewish refugees on the ship SS *St. Louis;* it is forced to return to Europe.

Leah Molton-Motulsky Kadden, her mother, and her brothers are among the passengers on the ship.

May 17

Great Britain issues the "White Paper," severely restricting Jewish immigration into Palestine. Jews in Palestine vow to challenge the White Paper through illegal immigration.

June

Walter Reed's parents send him at age fifteen to Belgium from Germany as part of a Belgian children's rescue operation.

August 23

Germany and the Soviet Union sign the Molotov-Ribbentrop Pact, a nonaggression agreement.

September 1

German troops invade Poland.

Miriam Studniberg Webster's family, along with other Jews, leaves the Kaminsko resort for Łódź to be farther away from the German border.

September 3

World War II begins as Great Britain and France, allies of Poland, declare war against Germany.

The Germans capture Miriam Studniberg Webster's hometown, Radomsko. They immediately confiscate her father's business and transfer it to a non-Jewish person.

September 8

The Gestapo arrests Gitta Horowitz Fajerstein's and Chaya Horowitz Roth's father and imprisons him in Sachsenhausen, where he is murdered ten days later.

September 17

Russia invades eastern Poland.

September 27

Polish Jews are forced to wear yellow stars. The occupying Germans force Jews to do slave labor and to establish *Judenräte* (local Jewish Councils) to facilitate German control.

Polish Jewish youths organize underground resistance movements.

Amos Turner and his family are among those forced to do slave labor.

October

Mass murder of Germans with disabilities is begun to strengthen the "German master race." German doctors carry out the killings, which are accomplished by starvation, lethal injections, and poison gas.

November 28

The first Polish ghetto is established in Piotrków.

December

Gitta Horowitz Fajerstein and Chaya Horowitz Roth are smuggled out of Berlin into Belgium.

The Gestapo confiscates Amos Turner's family property and other Jewish possessions in Zawiercie. Jews from Bohemia are deported to Poland and forced to move in with families, including the Turners, who have already been relocated into smaller quarters.

1940

January

Miriam Studniberg Webster and her family are evicted from their home in Radomsko, Poland, and forced into smaller quarters.

May 7

Łódź Ghetto is sealed, with between 165,000 and 230,000 inhabitants in about one-and-a-half square miles.

May 10

Germany invades the Netherlands, Belgium, and France.

May 14

Walter Reed and his children's refugee colony escape from Brussels to southern France.

June 22

France surrenders to the Nazis. The Vichy government is established.

August 5

Nicole Dreyfus Terry's father comes to Chambois and takes his family to France's unoccupied zone.

October

Italy invades Greece.

Isaac Daniel is attending school when Italy invades Greece.

November 15

The Warsaw Ghetto is sealed. It eventually holds five hundred thousand inhabitants, becoming the largest Polish ghetto.

November 24

Hungary, Romania, and Slovakia join the Axis. They pass antisemitic legislation.

Irma Morgenstern Grundland's family is forced into the Warsaw Ghetto.

1941

Jews in the conquered countries are segregated, marked, and banned from public schools and public places. Their businesses are confiscated.

Leonie Taffel Bergman and Olga Kirshenbaum Weiss are no longer in school.

April 6

Germany invades Yugoslavia and Greece, which is divided into three zones: German in the north, Bulgarian in the east, and Italian in the south. Salonika, with the largest Jewish population in Greece, is in the German zone. Athens is in the Italian zone.

Authorities arrest Isaac Daniel's family in both the German and Italian zones, but rescuers save them after both arrests.

Spring

Walter Reed and his children's refugee colony move to the Château de La Hille in France.

Ava Hegedis Kadishson Schieber escapes from Belgrade and hides in a farm in the country.

June

Einsatzgruppen mobile killing squads murder large numbers of Jews in Poland and Russia.

June 22

Germany invades the Soviet Union despite the nonaggression pact.

Summer

Pogroms massacre Jews in Lithuania and Latvia.

Walter Reed obtains a U.S. visa and arrives in New York on September 2.

September

Jews in countries occupied by the Third Reich are obligated to wear the yellow star.

The Nazis' first experiment with Zyklon-B gas to murder prisoners takes place at Auschwitz.

The Germans round up Edith Singer Turner and the rest of the Święciany Jews and send them to Poligon, an extermination site. Subsequently she and her family escape.

September 9

Sheila Taub Birger Gerber is born in the Kovno Ghetto in Lithuania.

September 29–30

The Einsatzgruppen shoot 33,771 Jewish men, women, and children at Babi Yar, a ravine near Kiev, Soviet Union.

Fall

The Nazis issue the order for deportation of German Jews to the east. Thousands die of starvation.

November 24

A new "model" camp is created at Theresienstadt for thousands of mostly central European Jews.

December 7

Japan launches a surprise attack on Pearl Harbor in Hawaii. The United States declares war on Japan. Germany and Italy declare war on the United States.

Winter

The Russians halt the German offensive outside of Moscow.

Leonie Taffel Bergman and Chaya Horowitz Roth are in the same first-grade classroom in Brussels, but they do not know each other.

1942

January

Underground resistance movements are organized in the Vilna and Kovno ghettos.

January 20

Nazi officials, industrialists, and academics convene at the Wannsee Villa, outside of Berlin, to organize the Final Solution, the systematic murder of European Jewry. Reinhard Heydrich announces a change in policy, from emigration to "evacuation to the east." Adolf Eichmann, chief of Jewish affairs and acting secretary of the conference, will be responsible for the rounding up and the deportation of Jews to the death camps.

March 1

As a result of the Wannsee Conference, *Aktion Reinhard,* the Nazi plan to murder Polish Jews, begins.

Extermination begins in Sobibor.

March 17

Extermination begins in Belzec.

Late March

Deportation and extermination begin at Auschwitz.

Spring

Gitta Horowitz Fajerstein and Chaya Horowitz Roth arrive in Nice, France, in the unoccupied zone.

All Jews in Belgium over the age of six, including Olga Kirshenbaum Weiss, must wear the yellow star.

June

Jewish partisans gather in Belarus forests.

Amos Turner escapes as the Germans evict two thousand Jews from Zawiercie and Jews from the neighboring villages are deported to Auschwitz.

June 1

Extermination begins in Treblinka.

June 15

Kurt Gutfreund's father is arrested, deported, and murdered at Maly Trostinec. Kurt and his mother go into hiding in Vienna.

July

Deportations from the Warsaw Ghetto to Treblinka begin.

Adele Laznowski Zaveduk's father is arrested and deported to Auschwitz. Adele's mother places her and her sister with a Catholic family in Brou, France, to hide them.

July 28

The Polish underground establishes Żegota (Council for Aid to Jews).

Summer

Deportation of Jews from Holland, France, and Belgium begins.

Throughout Nazi-occupied Europe, Jews in increasing numbers go into hiding, attempting to escape deportation. Among them are many Jewish children.

August

Word of the Final Solution reaches the United States.

Roundup of Jews in Brussels begins.

Olga Kirshenbaum Weiss and her family go into hiding.

Ida Paluch Kersz, Adam Paluch, and their family are forced into a selection line in the Środula Ghetto. Their mother commits suicide by jumping out a third floor window.

August 26

Chaya Horowitz Roth and her stepfather, Luzer, are caught in the Nice roundup and interrogated at the Auvarre barracks. Chaya is released, and her sister, Gitta, finds her.

September

Aaron Elster escapes a mass deportation in Sokołów, Podłaski, Poland.

While in hiding, Olga Kirshenbaum Weiss attends a private Catholic school in Belgium under a false name.

Adele Laznowski Zaveduk's mother is arrested and deported to Auschwitz.

Lillian Schreiber Zoloto's parents send her into hiding and do not know her whereabouts for four months.

October

Leah Molton-Motulsky Kadden, her mother, and her brother emerge from hiding and are smuggled to Switzerland with false papers. She is placed in Kinderheim Waldeck, a children's home, until it closes.

October 1

Miriam Studniberg Webster leaves her family, escapes the Radomsko Ghetto, and assumes a Polish Christian identity.

October 31

Marguerite Lederman Mishkin's father is taken to Malines and from there is deported to Auschwitz and murdered on November 28, 1942.

December

Kurt Gutfreund and his mother are arrested in Vienna.

Leonie Taffel Bergman goes into hiding in the Franciscan convent in Tervuren, Belgium.

December 24

Wilhelm and Jozefa Maj, a Polish Catholic couple, adopt Ida Paluch Kersz.

1943

January 8

Kurt Gutfreund and his mother arrive at Theresienstadt.

February 2

The Red Army wins the battle of Stalingrad; the war's momentum begins to shift against Nazi Germany.

February 11

The Gestapo shoots and kills Ida Paluch Kersz's adoptive father for smuggling ammunition for the Polish underground.

February 27

Irma Morgenstern Grundland escapes from the Warsaw Ghetto, becomes Barbara Nosarzewska, and goes into hiding.

March

Transports of Sephardic and Romaniot Jews from Salonika, the German zone, arrive in Auschwitz.

Among the Sephardic Jews arriving in Auschwitz are about fifty-five members of Isaac Daniel's family.

Judith Levy Straus's grandfather is deported and murdered upon arrival at Sobibor.

Edith Singer Turner and her family escape the Głębokie Ghetto.

April 19

The Warsaw Ghetto uprising begins.

The United States and Great Britain meet at the Bermuda Conference to find a plan to evacuate Jewish refugees who have reached neutral countries to safe havens. Nothing is achieved.

Spring

Isaac Daniel and his father escape the Greek police roundup during the Passover services in the Veria Synagogue. The entire family goes into hiding. Subsequently the Greek police arrest them and deport them to a transit camp, where Italians rescue them and take them to Athens.

June

The Nazis liquidate the Warsaw Ghetto after a valiant monthlong resistance by its last inhabitants.

Judith Levy Straus and her family are deported to Westerbork Transit Camp.

Himmler orders the liquidation of all Jews remaining in Polish and Soviet ghettos.

Summer

Leah Molton-Motulsky Kadden stays with a family in Basel, Switzerland, until the war's end.

August 2

Jewish slave workers revolt in Treblinka.

August 26

The Gestapo sends 4,500 Jews, including Amos Turner's parents and relatives, from the Zawiercie Ghetto to Auschwitz. Amos avoids deportation by hiding and subsequently escaping.

September

After the Italian surrender to the Allies, Gitta Horowitz Fajerstein, Chaya Horowitz Roth, and their mother escape southern France through the Alps into Italy.

September 8

Italy capitulates to the Allies. The Germans occupy Athens and all of southern Greece.

Isaac Daniel's family goes into hiding in Athens.

October

After Italy's surrender to the Allies, Germany reinforces troops in much of the northern part of Italy; Italian Jews are deported.

October 18

Jewish workers from the Luftwaffe factory in Zawiercie are deported to Auschwitz, but Amos Turner avoids deportation by hiding and subsequently escaping.

Winter

Deportation of Jews from Norway and Greece begins.

1944

January

United States President Roosevelt establishes the War Refugee Board, which will save thousands of Jews by funding the activities of rescuers, such as Raoul Wallenberg, or facilitating the escape of Jews to Switzerland or Palestine.

Sheila Taub Birger Gerber is smuggled out of the Kovno Ghetto in a basket and hidden with a Lithuanian farmer.

March

Deportations from southern Greece begin.

The Gestapo arrives at Isaac Daniel's house to arrest and deport the family, but his father bribes them to temporarily leave the family alone.

April

The Daniel family hides in Nea Smyrni, a suburb of Athens.

June 4

The Allies liberate Rome.

Gitta Horowitz Fajerstein's and Chaya Horowitz Roth's mother picks them up at the convent.

June 6

D-day: Allied forces land on the Normandy coast of France and begin the liberation of Western Europe.

Summer

The Russians liberate Belzec, Sobibor, and Treblinka.

July 23

The Russians liberate Majdanek.

Adam Paluch is among those liberated from Majdanek.

Late July

The Red Army crushes the German forces as it advances westward.

July 31

Leonie Taffel Bergman's parents and Marguerite Lederman Mishkin's mother are deported to Auschwitz from Malines, Belgium, and subsequently murdered.

August

Southern France is liberated.

The War Refugee Board asks that the Allies bomb railway lines leading to Auschwitz. The plea is rejected.

August 27

Nicole Dreyfus Terry's father hurries to the convent and finds that Nicole and her sister survived the bombing.

September

Olga Kirshenbaum Weiss and her family come out of hiding outside of Brussels.

Henry Stark and his family come out of hiding in Antwerp.

The Russians liberate Sokołów, Podłaski, Poland, Aaron Elster's hometown.

September 4

Judith Levy Straus, her father, and her mother are on the last transport from Westerbork to Theresienstadt. Three weeks later her father is deported to Auschwitz and murdered.

September 9

Belgium is liberated.

Olga Kirshenbaum Weiss, Leonie Taffel Bergman, Henry Stark, Lillian Schreiber Zoloto, and Marguerite Lederman Mishkin are among those liberated in Belgium.

October 7

Auschwitz inmates rebel and destroy one crematorium.

October 12

The Daniel family stays in hiding with Kyria Dimitra, a neighbor, until Athens is liberated.

November

The last deportation transport from Theresienstadt to Auschwitz occurs.

November 23

American and French forces liberate Alsace.

December

Civil war erupts in Greece.

December 16

The Battle of the Bulge in the Belgian Ardennes is Germany's last offensive in the west. It results in nearly twenty thousand Allied deaths.

1945

January 17

As the Red Army liberates camps in the east, the Nazis begin forced marches of prisoners, called death marches, in which many prisoners die.

Soviet forces liberate Częstochowa, where Ida Paluch Kersz lives.

January 27

Soviet forces liberate Auschwitz.

March

Nicole Dreyfus Terry and her family return to Paris.

March 22

Gitta Horowitz Fajerstein and Chaya Horowitz Roth sail on the Princess Kathleen *on Youth Aliyah for Palestine and arrive in Haifa on March 27, 1945.*

April

British troops liberate Bergen-Belsen, the first camp liberated by Western Allies.

The Red Army enters Germany from the east, while the rest of the Allied troops enter from the west. The Americans cross the Rhine River and liberate Buchenwald, Mauthausen, and Dachau.

Isaac Daniel and his family return to their home in Veria.

April 28

Mussolini is executed by Italian partisans.

April 30

Hitler commits suicide in his Berlin bunker.

May 7

Germany surrenders unconditionally.

May 8

The war in Europe is declared officially ended.

May 9

Soviet forces liberate Theresienstadt, where Judith Levy Straus and Kurt Gutfreund are imprisoned. After liberation, Kurt Gutfreund and his mother return to Vienna. Judith Levy Straus and her mother leave for Amsterdam.

Late Summer

Adele Laznowski Zaveduk's mother survives Auschwitz and returns to France to seek her family.

Summer–Fall

The Allies establish displaced persons camps for war survivors until they can return home.

Fall

Ava Hegedis Kadishson Schieber is reunited with her mother.

October 24

Representatives from fifty-one nations sign the United Nations Charter in San Francisco. Partly in response to the brutality committed during World War II, the UN will adopt the Universal Declaration of Human Rights.

November

The International Military Tribunal at Nuremberg begins to try high-ranking Nazis for their involvement in World War II. The court establishes the principle that "following orders" is not an acceptable defense for committing war crimes.

Despite British restrictions on immigration to Palestine, many Jewish refugees arrive there through clandestine channels, mostly with the help of the Jewish Brigade. Other Jewish refugees immigrate to other countries, primarily the United States.

Leah Molton-Motulsky Kadden, her mother, and her brother leave Switzerland and arrive in New York City on January 1, 1946.

1946

January

Irma Morgenstern Grundland is united with a distant cousin.

September

Lillian Schreiber Zoloto's parents retrieve her from her rescuers.

December 4

Leonie Taffel Bergman and her sister leave from Cherbourg, France, on the Île de France *and arrive in New York City on December 11, 1946.*

1947

Ida Paluch Kersz's father returns from Russia and retrieves her from the Maj family.

1948

The Displaced Persons Act of 1948 allows tens of thousands of Holocaust survivors to come to the United States throughout the late 1940s and early 1950s.

May 14

The new nation of Israel is established.

1949

Marguerite Lederman Mishkin's orphanage leaves for Israel.

Glossary

Aktion (German: "operation," plural *Aktionen*): The German roundup, deportation, and execution of Jews, especially in the Eastern European territories.

Aktion Reinhard or ***Einsatz Reinhard*** (German: "Operation Reinhard"): The German code name for the planned annihilation of Polish Jews. Named for SS General Reinhard Heydrich, the plan was approved at the Wannsee Conference in January 1942. (*See* Timeline, January 20, 1942.)

Aliyah (Hebrew: "ascent"): The immigration of Jews to Israel. *See also* **Youth Aliyah.**

Aliyah Bet (Hebrew): The name given to the illegal Jewish immigration from 1934 to 1948 to British-mandated Palestine in violation of the British White Paper of 1929, in contrast to the limited legal immigration allowed at that time, known as *Aliyah Aleph.*

Appell (German: "roll call"): A form of torture in which concentration camp inmates were summoned for "roll call" and forced to stand for hours regardless of weather.

Arbeit Macht Frei (German: "Work Makes One Free"): Slogan on a sign above entrance gates of some concentration and extermination camps, including Auschwitz, Dachau, and Theresienstadt, to deceive the prisoners into thinking that they were going to a labor camp and not a death camp.

bar mitzvah (Hebrew: "son of the commandments"): The religious ceremony of a Jewish boy upon reaching his thirteenth birthday, at which time he assumes the religious responsibilities of an adult. The same rite of passage for a girl is called a *bat mitzvah.*

Ben Shemen: An agricultural boarding school for children and youth founded in 1927 in central Israel.

Brundibár (Czech: colloquial, "bumblebee"): The title of a children's opera performed by the children at Theresienstadt Concentration Camp in 1944 to entertain Red Cross representatives who were inspecting the camp. This performance was part of a sham the Nazis presented to impress and mislead the visitors. The deception also included improving the appearance of the camp by beautifying the grounds and deporting many of the prisoners to Auschwitz.

brownouts: The dimming of street, home, and other lights to protect cities from air raids during World War II in the United States.

catechism: A summary of religious doctrine, typically presented in the form of questions and answers, used in Christian teaching.

cava: A shepherd's hut made out of the stone in the mountains.

challah (Yiddish: *khale*): A kind of yeast-leavened bread traditionally eaten by Jews on the Sabbath and on holidays. It is usually braided or twisted before baking, but it can also be formed into a round shape.

Comité Central Israélite: A Belgian organization that aimed to restore the Orthodox Jewish community in that country.

concarda: The Greek word for the yellow Jewish star that Jews were forced to wear at all times.

concentration camp (German: *Konzentrationslager, KZ*): An enclosed facility in which people were imprisoned without legitimate legal proceedings. Nazi concentration camps became notorious for the starvation, beatings, torture, and inhumane living conditions the prisoners there endured. These camps initially held political prisoners (1933–36). Later concentration camps (1936–45) also held nonpolitical prisoners—primarily Jews but also Roma (sometimes called Gypsies), homosexuals, and others deemed objectionable by the Nazis—as well as prisoners of war. Several million people perished in Nazi camps.

convent (Latin: *convenire*): A local community or dwelling of a religious order, especially an establishment of Roman Catholic nuns.

death marches: Evacuation of Nazi concentration camps during the winter of 1944–45, as Allied forces advanced from the east, in which the Nazis forced prisoners to march westward to other camps. Marching over long distances with little food and insufficient clothing for the weather conditions, many prisoners died along the way.

Einsatzgruppen (German: "Special Action Groups"): Mobile killing squads of SS troops that followed the German armies to the Soviet Union in June 1941 and systematically murdered the Jews in the area. The killing was done by mass shootings at first and later gassing prisoners with exhaust fumes in sealed vans.

Flemish: The language spoken in Flanders, a northern region in Belgium. It is a Germanic language considered a variant of Dutch.

Franconia (German: *Franken*): An area in south-central Germany that dates back to a medieval duchy in the kingdom of the Franks. The area includes the northern parts of the present-day German states of Bavaria, Baden-Württemberg, and Hesse.

gendarme (French: *gendarmes,* "armed people"): A police officer or a member of a body of soldiers serving as a police force to maintain public order, especially in France.

German American Bund: A pro-Nazi organization of ethnic Germans living in the United States. It became active in the mid-1930s, having among its chief goals promoting favorable opinions of Nazi Germany and keeping the United States out of World War II. After the United States entered the war on the side of the Allies opposing Germany, the German American Bund was outlawed.

Gestapo (German acronym for *Geheime Staatspolizei,* "Secret State Police"): The secret police force of Nazi Germany, established in 1933 and incorporated into Germany's regular police force in 1936. During World War II, the Gestapo had the authority in Nazi-occupied Europe to arrest and imprison people without legal consideration, and it became notorious for its terror tactics and brutality.

ghetto (Italian: *ghetar,* "foundry"): A section of a city where Jews settled or were forced to live. In Venice, Italy, during the early 1500s, Jews were forced to move onto an island within the city where a former iron foundry (called a *gèto*) had stood. Jews also were segregated in other cities. Most enforced segregation of Jews had ended by the 1800s, but in the 1930s the Nazis reinstituted ghettos. These ghettos were overcrowded and had unsanitary conditions, little food, and few medical resources. Ghetto inhabitants sometimes were forced to do hard labor. During World War II, the ghettos served as holding areas for Jews before they were deported to concentration camps and murdered.

Greek civil war: Armed internal conflict between Communists and royalists in Greece from 1944 to 1949.

grogger (also spelled *gragger* or *gregger*): A noisemaker used during Purim services every time Haman's name is mentioned, to drown out his name.

Haman: Prime minister of Persia under King Ahasuerus. As described in the biblical book of Esther, Haman plotted unsuccessfully to kill all the Jews of Persia and was hanged.

Hashomer Hatzair: A Zionist youth group started in 1913 in Poland. Members of the group helped in the resistance movement during the German occupation of Poland in World War II. *See also* **Zionist.**

Hasidism (also spelled *Chasidism;* Hebrew *asidut:* "loving-kindness"): A mystical religious movement in modern Judaism that encourages spirituality and joy in worship. It was founded by the Jewish teacher Ba'al Shem Tov and his followers in the mid-1700s as a reaction against traditional Judaism. The Hasidic movement spread throughout Eastern Europe and is practiced today by some Jews in Israel and the United States as well.

HIAS: Hebrew Immigrant Aid Society: A Jewish organization established in the United States in 1881 to support and aid Jews and other people who seek to escape oppressive governments.

Holocaust (from Greek *holokauston,* "a sacrifice consumed by fire"): The systematic murder of Jews and others in Europe that was planned and carried out by the Nazis between 1933 and 1945. The Holocaust wiped out six million Jews—more than two-thirds of the Jews in Europe. About five million others were killed, including Germans who had physical or mental disabilities; Roma (also known as Gypsies), Slavs, and other ethnic groups the Nazis considered inferior: Soviet prisoners of war; homosexuals; priests and ministers; labor union members; and Communists and other political opponents. Many Holocaust victims were taken to Nazi concentration camps and killed in gas chambers, after which their bodies were incinerated.

hora (Hebrew: *horah,* from Romanian: *horă*): A circle dance that originated in Romania and became popular in Israel as well.

Israel and Sarah: Names Jewish men and women, respectively, were required to add as middle names on their passports and other legal documents. (*See* Timeline, August 17, 1938.)

JDC (American Jewish Joint Distribution Committee, or "Joint"): Organization founded on November 27, 1914, by representatives of forty U.S. Jewish organizations to aid starving Jews in Europe and Palestine during World War I. During World War II, the JDC helped rescue and relocate European Jews endangered by the Nazis. Today the JDC continues to support Jewish communities around the world.

Jewish Council: *See* ***Judenrat.***

Joint: *See* **JDC.**

Judenrat (German: "Jewish Council," plural *Judenräte*): The governing body of Jewish leaders in a Jewish ghetto established by the Nazis during World War II. To keep the ghetto population under control, the Nazis appointed Jewish leaders to enforce the Nazi rules and regulations. The Jewish Councils tried to secure necessities for the people living in the ghetto. Sometimes the Nazis ordered the council to provide names of ghetto residents to be deported to the death camps.

Judenrein (German: "cleansed of Jews" or "free of Jews"): Nazi term for the complete removal of all Jews from an area through emigration, extermination, or a combination of the two. The Nazis succeeded in killing about two-thirds of Europe's Jews before World War II ended.

kashruth (also spelled *kashrut* or *kashrus;* Hebrew: "fitness"): The Jewish dietary laws and types of food that are sanctioned as *kosher,* or fit for use.

kibbutz (Hebrew: "gathering, clustering," plural *kibbutzim*): A Jewish communal settlement in Israel based on joint ownership and social equality. Kibbutzim are governed by officials elected from among the members, but everyone in the kibbutz votes to approve its rules and regulations. The first kibbutz was founded in Palestine in 1909, about forty years before the state of Israel was established.

Kristallnacht (German: "Crystal Night," known in English as the "Night of Broken Glass"): A riot against Jews throughout Germany, sanctioned by the Nazi government, on the night of November 9–10, 1938. Nazi Party members attacked Jews in public and in their homes and destroyed Jewish property, including synagogues, homes, stores, cemeteries, hospitals, and schools.

kosher: *See* **kashruth.**

Ladino (also known as **Judeo-Spanish**): A language based on medieval Spanish, with mixtures of Hebrew, Portuguese, Italian, Turkish, and Greek, used by Sephardic Jews, especially in Greece, Turkey, and other parts of the Balkan Peninsula.

Luftwaffe: The German air force.

Malines (Mechelen): A city in Belgium about halfway between Brussels and Antwerp. During World War II, a military building in Malines served as the Mechelen Transit Camp prison for Jews deported by the Nazis from Belgium to Auschwitz. (*See* **Mechelen** in the section Extermination and Concentration Camps.)

matzo: Unleavened bread, eaten especially during Passover as part of the seder to symbolize the flat bread eaten by the Israelites fleeing Egypt who did not have enough time to let their bread dough rise (*see* **Passover, seder**).

megillah (Hebrew: "scroll"): A religious scroll containing the book of Esther from the Bible, which is read in synagogues during Purim (*see* **Purim**). The book describes the persecution of the Jews in the Persian Empire.

Mischling (German: *Mischling,* "mongrel," plural *Mischlinge*): Nazi classification for a person of "mixed race" rather than the "pure" German blood of so-called Aryans; someone who was part Jewish.

Nazi Party (National Socialist German Workers' Party): German Fascist party led by Adolf Hitler that controlled Germany from 1933 to 1945. The party was founded on doctrines of nationalism, racism, and antisemitism.

ORT (Russian: *Obschestvo Remeslenovo i zemledelcheskovo Trouda,* "Society for Trades and Agricultural Labor"): The world's largest Jewish education and vocational nongovernmental training organization. It was started by a group of Jews in czarist Russia in 1880.

Orthodox (Greek: *orthos,* "straight, correct," and *doxa,* "opinion"): A branch of Judaism that strictly adheres to the laws of the Torah and the Talmud, including dietary rules, daily prayer, and observance of the Sabbath and other Jewish holidays. Orthodox Jews follow traditional Jewish customs. Men wear skullcaps or hats at all times, and men and women sit in separate sections of the synagogue.

Palestine: Historic region bordering the eastern end of the Mediterranean Sea. The region is considered a sacred land in Judaism, Christianity, and Islam; and as a result, it has been the site of much conflict among religious groups over the centuries. By about 1500 B.C.E. the ancient Hebrews had moved into the region from Mesopotamia. They became known as Israelites. The ancient Kingdom of Israel was created about 1000 B.C.E. The kingdom later fractured, and the Israelites living in the southern state of Judah became known as Jews. In 63 B.C.E. Judah was conquered by the Romans, who renamed it Judea. Muslim Arabs controlled Palestine from the 600s C.E. through the early 1900s. The British mandate of Palestine existed from 1922 to 1947, when the region was divided into Arab and Jewish areas under the post–World War II partition plan of the United Nations. In 1948, the Jewish area became the independent nation of Israel.

Passover: A Jewish holiday celebrating the Israelites' exodus out of Egypt and recounting the story of the Jews gaining freedom from enslavement as told in the book of Exodus in the Bible. The celebration lasts seven or eight days and includes the seder (*see* **seder**). Passover begins in March or April on the day corresponding to the fifteenth day of the month of Nisan in the Hebrew calendar.

pogrom (Yiddish, from Russian: "devastation"): An organized massacre, particularly a massacre of Jews. Pogroms against Jews were carried out in the late 1800s, first in Russia and then in other parts of Eastern Europe. Such attacks included looting of property, murder, and rape. Kristallnacht in 1938 was a pogrom carried out by the Nazis in Germany (*see* **Kristallnacht**).

Purim (from Hebrew: *pur,* "lot"): A Jewish holiday commemorating the events described in the book of Esther, in which the Jews of Persia were rescued through the bravery of Persia's queen, Esther, from a plot to kill them. The biblical story is recounted by reading it from the megillah (*see* **megillah**). Purim is celebrated in February or March, on the day corresponding to the fourteenth day of the month of Adar in the Hebrew calendar. It is a joyful holiday in which children dress up in costumes and people give gifts to the poor.

Righteous Gentiles: Term used to describe non-Jews who risked their lives to save Jews from Nazi persecution during the Holocaust. Those so designated by Yad Vashem have been honored at the museum by having trees planted in their names.

Rosh Hashanah (Hebrew: "head of the year"): A Jewish holiday marking the start of the Jewish New Year. It is a solemn occasion during which Jews attend services at the synagogue to recognize God's annual judgment of humankind and pray for God's forgiveness. Rosh Hashanah usually begins in September, on the date corresponding to the first day of the month of Tishri in the Hebrew calendar. It is a two-day holiday but also the start of the Ten Days of Penitence, which end on Yom Kippur (*see* **Yom Kippur**). Rosh Hashanah and Yom Kippur together are known as the High Holidays because they are the holiest days in the Jewish calendar.

SA (abbreviation of German: *Sturmabteilung,* "storm division"): Nazi Party paramilitary group, commonly known as storm troopers or as *brownshirts* because their uniforms included brown shirts. The SA served as the private army of Adolf Hitler. From 1923 to 1934, Hitler's storm troopers threatened the German people and helped him and his party take control of Germany.

seder (Hebrew: "order"): The ceremonial meal that begins the Jewish holiday of Passover (*see* **Passover**). It includes unleavened bread called matzo (*see* **matzo**) and other foods symbolizing aspects of the Passover story. The seder includes the youngest child present asking four questions that allow the leader of the ritual to retell the story of Passover.

Sephardic Jews: Jews who trace their ancestry through what are now Spain and Portugal. The term "Sephardic" is used more broadly to further encompass all Jews whose ancestry is traced through Arab and Persian countries, in contrast to the Ashkenazi Jews, whose ancestry is traced through northern and central Europe. Sephardic Jews have their own language, Ladino (*see* **Ladino**).

Shema: *See* ***Shema Yisrael.***

Shema Yisrael (Hebrew: "Hear, O Israel"): The Hebrew words that begin the traditional Jewish prayer affirming the existence of one supreme God—"Hear, O Israel: the Lord our God, the Lord is one"—and a shorthand phrase used to refer to that prayer.

Shoah (Hebrew: "catastrophe"): Term used as a synonym for the Holocaust (*see* **Holocaust**).

shtetl (Yiddish: diminutive for *shtot,* "town or city," plural *shtetlach*): A village or small town in Eastern Europe with a predominantly Jewish population.

SS (abbreviation of German: *Schutzstaffel,* "protection squad"): An elite security force of the Nazi Party. During World War II, the SS became the most powerful and most feared organization in Germany and Nazi-occupied Europe. It also ran the concentration camps.

Stalag (from German: *Stammlager,* "base camp"): A German prison camp for noncommissioned officers or enlisted men taken as prisoners of war.

sukkah: A small temporary hut in which Jews are expected to eat and sleep, in accordance with Jewish law, during the holiday of Sukkoth (*see* **Sukkoth**).

Sukkoth: A Jewish holiday that commemorates the ancient Hebrews' wandering in the desert for forty years in biblical times. Also called the Feast of the Tabernacles, it is a seven-day harvest festival that includes joyful parades in synagogues and meals eaten in sukkahs (*see* **sukkah**). Sukkoth begins in September or October on the date that corresponds to the fifteenth day of Tishri in the Hebrew calendar.

Theresienstadt children: Jewish children confined to the Theresienstadt Concentration Camp, which had a special section for children. (*See* "Theresienstadt" in the section Extermination and Concentration Camps.)

UNRRA: An acronym for United Nations Relief and Rehabilitation Administration, an agency established by the Allies in 1943. Its mission was to assist homeless and displaced people after World War II ended.

Vaad Hatzala (Hebrew: Rescue Committee): An organization established in 1939 by the Union of Orthodox Rabbis of the United States and Canada to rescue rabbis and religious students. It soon expanded its mission to assist all Jews.

Vichy: City in southern France from which the area that remained supposedly under French control was governed after the defeat of the French Army by Nazi Germany in 1940 and subsequent Nazi occupation of the northern two-thirds of France. Marshal Henri Philippe Pétain, a Nazi sympathizer, led the Vichy government.

Volksdeutsche (German: "German people"): Nazi term for ethnic Germans living outside Germany. Nazi leader Adolf Hitler envisioned the *Volksdeutsche* as part of a new Europe that would be dominated by "pure" Germans, whom he considered racially superior to other forms of humanity, and free of Jews (*see* ***Judenrein***).

Yad Vashem: The official museum and memorial in Israel dedicated to the Jewish victims of the Holocaust. An additional section of the museum honors those designated Righteous Gentiles, who risked their lives and their families' lives to save Jews.

yeshiva (also spelled *yeshivah;* Hebrew: *yeshibhah*): An Orthodox Jewish religious educational institution where Jewish men devote themselves to the advanced study of the Torah and Talmud and can be ordained as rabbis. The term also is used more generally to mean a school for Talmudic study or a Jewish day school providing both religious and secular instruction.

Yiddish: A Germanic language written in Hebrew characters that is the traditional language spoken by most Ashkenazi Jews of central and eastern European ancestry.

yizkor (Hebrew: "remembrance"): Judaism's memorial prayer for the dead. On such Jewish holidays as Yom Kippur and the last day of Passover, the prayer is recited in the synagogue for the departed.

Yom Kippur (Hebrew: "Day of Atonement"): A Jewish holiday known as the Day of Atonement, which is considered the holiest day in the Jewish calendar. It is a solemn occasion observed by fasting for twenty-four hours. Jews confess their sins and ask for forgiveness from God and one another. Yom Kippur occurs in September or October, on the date corresponding to the tenth day of the Hebrew month of Tishri—ten days after the holiday of Rosh Hashanah (*see* **Rosh Hashanah**).

Youth Aliyah: A program started in 1933 and sponsored by the United States–based Jewish women's organization Hadassah to rescue Jewish children from the Nazis and relocate them to Jewish settlements in Palestine. The American social worker Henrietta Szold founded Hadassah in 1912. A century later, Hadassah is the largest Jewish women's organization in the world, and the Youth Aliyah program continues to aid refugee children.

Zionist: A follower of Zionism—a movement to establish an independent Jewish nation in Palestine, the ancient Jewish homeland known as Zion (*see* **Palestine**). The movement began in the late nineteenth century, as antisemitism increased in Eastern Europe and some European Jews seeking to escape persecution immigrated to Palestine and established Jewish farm colonies, which later developed into *kibbutzim* (*see* **kibbutz**). At the World Zionist Conference held in Basel, Switzerland, in 1897, the Austrian journalist Theodor Herzl officially launched the Zionist movement on a worldwide scale. After a long struggle, the Zionists reached their goal in 1948 when the independent nation of Israel came into existence.

Extermination and Concentration Camps

During the Holocaust the Nazis established numerous concentration and death camps throughout Europe. Six of these camps were extermination camps in Poland, set up to efficiently murder large numbers of Jews. Some were slave labor camps, where prisoners were starved and worked to death. A few were transit camps, where families were gathered and held pending deportation to the extermination or labor camps.

The six extermination camps in Poland, responsible for the mass murder of about three million Jews—half of the six million Holocaust victims—were the following: (1) Auschwitz-Birkenau (September 1941–January 1945), more than 1 million killed; (2) Belzec (March 1942–November 1943), more than 600,000 killed; (3) Chelmno (December 1941–Summer 1944), 152,000 killed; (4) Majdanek (July 1941–October 1943), 60,000 to 80,000 killed; (5) Sobibor (March 1942–December 1943), 250,000 killed; and (6) Treblinka (1941–November 1942), more than 800,000 killed.

The following twelve camps are described in detail here because they are mentioned in the stories told in this book. Five of the twelve were partially or wholly extermination camps—from which there was no hope of return.

Auschwitz (Extermination and Concentration Camp; Poland, west of Kraków, near what is now Oświęcim): The Auschwitz Concentration Camp complex, opened May 26, 1940, was the largest of its kind established by the Nazi regime. The huge complex encompassed three camps: (1) Auschwitz I, built in 1940; (2) Birkenau, or Auschwitz II, built in 1941; and (3) Monowitz, or Auschwitz III, built in 1942. More than a million Jews died at Auschwitz between September 1941 and January 1945, some from starvation or disease but most from mass execution by poison gas.

At the height of the war, trains arrived at Auschwitz frequently with transports of Jews from virtually every country in Europe occupied by or allied with Germany. Above the entrance gates was a sign with the slogan Arbeit Macht Frei (Work Makes One Free), intended to create the impression that Auschwitz was a labor camp rather than a death camp. Transports arrived from 1942 to the end of summer 1944. Newly arrived prisoners at Auschwitz underwent "selections" by SS personnel. Those who were judged unfit for forced labor—that is, anyone who was not an able-bodied young adult; in other words, the majority of the prisoners—were sent immediately to the gas chambers, which were disguised as shower rooms to deceive the victims.

On October 7, 1944, several hundred prisoners slated for disposal at Crematorium IV at Auschwitz-Birkenau rebelled after learning that they would be killed. During the uprising, the prisoners killed three guards and blew up the crematorium and adjacent gas chamber using explosives that had been smuggled into the camp by Jewish women who had been assigned to forced labor in a nearby armaments factory. Only a few of the prisoners escaped. The Nazis killed all of the remaining prisoners who had been involved in the rebellion. The women who had smuggled in the explosives were publicly hanged in January 1945.

In November 1944, as the Allies advanced through Europe and Germany seemed more likely to lose the war, SS leader Heinrich Himmler ordered gassings to stop and a "clean-up" operation to begin, to conceal traces of the mass murder. In January 1945, to remove witnesses to their cruelty, the Nazis evacuated fifty-eight thousand prisoners from the Auschwitz complex and forced them to march westward toward other camps (*see* **death marches** in Glossary). The Nazis left behind about seven thousand sick or incapacitated prisoners too weak to march, who were not expected to live for long. Few of them were still alive when Soviet forces arrived to liberate the camp. The site of the camp remains today as a museum and archive preserved by the Polish government.

Bergen-Belsen (Concentration Camp; northwest Germany, near Hannover): In 1943 Bergen-Belsen was converted from a detention camp into a concentration camp. During the winter of 1944–45, tens of thousands of prisoners from other camps arrived at Bergen-Belsen on foot after agonizing death marches (*see* **death marches** in Glossary).

The camp could not accommodate so many prisoners, and all basic services—food, water, and sanitation—collapsed, leading to the outbreak of disease. The young German Jewish diarist Anne Frank and her sister, Margot, were among the many prisoners who died in March 1945 as the result of a typhus epidemic. Bergen-Belsen had no gas chambers, but nearly fifty thousand people died there of starvation, disease, overwork, brutality by the guards, and cruel medical experiments. When British forces liberated the camp on April 15, 1945, they found about sixty thousand starving prisoners and more than ten thousand unburied corpses.

Dachau (Concentration Camp; southeastern Germany, at the edge of the town of Dachau, near Munich): Established in March 1933, the Dachau Concentration Camp was the first permanent concentration camp established by the Nazi government. The Dachau camp served as a training center for SS guards, and the camp became the model for all other Nazi concentration camps.

The number of Jewish prisoners at Dachau rose following the widespread violent persecution of Jews on Kristallnacht, November 9–10, 1938 (*see* **Kristallnacht** in Glossary). After Kristallnacht, more than ten thousand Jewish men were interned there. After 1942, many of the prisoners were forced to work as slave laborers in weapons factories or on farms near the camp.

In Dachau, as in other Nazi camps, German physicians under SS command performed cruel medical experiments on prisoners, including high-altitude experiments using a decompression chamber; hypothermia experiments that subjected victims to extreme cold; and malaria and tuberculosis experiments that infected victims with those diseases. Prisoners were also forced to test new medications and methods for making seawater drinkable and for halting excessive bleeding. Most of the more than thirty-five hundred prisoners who were subjected to these experiments died.

As Allied forces advanced toward Germany in 1945, the Nazis began to evacuate prisoners from camps near the front to prevent their being liberated and bearing witness to the mass murder that the Nazis had been perpetrating. Transports carrying thousands of prisoners from the evacuated camps arrived at Dachau, resulting in severe overcrowding that led to food shortages and a dramatic deterioration of sanitary conditions. Typhus epidemics broke out and led to many deaths. More than twenty-eight thousand prisoners died as a result of disease, starvation, or murder. When United States forces liberated the camp on April 29, 1945, they found more than thirty-two thousand starving prisoners and about ten thousand corpses.

Drancy (Transit Camp; northeastern suburb of Paris): Drancy was a detention camp established after a mass roundup and arrest of about four thousand Jews in Paris in August 1941. The camp was operated by the Vichy government of Philippe Pétain. Drancy remained under the control of the French police, who conducted additional roundups, until July 3, 1943, when Nazi Germany took control as part of an acceleration of mass exterminations of Jews. Living conditions at Drancy were harsh; prisoners suffered from inadequate food, unsanitary conditions, and overcrowding. Drancy was designed to hold seven hundred people, but at its peak it held more than seven thousand.

Upon arrival at Drancy, children were separated from their parents by the French police. The parents were transported to the Auschwitz death camp and gassed. The children remained at Drancy, sometimes for weeks, without proper care or adequate food. Eventually all the children were also transported to Auschwitz and sent to the gas chambers. More than six thousand Jewish children from all regions of France were arrested, detained at Drancy, and transported to their deaths between July 17 and September 30, 1942. Altogether, nearly sixty-five thousand Jewish men, women, and children were held at Drancy. Fewer than two thousand of them survived the war.

On August 15–16, 1944, with Allied forces approaching, the Nazi authorities at Drancy burned all the camp documents and fled. The Swedish consul general Raoul Nording took over the camp on August 17 and asked the French Red Cross to care for the fifteen hundred prisoners who remained.

Majdanek (Extermination and Concentration Camp; Lublin, Poland): Throughout its entire existence, Majdanek camp was under construction. The majority of its prisoners were sent there as forced laborers. Conditions in the camp during the bitterly cold winter of 1941–42 were lethal. The SS guards routinely took prisoners who were too weak to work and shot them to death. Others died as a result of the inhumane living conditions. Estimated total deaths range from sixty thousand to eighty thousand. Majdanek also housed storage facilities for clothing and personal items taken from Jews before their deaths at other extermination camps.

Maly Trostinec (Extermination and Concentration Camp; outside Minsk, Belarus): Maly Trostinec was established to eradicate the Jewish population of Minsk and the surrounding areas, using mobile gas chambers. Thousands of Viennese Jews also were deported to Maly Trostinec and murdered. The first transport of Jews arrived at the camp on May 10, 1942. However, many Jews were killed even before they reached the camp. As they were brought to the nearby forests, the victims were forced to strip naked and line up in front of large pits. SS guards shot them, and their dead bodies fell into the pits, which were then covered over and flattened by tractors. Prisoners in the camp were forced to sort through the victims' possessions and maintain the camp.

In 1943, the Nazis shifted away from forced labor and began to carry out mass extermination of the prisoners in the camp. On June 28, 1944, as Germany was losing the war and the Red Army was approaching the region, the Nazis bombed the camp in an attempt to wipe out evidence of its existence. They locked up the remaining prisoners and burned the buildings to the ground.

Mechelen (Transit Camp; Mechelen, Belgium): Halfway between Antwerp and Brussels, two urban centers that were home to most of the Jewish residents of Belgium, the city of Mechelen (called Malines in French) was considered by Nazi Germany to be an ideal location from which to deport the Jews of Belgium to extermination camps in Poland. The Nazis converted the Dossin de Saint-Georges military barracks in Mechelen into a transit camp for this purpose.

The first group of Jews arrived in the Mechelen camp from Antwerp on July 27, 1942. Once a week between August and December 1942, two transports with about 1,000 Jews each left the camp, bound for the gas chambers at Auschwitz. Between August 4, 1942, and July 31, 1944, a total of twenty-eight trains carrying 25,257 Jews departed Mechelen for Poland, most of them headed for Auschwitz. More than half of the Belgian Jews murdered during the Holocaust were on those transports.

Several trains carrying Jews from the Mechelen camp to Auschwitz during 1942–44 were derailed by the Belgian Jewish underground, assisted by the Belgian resistance. Although most of the Jews on those trains were deported in later transports, about five hundred Jewish prisoners managed to escape. In April 1943, about a quarter of the Jews in one transport tried to escape from the train; 208 of them succeeded, and 23 were shot dead by SS guards. Several liberation attempts at the camp were made by members of the Committee for Jewish Defense (CDJ), which was in contact with the Belgian resistance movement. The organized Jewish community sent in packages to help ease the harsh living conditions in the camp. In September 1944, as Germany was losing the war and Allied forces were approaching, the Nazis closed the Mechelen camp.

Sachsenhausen (Concentration Camp; Germany, outside Berlin): Sachsenhausen Concentration Camp was built in July 1936. Near the administrative center for all the concentration camps, it became a central training facility for SS officers, many of whom would oversee the camps. The entrance gates to Sachsenhausen bore a sign with the infamous slogan ARBEIT MACHT FREI (WORK MAKES ONE FREE; *see* ***Arbeit Macht Frei*** in the Glossary).

Prisoners suffered from inadequate food and poor sanitation. The first typhus epidemic of many broke out in November 1939. The SS refused to provide medical care, and hundreds of prisoners died in the following weeks. At first, corpses were sent to crematoriums in Berlin. Starting in 1940, crematoriums were built at the Sachsenhausen camp to dispose of the bodies on site.

Living conditions at the Sachsenhausen camp were barbaric. The SS carried out daily executions by shooting or hanging, and many more prisoners died as a result of routine brutality.

In addition to its role as a camp, Sachsenhausen was the site of the Nazis' largest currency counterfeiting operation. The Nazis forced Jewish artisans to forge American dollars and British pound notes as part of a Nazi plan to undermine the economies of the United States and Great Britain.

In the spring of 1945, as Germany was losing the war and the Red Army was advancing toward Berlin, Sachsenhausen was prepared for evacuation. On April 20–21, the Sachsenhausen SS ordered thirty-three thousand prisoners on a forced march northeast. The SS planned to load the prisoners onto ships, put the ships out to sea, and then sink them. However, thousands of the prisoners did not live long enough to reach port; they died along the way from exhaustion or were shot by SS guards if they collapsed.

Sobibor (Extermination Camp; southeastern Poland): The Nazis opened Sobibor in spring 1942. Trains of forty to sixty freight cars full of Jewish men, women, and children regularly arrived at the Sobibor railway station. SS guards ordered the Jews to hand over all their valuables, enter the barracks, undress, and run into the tunnel-like "tube," where women made an additional stop to have their heads shaved. The tube led directly into gas chambers labeled as showers. Then the chamber doors were sealed, and the guards outside started an engine that piped in carbon monoxide, killing everyone inside. The bodies were buried in mass graves.

In late 1942, the Nazis decided they wanted to wipe out all traces of mass murder at Sobibor. SS guards directed Jewish forced laborers to exhume the mass graves and burn the bodies on open-air "ovens" made from rail track. Any bone fragments that remained were ground into powder by a machine.

In June 1943, Heinrich Himmler, head of the German police, ordered that Sobibor be converted into a concentration camp. Understanding that this order was essentially a death sentence, Jewish prisoners under the leadership of Leon Feldhendler organized a resistance movement and worked out an escape plan. The prisoners' revolt began on October 14, 1943. Eleven SS members and a number of Ukrainian guards were killed in the fighting. Three hundred Jews escaped, but dozens were killed in the minefield around the camp and dozens more were subsequently hunted down. Fifty of the escapees survived. The Nazis liquidated the camp in October 1943 and disguised the site as a farm.

The Sobibor uprising was the most successful escape attempt from any Nazi camp during World War II, according to Thomas Toivi Blatt in his book *Sobibor—*

The Forgotten Revolt (Issaquah, Wash.: H.E.P., 1998). A feature film based on events at the camp, *Escape from Sobibor* (1987), starred Alan Arkin as Leon Feldhendler.

Theresienstadt (Concentration Camp; Terezin, Czechoslovakia [now Czech Republic], near Prague): Although classified here as a concentration camp, Theresienstadt was a unique facility that also incorporated elements of transit camps and ghettos during its existence from November 24, 1942, to May 9, 1945. It served as a transit camp for Czech Jews whom the Germans deported to death camps, concentration camps, and forced-labor camps; and it served as a ghetto and labor camp in which the SS imprisoned certain categories of Jews based on their age, disability as a result of past military service, or achievements in the arts and other cultural life. It was expected that the poor living conditions at Theresienstadt would hasten the deaths of many deportees, and those who survived were sent to death camps in the east. Of the many thousands of children who passed through Theresienstadt, about 90 percent were murdered in the death camps. Yad Vashem estimates that 1,234 children survived.

The high concentration of prisoners who had talent in the visual and performing arts gave Theresienstadt a cultural element that other Nazi camps lacked. Concerts, theatrical performances, author lectures, and art displays were presented at Theresienstadt. Some paintings and drawings depicting the harsh reality of the prisoners' incarceration were hidden from the Nazis. However, the Nazis exploited Theresienstadt's robust cultural life in perpetrating an elaborate hoax on the outside world. Succumbing to pressure following the deportation of Danish Jews to Theresienstadt, the Nazis allowed the International Red Cross to visit in June 1944 to inspect living conditions there. In preparation for the visit, the Nazis intensified deportations from the ghetto to make it less crowded and rid it of the weakest, sickest prisoners. They also ordered that the ghetto itself be "beautified" so that both the grounds and the residents who were allowed to be seen by the visitors would look more attractive. When the Red Cross group visited, the operetta *Brundibár* was performed by the prisoners for them (*see* ***Brundibár*** in the Glossary). The Nazis also produced a propaganda film showing some well-chosen Theresienstadt prisoners. After the filming was completed, all the participants were deported to Auschwitz, where they were sent to the gas chambers upon arrival.

Treblinka (Extermination Camp; northeastern Poland, near Warsaw): Two facilities made up the Treblinka camp. Treblinka I, opened in 1941, held Jews and Polish political prisoners, who were used as forced laborers in a nearby quarry. Treblinka II, opened in July 1942, was strictly a killing center designed for the mass murder of Jews. Using an efficient two-hour process similar to that used at Sobibor (see previous **Sobibor** entry), the Nazis murdered more than 800,000 Jews who arrived in train transports and went straight to the gas chambers at Treblinka II during its thirteen months of existence.

Initially the bodies of the people killed at Treblinka II were buried in mass graves. In late 1942, SS guards began to order Jewish forced laborers to exhume the corpses and burn them on open-air "ovens" made of rail track and placed in large trenches. On August 2, 1943, the forced laborers seized weapons from the camp armory and set fire to Treblinka II, but they were discovered by SS guards before they could take control of the camp. Hundreds of prisoners stormed the main gate in an attempt to escape, and many were killed by machine-gun fire. However, more than three hundred prisoners did escape—though two-thirds of them were eventually tracked down and killed by the SS and the police as well as military units. The surviving prisoners were forced to dismantle the remaining buildings to obliterate all evidence of the camp, and were shot to death after they completed the task. By November 1943, the grounds had been cleared, leveled, and planted with crops to give the site the appearance of a farm. Survivor accounts, documents, and postwar testimony of camp officials who were tried for war crimes substantiated the existence of the camp.

Westerbork (Transit Camp; northeastern Netherlands): From 1942 to 1944, Westerbork served as a detention center for Dutch Jews before they were deported to extermination camps in German-occupied Poland. Altogether, about one hundred thousand Jewish men, women, and children were held at Westerbork. Under Nazi orders and often supervised by Dutch police, members of a Jewish security service who feared for their own lives selected the Jews to be deported on the trains that departed for the east every Tuesday. Most of those deported to the Auschwitz and Sobibor camps were killed upon arrival.

Hidden Children/Child Survivors Chicago Mission Statement

Definition

The Hidden Children group consists of Jewish adults who were hidden during World War II's Holocaust in order to survive it. Like other child survivors, we are the last living generation to have witnessed the Holocaust.

History

A generation of Jewish children disappeared during the Holocaust. Where they weren't killed outright, they died of hunger, disease, or other Holocaust-induced causes. Yet a handful of children did survive.

To survive, most of we children were hidden in some fashion, sometimes with their families but mostly alone. We lived with Christian families, or in convents, or on farms, or roaming the forests, or in the mountains, or in underground caves, attics, or other makeshift shelters. We are those children.

Silent for a long time, possibly because our parents could not break their silence, some of us began to speak about forty-five years after the end of the war. The relief we found in speaking led us to other hidden children with experiences similar to ours. These connections grew worldwide, and in 1991, the first international gathering of sixteen hundred Hidden Children was held in New York, organized by the Hidden Child Committee, with the help of the Anti-Defamation League (ADL).

Hidden Children/Child Survivors Chicago

In 1992, a Hidden Children group was formed in Chicago, with the following initial objectives:

1. Hearing one another's wartime childhood experiences and thereby learning to understand the strengths and coping capacities, as well as the difficulties we experienced as children and as adults, and

2. Educating ourselves about Jewishness, the Holocaust, antisemitism, and related topics.

These topics have included the nature of our vulnerability and resilience, hiding as a form of resistance, our rescuers, our self-image as parents, and ourselves as children of our parents.

Toward these ends, we met every other month. The meetings were generally attended by twenty-five to thirty people, though this number has declined of late. On some occasions we met with another child survivor group; and on other occasions, we invited our own children to meet with us and discuss how our experience affects their lives. We've had several social events. Some of us also attended, and brought news from, international conferences about hidden children.

In 1995, an informal self-survey suggested that our attendees were satisfied with these gatherings that focused on support, education, and social contact.

Members of the speakers' forum speak at public and private schools, churches and synagogues, civil service gatherings, and other community sites. The Illinois Holocaust Museum & Education Center has now taken over this function.

Mission Statement

Since the inception of the group, our goals remain basically the same, with the added goal of more formally educating others.

1. To support one another while we learn from one another, regarding not only what happened to us but also what we've done with those happenings.

2. To educate ourselves as to the larger picture—of ourselves as Jews and human beings, of the war, of past and the present attitudes about us, of our relationship to our parents and children—a picture of who we were and are, in the context of the rest of the world; and to try to make sense of that picture.

3. To remember those who have perished and their circumstances, and to try to understand them and how our relationship with them in the past, and now, still affects us.

4. To educate others, first by faithfully telling or writing our stories and then by means of speaking, with the restraint and dignity we have attained over time, to a variety of audiences, including children.

Contributors

Leonie Taffel Bergman was born in Berlin, Germany. Seeing the danger of remaining in Berlin, her family left for Belgium in 1938, hoping for security there. A new daughter, Clara, was born in 1940. Soon war broke out in Belgium, and in 1942 Leonie and her sister were hidden for safety. Leonie was eventually placed in a convent, where she remained for more than three years. Her sister was nearby, with a farming family. Their parents died in Auschwitz in 1944. At the end of 1946, the sisters arrived in New York. Within a few months they were "given" to strangers. Life with this family became unbearable for Leonie, and at age fourteen she was sent to the couple in Chicago who ultimately adopted her. Leonie earned bachelor's and master's degrees and taught in the Chicago Public Schools for many years. Her husband, Howard Bergman, is also a Holocaust survivor. Leonie and Howard have two children and four grandchildren.

Isaac M. Daniel was born in Thessaloniki (Salonika), Greece, and grew up speaking Ladino and Greek. After the Germans invaded Greece in 1941, the family had many narrow escapes. Isaac became the valedictorian of his high school class and entered the National Technical University of Athens in 1952. He immigrated to the United States with his family in 1955. They settled in Chicago, and Isaac transferred to the Illinois Institute of Technology, where he obtained B.S., M.S., and Ph.D. degrees. He joined the IIT Research Institute and then the IIT teaching faculty as a full professor in 1982. He is currently the Walter P. Murphy Professor of Theoretical and Applied Mechanics and director of the Center for Intelligent Processing of Composites at Northwestern University. He and his wife, Elaine Krule Daniel, have three children.

Aaron Elster was born in the small northeastern Polish village of Sokołów-Podłaski. Aaron lived in the Sokołów Ghetto with his two sisters, mother, and father until the liquidation in September 1942. He escaped and hid in surrounding farms, eventually finding refuge in the attic of a Polish family, where he hid for two years until the war's end. After the war Aaron lived in several orphanages, and eventually was smuggled out of Poland to displaced persons camps in West Germany. Aaron and his older sister came to the United States in 1947. He was educated in Chicago and served in the U.S. armed forces in Korea. Married with two sons and three grandchildren, he worked for more than forty years in sales and management in the insurance industry. He serves as cochairman of the Speakers' Bureau and vice president of the Illinois Holocaust Museum & Education Center. In addition, he served as chairman of the Speakers' Bureau for Hidden Children/Child Survivors Chicago. He is the coauthor of *I Still See Her Haunting Eyes* (2007), which chronicles his Holocaust experiences.

Gitta Horowitz Fajerstein was born in Berlin into an Orthodox Jewish family. In 1939, the Gestapo arrested all Jewish men born in Poland, including her father, who was sent to the Sachsenhausen Concentration Camp and beaten to death. Gitta and her sister, Chaya, were smuggled into Holland, then to Belgium and France, finally crossing the Alps into Italy. Chaya and Gitta hid in a convent in Rome until the Allies liberated the city in 1944. Under the auspices of Youth Aliyah, Gitta and Chaya went to Palestine in 1945. The sisters spent a year and a half in Ben Shemen, a Youth Aliyah children's village. Today, Gitta is a licensed clinical social worker in private practice. She is a member of the Holocaust Community Services Committee of Jewish Child and Family Services, a cofounder and member of the Holocaust Educational Foundation, a past director of a senior center of the Jewish Community Centers, a past chapter president of Hadassah North Shore, and cofounder of the Hidden Children/Child Survivors Chicago. Gitta is the mother of three children and grandmother of eight.

Elaine Saphier Fox is a former partner, now of counsel, at the Chicago office of Seyfarth Shaw LLP, and has more than thirty-five years of experience in labor and employment matters nationwide. She coedited the seventh edition of *How to Take a Case Before the NLRB* (2000) and its supplements and has written numerous articles on labor and employment. She is a member of the American and Chicago bar associations and of the ABA Foundation and an inducted fellow of the College of Labor and Employment Lawyers. She has served as chair of the 2010 conference of the World Federation of Jewish Child Survivors of the Holocaust, president of the Jewish Vocational Service, and national vice president of the American Jewish Congress. She and her husband, Alan A. Fox, have three daughters, nine grandchildren, and three great-grandchildren.

Sheila Taub Birger Gerber was born in Kaunas, Lithuania. She was raised as the daughter of Rosa and Daniel Birger, Holocaust survivors, who also had two sons. For much of her life, Sheila sensed, and finally at age twenty-six learned, that she was not the Birgers' daughter but their niece. Sheila and her father (uncle) immigrated to the United States in 1950 and settled in Chicago, followed by her mother (aunt) and two brothers (cousins). She went to college, became a teacher, taught for many years, and retired in 1998. In 1962, Sheila married Larry Gerber. They have two children and four grandchildren. Sheila is active in the local PTA, in her synagogue, and in other Jewish organizations. In 1980, in Israel for her daughter's bat mitzvah, she was reunited with Shira, her long-lost sister. She also found two aunts and two cousins.

Irma Morgenstern Grundland was born in Warsaw, Poland. In 1940, the Nazis forced her and her family into the Warsaw Ghetto. Irma escaped in 1943 and hid in Poland and Ukraine until the war's end. Her grandfather's cousin, Emilia, found Irma and cared for her until her own death in 1950. A Warsaw company, Centrala Import Export Chemicals (CIECH), hired Irma for office work. After a while, Irma asked CIECH to send her to the evening university to learn a trade. CIECH agreed, if she would work for the company for ten years after she obtained her degree. In 1954, she married her husband, Ted. The couple left Poland in 1959 and settled in Chicago. Irma took courses in accounting at Oakton Community College and worked in the field. She and Ted have two children and four grandchildren.

Kurt Gutfreund was born in Vienna, Austria. In June 1942, the Germans arrested and transported Kurt's disabled father to Maly Trostinec, a death camp, where he was murdered. Kurt and his mother went into hiding. In December 1942, they were arrested and shipped to Theresienstadt, where they stayed until the Russians liberated them in 1945. Kurt immigrated to the United States. He opened his own business, M & L International, a manufacturer of children's jackets, snowsuits, and other outerwear. Kurt has a son and daughter with his first wife. After many years of marriage, they divorced. Later, his daughter introduced him to the woman who became his second wife, Nancy Schwartz, with whom he had another daughter. Kurt also has two grandchildren. Kurt frequently returns to Vienna. He has visited Maly Trostinec, where his father was murdered, and Treblinka, where his grandfather and step-grandmother died.

Leah Molton-Motulsky Kadden was born in Fischhausen, East Prussia, Germany. After debarking from the SS *St. Louis* in Antwerp, Belgium, in 1939, Leah and her family were assigned to live in Brussels. After Germany invaded Belgium in 1940, her oldest brother Arno was sent to Gurs, a concentration camp in southern France. In 1942, Leah, her mother, and her brother Lothar went into hiding. Eventually, they crossed into Switzerland, where they remained until the war's end. In 1946, landing in New York Harbor, Leah was reunited with her father and Arno. Leah attended Wilson Junior College in Chicago. She married Herbert Kadden, and they raised two children. When the children grew older, Leah joined the National Opinion Research Center (NORC) at the University of Chicago as a field supervisor. After twelve years at NORC, Leah became office manager for her husband, serving in that role until they retired and closed the office in 1989.

Ahlyce Goldman Kaplan was born and raised in Paris. Her father, drafted into the French Army in 1942, became a prisoner of war in a camp near Frankfurt, Germany. During the war, Ahlyce cared for her younger disabled sister, Nicole, and herself, living on the run to escape German detection. She and her sister were later reunited with their mother in free France. They returned to Paris after the war, when their father rejoined them. The family eventually came to the United States. Ahlyce attended the University of Chicago, where she studied humanities. She has worked as a substitute French teacher, a guide at the International Visitors Center, a designer of clothes, and a concierge at a luxury hotel. She became vice president of the American chapter of the international association of concierges, *Les Clefs d'Or.* She and her deceased husband, Marvin Kaplan, have three children and four grandchildren.

Ida Paluch Kersz and her twin brother, Adam, were only four months old when the German Army occupied Poland. Their family lived in Sosnowiec, Poland. In 1942, Wilhelm Maj, a Christian, rescued Ida from the ghetto and took her to Częstochowa. After the war, her father returned from Russia and placed her in an orphanage in Zabrze. Later he took her to Wrocław, where Ida attended a Jewish school. Ida emmigrated to Israel in 1957. She married and had a daughter. Ida left Israel with her family in 1963 and came to the United States. She studied computer programming and bookkeeping at Oakton Community College in the evenings. In 1973, Ida moved to Skokie, Illinois. She joined the Illinois Holocaust Museum as a volunteer and became a director on the museum's board. She also joined a group of Holocaust child survivors who met at the Skokie Jewish Community Center. In 1987, the group sent Ida to represent them at a meeting of Holocaust child survivors in Lancaster, Pennsylvania. There they made a decision to organize a yearly gathering of hidden child survivors. In 1995, Ida found her long-lost twin brother, Adam, in Poland. He now lives in Illinois. Ida also has two grandsons.

Phyllis Lassner is a professor at the Crown Family Center for Jewish Studies and in the Writing and Gender Studies programs at Northwestern University. She teaches courses in Representing the Holocaust in testimony, literature, and film, as well as from the perspective of gender and race; and on children's experiences and fiction for young readers. In addition to two books on the Anglo-Irish writer Elizabeth Bowen and many articles on interwar and World War II women writers, her writings include *British Women Writers of World War II: Battlegrounds of Their Own* (1998), *Colonial Strangers: Women Writing the End of the British Empire* (2004), and most recently, *Anglo-Jewish Women Writing the Holocaust: Displaced Witnesses* (2008). Professor Lassner has served as president of the scholarly society The Space Between: Literature and Culture 1914–1945. She has also lectured on her research in Holocaust writing and film in Israel, Britain, and Europe.

Marguerite Lederman Mishkin was born in Brussels. She and her sister, Annette, survived the war as hidden children with a family in rural Belgium after their parents were murdered in Auschwitz. After the war, Marguerite and her sister were put into a Jewish orphanage. Several years later they were adopted by Rabbi Leonard Mishkin and his wife, Leah, of Chicago. The sisters arrived in the United States in 1950. Marguerite received her B.A. from Roosevelt University. After teaching in California for a year, she began her lifelong career in the Chicago Public Schools. She earned her master's degree in guidance and counseling from Northeastern Illinois University and her master's in social work from Loyola University. After working as a teacher, counselor, and teacher mentor in the Chicago Public Schools for thirty-five years, Marguerite retired. An expert in needlework, she now works part time in a needlepoint shop. She is one of the founders of the Hidden Children/Child Survivors Chicago. Marguerite often speaks on the Holocaust and her experiences to school, college, and community groups.

Adam Paluch lived through the German occupation in Polish ghettos with his mother, his twin sister, Ida, and his older sister, Genia. In 1942, separated from his family, he was incarcerated in the death camp at Majdanek, where he may have been subjected to medical experiments. Placed in an orphanage in Lublin, Adam was then taken by a foster family, who changed his name to Jurek Janusz Dolebski. He attended the University of Łódź, then transferred to the University of Kraków, but had to go to work to support his family. In 1963, Adam married Danuta Mis. Adam worked for the Rescue Marines, traveling around the world looking for his Jewish roots. Later he worked for the Government Agricultural Corporation, then opened his own business. In 1991, he became a member of a child survivors group. In January 1995, he learned that his twin sister was looking for him. Three months later, they were reunited in Warsaw. Adam went to the United States to meet more of his family and decided to remain in the States. He has sons and grandchildren in Poland and visits them often.

Walter Reed was born in Würzburg, Germany, and grew up in a small Bavarian village. He was arrested as a fourteen-year-old during Kristallnacht and escaped to Belgium in 1939, then to southern France in 1940, where he became part of a Jewish children's refugee colony known as "The Children of La Hille." In 1941, he immigrated to the United States. He became a U.S. citizen in 1943 and changed his name from Werner Rindsberg to Walter Reed. Drafted in 1943, he served in the U.S. Army, landed in Normandy in June 1944, and was assigned to Military Intelligence, interrogating German prisoners at the front. He was discharged as a staff sergeant in early 1946. Graduating from the University of Missouri School of Journalism, he worked for eight years as a fund-raising consultant in Kansas City and then became director of public relations of the National Automatic Merchandising Association in Chicago in 1958. After he retired in 1989, Reed established an international consulting firm with clients in Europe, Asia, and the United States. Reed and his wife, Jeanne, have three sons. Reed has long been active in civic affairs and is a member of the Speakers Committee of the Illinois Holocaust Educational Foundation. After years of research, he has written a history of his wartime refugee children's colony: "The Heroes of La Hille—How Almost One Hundred Jewish Children Foiled the Nazi Murder Machine (1939–1945)."

Chaya Horowitz Roth was born in Berlin. After the Nazis murdered her father, Chaya lived on the run or in hiding, carrying forged papers. In 1953, she came to Chicago and graduated from Roosevelt University in 1955. She received her doctorate from the University of Chicago in 1960. She trained in psychoanalysis and child development and was appointed professor of clinical psychiatry at the University of Chicago. She maintained a private practice from 1979 until 2005. Roth developed a new concept for parent-infant treatment, which she described in her book *The Multiple Facets of Therapeutic Transactions* (1997). She was most recently a clinical professor of psychiatry at the University of Illinois at Chicago and Institute of Juvenile Research. Her most recent book is *The Fate of Holocaust Memories: Transmission and Family Dialogues* (2008). Roth is a fellow of the American Orthopsychiatric

Association and a member of the American Psychological and Jewish Studies associations. She was a cofounder and board member of the Holocaust Educational Foundation and cofounder of Hidden Children/Child Survivors Chicago. Walter and Chaya Roth are the parents of three and the grandparents of seven.

Ava Hegedis Kadishson Schieber was born in Novi Sad, Yugoslavia. Ava survived World War II on a farm in Serbia posing as a person who was deaf and could not speak. After the war she studied at the Art Academy in Belgrade. She left Yugoslavia in 1949 for Israel, where she raised a family and worked as a theatrical set designer in Tel Aviv. She founded and co-owned the Theater Club, a political satire theater. After her husband's death, she exhibited her paintings in the United States. She married again in 1984 and settled in Chicago. Ava's book *Soundless Roar* was published by Northwestern University Press in 2002. Her artwork is displayed at the United States Holocaust Memorial Museum in Washington, D.C., and at the Illinois Holocaust Museum & Education Center in Skokie, Illinois.

Henry Stark was born in Antwerp, Belgium. The family immigrated in 1949 to the United States, where Henry attended an Orthodox yeshiva. After earning a degree in electrical engineering from the City College of New York, he married an American Jew, Alice, in 1960. They raised two sons. Subsequently, Henry earned a doctorate in engineering from Columbia University. He was department chairman at the Illinois Institute of Technology for ten years. During 1969–70, he and his family resided in Israel, where he was associated with the Weizmann Institute of Science. His book *Probability and Random Processes with Applications to Signal Processing* (2002) is used in research universities throughout North America. Upon retiring from teaching, he wrote two children's books: *The Adventures of Jasmine Turmalina* and *Heart Lessons* (both 2008).

Judith Levy Straus was born in Dortmund, Germany, in 1933, a few days after Adolf Hitler came to power. Her parents, fearing the future, moved to Amsterdam, Holland, for greater safety. In 1940, Hitler and his armies invaded the Netherlands, and the persecution of Dutch Jews soon began. Judy and her parents were caught in a roundup in 1943 and spent the next two years in the Westerbork Transit Camp (in the Netherlands) and the Theresienstadt Concentration Camp (in Czechoslovakia). In 1944, Judy's father was put on a transport to the "east"—that is, to Auschwitz, where he was murdered upon arrival. Judy and her mother were liberated from Theresienstadt by the Red Army in May 1945 and returned to the Netherlands in June of that year. In 1949, mother and daughter moved to the United States. Judy finished college and graduate school with a degree in social work. Judy and her husband, Henry, married in 1955. They have three children and six grandchildren. Judy worked as a social worker with children and their families until she retired in 1999. She is presently part of the Speakers' Bureau of the Illinois Holocaust Museum & Education Center, where she shares her memories of her childhood experiences with school-age children.

Nicole Dreyfus Terry was born in Strasbourg, France, and grew up in a Paris suburb. Except for a twenty-one-year-old cousin in the French underground who was murdered, her family survived the war. Nicole studied to be a kindergarten teacher. She worked with a student of Maria Montessori who created an experimental school for mentally challenged children. In her twenties she spent two years in Israel with a Jewish agency, first as a student, and then as part of a working team. Upon her return from Israel, she and others created Torah Ve Zion, an organization to locate Jewish Moroccans, Tunisians, and Algerians, in Paris and its vicinity and to integrate them into the Jewish community. In 1962, in Israel, she met Eugene Terry, a Chicago attorney. They married in Israel, and their first daughter, Elisa, was born there. In 1965 they returned to the Chicago area, where their second daughter, Kathryn, was born. Nicole created a successful business, importing from Israel quality control instruments used in metallurgy. In 1984, her younger sister Simone died. Simone's children Philippe and Chantal became part of Eugene and Nicole's family. Gene and Nicole have eight grandchildren, including Simone's grandchildren. Nicole speaks about the Holocaust in schools and is active with Hidden Children/Child Survivors Chicago.

Amos Turner lived in Zawiercie, Poland, with his parents from 1926 until 1939. His childhood was interrupted by the German occupation of Poland in 1939. Amos hid to avoid forced labor. In 1943, Amos escaped and pretended to be a Pole, obtaining work as an electrician in a shoe factory in Ottmuth, Germany. After the war ended in 1945, Amos reunited with his father and surviving members of his family in Munich, Germany. Amos studied and obtained a Bachelor of Science degree in electrical engineering. He left Germany for the United States in 1950. He lived in Chicago with his father and studied at Illinois Institute of Technology for a master's degree in electrical engineering, which he received in 1954. He had met Edith Singer on the ship coming to the States in 1950, and they married in 1954. They have three children and four grandchildren. Amos worked for a number of engineering companies. In 1962, Amos and two partners started their own engineering and construction company, Hoyer-Schlesinger-Turner, Inc. After a forty-year career, he retired in 2002. Amos works as a volunteer for the Jewish United Fund, Israel Bonds, and his synagogue.

Edith Singer Turner was born in Vilna, Poland, now Vilnius, Lithuania. When World War II broke out in 1939, she and her family moved to the small town of Święciany, Poland. They survived the Holocaust living through many life-threatening and difficult situations. After the war they traveled to the American Zone of Germany with the help of Aliyah Bet. Edith enrolled in the University of Munich for premedical studies. Edith immigrated to the United States in 1950 and became a medical records librarian. Edith is a past president of the Highland Park and North Shore (Illinois) chapters of Hadassah. She is a board member of the Great Plains Region of Hadassah and the chair of Holocaust Studies. Edith is married to Amos Turner. She is the mother of three children and grandmother of four.

Miriam Studniberg Webster was born in Łódź, Poland. She grew up in Radomsko, Poland, and lived there with her parents and younger brother until the German invasion in 1939. Her father was forced to turn over his business to a Christian, who volunteered to help Miriam escape. In 1942, when the Radomsko Ghetto was about to be liquidated, he got her onto a train. Eventually, disguised as a Polish peasant, she made her way to Mannheim, Germany. She worked for a German family until 1945, when the Americans invaded Germany. While in Germany, she worked for the United Nations Relief and Rehabilitation Administration (UNRRA). She helped teach English to survivors and gave them information on how to contact other helpful agencies. In 1949 Miriam came to Chicago, where she worked with the Travelers Aid Society helping new immigrants from Europe. Miriam also worked as a bookkeeper. She and her husband have two sons and six grandchildren. Miriam speaks regularly to groups and schools about her experiences during the Holocaust, keeping a promise she made the day she left her family in Radomsko. She vowed that if she survived the war, she would tell their story to the world.

Olga Kirshenbaum Weiss was born in Antwerp, Belgium. She and her parents immigrated to Chicago in 1950. Olga graduated from the University of Chicago with a degree in biochemistry. She completed a graduate program in art history at the Art Institute of Chicago in 1983. In 1959, she married Gerald Weiss. In 1976, Olga began working at the Spertus Museum of Judaica, where she eventually was appointed curator for collections and exhibitions. She retired in 2005. After her husband died, she remarried George Honig in 1998. Olga has three children and eight grandchildren. George has three children and five grandchildren. Olga is a member of the Art Collections and Exhibition Committee of the Illinois Holocaust Museum & Education Center in Skokie. She is a past member of the Steering Committee of the Council of American Jewish Museums. Olga was a cofounder of Hidden Children/Child Survivors Chicago.

Adele Laznowski Zaveduk was born in Paris. She was three years old when the German Army occupied France. Her mother left her and her two-year-old sister with a Christian Catholic widow in a small town in the countryside. After the war Adele and her sister were reunited with their parents, who survived Auschwitz Concentration Camp. The family returned to Paris and lived there until she was about fifteen years old, when they immigrated to Buenos Aires, Argentina. There she met and married Ben Zaveduk. Ten years later, they decided to move to the Chicago area. Adele is a speaker for the Illinois Holocaust Museum & Education Foundation, the Spertus Museum of Judaica, and Chicago's Facing History and Ourselves, an organization that combats racism, antisemitism, and other forms of prejudice. Adele has held a number of offices at Congregation Beth Shalom of Northbrook, Illinois, and served as planning committee member and treasurer of the 2010 conference of the World Federation of Jewish Child Survivors of the Holocaust. Adele is the mother of two sons and grandmother of two.

Lillian Schreiber Zoloto was born in Brussels, Belgium. In 1942, with roundups escalating in Brussels, Lillian was placed in hiding with a Christian family, Josine and Jean Opdebeeck. The Opdebeecks, head of a resistance group, cared for Lillian as part of their family. At the war's end, the Opdebeecks returned Lillian to her parents. When Lillian's parents decided to immigrate to the United States, Lillian was devastated to leave her adopted family. Lillian attended night classes at Roosevelt and Northwestern universities, married, and raised three children. In addition to her three children, Lillian has seven grandchildren. Yad Vashem in Jerusalem recognized the Opdebeecks as Righteous Among the Nations.